Ari Means Lion

A Memoir by Ari Rath

Ari Means Lion
A Memoir by Ari Rath

Recorded by Stefanie Oswalt
Translated by Laura Radosh

Ariadne Press
Riverside, CA

Ari Means Lion
A Memoir by Ari Rath

Afterword by Stefanie Oswalt
Translated by Laura Radosh

Originally published as *Ari heißt Löwe • Erinnerungen*
© 2012 Paul Zsolnay Verlag, Vienna

Studies in Austrian Literature, Culture and Thought, Translation Series
© 2024 Ariadne Press
Riverside, CA

Photographs courtesy Ari Rath, unless otherwise noted; see Photo Credits page.
Typesetting: Carrie Paterson

Ariadne Press would like to express appreciation for assistance in publishing this book. This translation was made possible by grants from the Moses Mendelssohn Foundation, Berlin, Germany and GBI Group, Germany. The index of this book was made possible by a grant from Saleh Turujman, Washington, D.C.

Publisher's Cataloging-in-Publication data

Names: Rath, Ari, 1925-2017, author. | Oswalt, Stefanie, 1967-, author. | Radosh, Laura, translator.
Title: Ari means lion : a memoir / by Ari Rath; recorded by Stefanie Oswalt; translated by Laura Radosh.
Series: Studies in Austrian Literature, Culture and Thought, Translation Series
Description: Originally published in 2012 as Ari heißt Löwe, Erinnerungen, Paul Zsolnay Verlag, Vienna | Riverside, CA: Ariadne Press, 2024.
Identifiers: LCCN: 2023921986 | ISBN: 978-1-57241-236-1 (hardcover) | 978-1-57241-237-8 (paperback) | 978-1-57241-238-5 (ebook)
Subjects: LCSH Rath, Ari, 1925-. | Journalists--Israel–Biography | Journalists--Austrian–Biography. | Newspaper editors--Israel–Biography | Jews, Austrian--Israel--Biography. | Israel--History--20th century | BISAC BIOGRAPHY & AUTOBIOGRAPHY / Editors, Journalists, Publishers | BIOGRAPHY & AUTOBIOGRAPHY / Jewish
Classification: LCC DS125.3.R38 A3 2024 | DDC 079.5694/92--dc23

For my mother Laura, whom I never really knew

לאמי לאורה שלא היכרתי.

Contents

Prologue | Coming Full Circle	9
A Viennese Childhood	14
Leaving Austria	36
The Ahava Youth Home	48
The Young Kibbutznik	69
Political Baby Steps	81
Youth Movement Delegate	90
New Duties, New Paths	111
Journalist at the *Jerusalem Post*	146
Managing Editor in Turbulent Times	170
The Grand Old Man's Personal Aide	190
Between the Front and My Desk	205
The Yom Kippur War and Its Aftermath	268
Hopes and Setbacks	287
Epilogue | Between Jerusalem and Vienna	348
Acknowledgements	371
Editorial Note	373
Afterword to the English Edition	376
Index of Names	383
Photo credits	393

Im Meer, am 2.XI.

Liebe Alle!

Ich schreibe ja unerhört fleissig einer Karte hat'ich schon geschrieben und jetzt der Brief. Alles in einem Tag. Die Bahnreise war ganz angenehm. Zollrevision hatten wir überhaupt keine. Also nach den langersehnten 13 Stunden kamen wir in Triest an. Auf der Bahn noch fielen uns die vielen italienischen Uniformen auf. In Triest angekommen wurden wir dann in einen Raum geführt in dem in 16 Sprachen

Ari Rath's letter to his friends in Vienna, written on November 2, 1938 aboard the Galilea *on the journey from Trieste to Haifa.*

Prologue
Coming Full Circle

In November 1938, eight months after the Anschluss, the Nazi "annexation" of Austria, I was ousted from my childhood home of Vienna. Everything that I had loved, all that had been important to me, was snatched from me on March 11, 1938, before my fourteenth birthday, because I am Jewish. The earth in which my mother Laura was buried in the Central Cemetery—at a very young age— became foreign soil. Jews were suddenly no longer allowed to enter my favorite playground in Liechtenstein Park near Porzellangasse in the ninth district, the setting of my childhood. From one day to the next, my father Joseph's successful business was taken over by a Nazi Commissioner. Overnight, we had become fair game, outside the law.

At the eleventh hour, together with my brother Maximilian/ Meshulam, three years my senior, I managed to emigrate to Palestine in the land of Israel. With much physical and even more mental effort, I built a new life for myself there. It doesn't bear thinking about what might have happened had I missed the train from Vienna to Trieste on the first of November that year. This is not simply idle speculation: the day before our departure I made a narrow escape from the Nazis. We had just said tearful good-byes to our classmates at the Jewish school on Schiffamtsgasse, and I had been walking quickly home with my two best friends through the dark and narrow streets. Suddenly, we were surrounded by a gang of Hitler Youth on bicycles. They screamed "*Judenbuben! Judenbuben!*" at us and forced us "Jew boys" to climb onto a truck whose cab was covered with a large banner that read "Hermann Göring Scrap Metal Collection." They drove us to a large courtyard where we were to be loaded onto a new truck and transported to Lobau, an industrial area across the Danube River. There, the next morning we were meant to begin forced labor sorting scrap metal. While SA men were shouting "get off" and "climb up," I gathered my wits about me and called out to Paul and Herbert: "Run for it!" As fast as we could, we sprinted through the dark to the large gate that led to the street and ran down Ausstellungsstrasse to Praterstern. Luckily, the Nazis only screamed after us and did not shoot. We were safe.

◆

In February 2011, in the best tradition of public university health care, the Vienna General Hospital saved my life. At the end of a lecture tour, I had suddenly begun suffering terrible pain that stemmed, it turned out, from a burst appendix. After an emergency operation, I also developed a pulmonary infection. For thirty-six hours, without my conscious knowledge, I hovered at the brink of death—a strange feeling, even after the fact. Later, the wonderful General Hospital doctors explained that my strong will to live had helped me to weather those critical hours. During the twelve weeks of rehab in the new Maimonides Center on the Danube, every day I looked out of my fifth-floor window across the Prater Bridge and over to the Lobau. To this day, the name has a threatening sound. Never in my wildest dreams would I have believed back then that one day I would again spend so many years in Vienna. For 73 years, if I visited Austria at all, it was only for a very short stay. But for many years now, I have been at home on three continents. And Vienna, with its classical middle-European culture, was always with me and in me, even if, after the terrifying events of 1938, I had repressed my connection to the city of my birth and all but forgot my mother tongue, German. To this day I speak Hebrew with my brother. We had solemnly promised each other to do so after arriving in Palestine, even though our knowledge of the language had been rudimentary at best. Neither did any of my nieces or their children ever learn German. But after the Waldheim affair in 1986, Austrians began to deal with their past in earnest, making it possible for me to reconnect with Vienna. I got to know many politicians, writers, and artists from a new generation—people who took part in the weekly protests against Waldheim. I am still friends with many of them to this day.

Ever since the kibbutz movement sent me from Jewish Palestine to New York in November 1946, I have also felt at home in the United States. I was 22 years old and had been given the task of recruiting young American Jews for a life in Palestine. The 21 months that I spent in the United States introduced me to many facets of the English-speaking world that I had known nothing about. In Palestine, English was the language of the policemen, soldiers, and colonial administrators in the British Mandate government, which we rejected and even hated. During the three-week journey by ship from Haifa to New York, every day I read articles in old editions of the *Palestine Post* (renamed the *Jerusalem Post* in 1950), the only

English-language newspaper in the country until the 1990s. Since there is no such thing as coincidence in life, it is probably unsurprising that twelve years later I would begin my career as a journalist at the *Jerusalem Post*. When I became the paper's editor-in-chief, I was most likely the only person at an English-language newspaper to hold that title without ever haven taken an English class in their life.

But despite my roots in Europe and in the New World, the trunk of my tree of life is without a doubt the land of Israel. Israel is the center of my personal, political, and cultural interests and connections. It is where my family lives and since 1957, Jerusalem has been my home town. The years of my youth at the Ahava school in Haifa, my time building the Hamadia kibbutz, my service as a reserve soldier in the Israeli army, and most of all my many years with the *Jerusalem Post* all tie me inextricably to Israel. Often, I was an eyewitness to the country's eventful history. I was there when our dream of a Jewish state of our own became true in 1948, and when that state repeatedly had to be defended over the decades that followed. I am proud of my work for David Ben-Gurion and Teddy Kollek, and look back with wonder at key encounters with leading politicians including Yitzhak Rabin, Moshe Dayan, Golda Meir, and Shimon Perez.

In retrospect, my thirty-one years at the *Jerusalem Post* were my most important and productive years. In the pre-digital age, newspapers had a different meaning than they do today. We not only informed our readers about world events, as the only English-language and back then also liberal Israeli newspaper, the *Post* gave outsiders a window into the society of the young state. The highlights of my life as a journalist encompass personal conversations with leading international politicians including Indira Gandhi, Olof Palme, Henry Kissinger, Konrad Adenauer, and Bruno Kreisky.

It is my firmly-held belief that Israel's future depends on a lasting and just peace with the Palestinians. The historic visit by Egyptian president Anwar Sadat in Jerusalem in November 1977 was covered euphorically by the *Jerusalem Post*. Until I left the paper in 1989, it supported various initiatives for peace to the best of its abilities. During those years, I met many leading Egyptian and Palestinian politicians and am still in touch with many of them today. Sadly however, it seems to me that peace is further away than ever. I am deeply saddened by the demise of the once mighty labor movement, which played such a key role in the founding of the state. It is with great distress that I observe the increasing influence of the religious settlers' movement on the military, as well as the general swing to the right within Israeli society. But although prospects are dim, in the evening of my life I have no intention of giving up the hope that I may yet experience the dawn of a peaceful future.

I have been blessed in that I have never lost my natural curiosity, my good memory, or my optimism. Thankfully, I look back on a treasure trove of memories and am myself amazed at how many of them are linked to key political moments of the twentieth century. The time has come to finally write them down.

A Viennese Childhood

My parents are from Galicia; my mother Laura, née Gross, was born in 1889 in Stryi, a city south of Lviv (then Lemberg), and my father, Josef Rath, was brought into this world in Kolomyia near Czernowitz, on the border between Galicia and Bukovina. Back then, both Stryi and Kolomyia were part of the Habsburg monarchy; today, they are in Ukraine.

Despite decades of communist rule, the Austrian origins of the cities of Lviv and Czernowitz are still easily recognizable. When I visited Lviv for the first time in September 2008, to search for the lost world of my parents, I was reminded very much of Vienna. Old-fashioned street cars drive through cobblestone streets, many historic city palaces are still standing, and here and there a few traditional coffee houses have reopened.

When the First World War broke out, my father enlisted in the Austrian military. He had just graduated from a German-language Gymnasium in Kolomyia and earned his Matura, the qualification for a university education. Because of his slender and rather delicate physique, he was given a civil servant position at the Ministry of War in Vienna. I do not know why my mother left Stryi for Vienna. My parents' families had been acquainted in Galicia, but my parents first got to know one another better during the First World War in Vienna, and they married after the end of the war. In November

1921, my brother Maximilian (Maxi) came into the world, and I was born a little more than three years later on January 6, 1925. Since that is Three Kings' Day, or Epiphany as it's called in Catholic Austria, my birthday was always a school holiday. According to the Jewish calendar, which follows the moon, my birthday was on the tenth of Tevet, a day of fasting for strictly religious Jews, as it is the day the Babylonian army breached the first city walls of Jerusalem.

When I was born, we lived in the eighth district on Piaristengasse 46, around the corner from the Theater in the Josefstadt. My brother claims he can remember our father coming home in a taxi with a small bundle in his arms, in which I was wrapped. A few months after my birth, we moved to Porzellangasse 50 in the ninth district, near the Franz Josef train station. My father and his brother Jakob Fried (although they shared the same parents, they had different surnames due to a mistake made by the Austrian municipal administration in Kolomyia) founded a wholesale paper company, Fried & Rath, at first housed in a small store in the city center. After a few years, they moved to larger premises across the street from the Ministry of War on Wiesingerstrasse. I remember playing in the freight elevator as a child, which was used to bring the huge rolls of paper from the street-level delivery trucks to the basement storerooms. As a reward for "helping" in the warehouse, I was allowed to go to the coffee house across the street and order myself a Linzer torte or a *Baiser mit Schlagobers*—meringue topped with whipped cream.

Business must have been good, since my father and uncle invested their profits in the late twenties and early thirties in Berlin, where they bought five multi-unit buildings that they rented out. But they fought often; my father was ten years younger than his brother, and was impatient by nature and sometimes quick to anger. Even as

Left: Ari 1929. Right: Ari with his father (left), Uncle Jakob (right), and governess 1931 on the Hermannskogel in the Vienna Woods.

a child, I was drawn to my kind Uncle "Jakub" and felt very close to him. The brothers' repeated fights led them to end their tenure as business partners, although the company kept both names, Fried & Rath, until the end, after the Anschluss in March 1938. From his share of the paper wholesaler profits, Jakob Fried bought a large fur tannery on Muthgasse in the 19th district. But Schlammerdinger, as the company was called, did not last long. In 1935, after Hitler had already come to power, Uncle Jakob, with his wife Bassia and their daughters Dolly and Lore, moved to Berlin to see after the family properties. He retained ownership of the house on Muthgasse until it was foreclosed by the Nazis in 1939. To this day, his family has not been able to regain ownership, even though they have all of the paperwork from the forced sale. For this reason we know that the house was bought by an architect named Pichler for 17.100 reichsmarks, plus a "de-Jewification" surcharge of 1800 reichsmarks, which was paid directly to the Gestapo. In Austria, the original Jewish owners or their rightful heirs only have a right to property that is owned by the municipal, state, or national government. The descendants of "Aryanizers" are still profiting from Nazi theft.

My first clear childhood memory is also one of the saddest moments of my life. During Passover, in April 1929, my mother died. Despite otherwise very good recall of my past, I have no memory of her and do not know what she looked like. The only photo that I have of her is from the bound black memorial album that the *chevra kadisha*, the Jewish burial society, gave to our family after her death. It must be one of the last pictures of my mother, since her face and neck are swollen, characteristic symptoms of Basedow's disease. The thyroid and cardiovascular disorders associated with the illness can lead to severe depression and could not be treated effectively at the time. I remember the fateful day very well. My seven-and-a-half-year-old brother Maxi and I, four and almost four months at the time, were in what was known as Beserl Park near Franz Josef train station with our governess while the family was preparing a celebratory midday dinner for our cousin Dolly's eighteenth birthday. Suddenly, our cook ran up to us all flustered and whispered something in our governess's ear. Both women began to cry, and then our governess took us by tram to our uncle Jakob's apartment on Kaiserstrasse in the 7th district, where we stayed for several weeks. My brother and I had no idea why we suddenly had to live with Uncle Jakob and his family. Not until forty years later, when Dolly visited Israel for the first time, did I learn about the dramatic events that made up the worst day of my life. Dolly had taken the tram to our house, and as soon as she stepped down she

Bothers Max (left) and Ari, 1929.

could see the ambulance and the many police officers blocking the entrance to our house. After insisting to be let in as a close relative of the Rath family, she learned the horrible truth. Shortly before the planned birthday meal, my mother Laura ran to the fourth floor and threw herself out of the window into the courtyard. She died on impact. We children were told that our mother had contracted pneumonia and was in the hospital, where we were not allowed to visit. My family lied to me for an entire year, something you should never do to a bright child, which I was.

One year later, on my mother's first yahrzeit, I was allowed to accompany the family to the unveiling of the gravestone in the Jewish cemetery at the fourth entrance to Vienna's Central Cemetery. It is an enormous graveyard, with thousands of Jewish tombstones, all of which have survived both Nazi rule and the war. I have never understood why the Nazis murdered millions of Jewish people but left Jewish cemeteries intact. My mother's original gravestone was a round white marble pillar, cut off diagonally in the middle to symbolize the early interruption of her life. During the final battles for the liberation of Vienna, this gravestone was damaged badly by cannons. My brother had it replaced by a simple, grey rectangular stone during his first post-war visit to Vienna in December 1947. I visit my mother's grave whenever I am in Vienna. I lay a small stone on her gravestone and place a potted flower on the grave. I have to buy the flower at the second gate, there is no flower shop at the entrance to the Jewish cemetery—too few people come to visit. I always bring my small black siddur with me to say the Kaddish, the traditional Hebrew and Aramaic mourner's prayer. It begins with the words *"Yitgadal v'yitkadash sh'mei raba"* (May his great name be blessed forever and to all eternity). In it, the Holy one is exalted in magnificent adjectives and extolled as "He who creates peace in His celestial heights, may He create peace for us and for all Israel." The Kaddish is a prayer praising God and not an expression of individual mourning. For that reason I always also recite "El Maleh Rachamim," the prayer recited to God of compassion, which names the person who has passed and asks that they be granted eternal rest in paradise.

My mother Laura's early death, the loss of the most important person in my life, made a deep mark on me, and has most certainly determined my relationships to women. Right after the burial, my maternal grandmother, Omama Frimtsche, moved in with us. She was a loving and generous woman, but she could not replace a mother's love. I was a child unable to say "Mama." For me, the word "mother" meant only a dark grave. Aside from Omama Frimtsche, I did not have a constant relationship with any woman, as our governesses were always changing. As soon as I had gotten used to one, she was sent away again. My somewhat spoiled brother, who hated all sports, complained incessantly to our father about being made to go mountain climbing or swimming during summer vacation, until my father caved and fired the offending governess. Impatient as my father was, he most likely simply wanted some peace and quiet, and by giving in hoped to not be bothered—until the next governess came along. My brother and I had at least seven different caretakers in seven years. Already as a child, I had to acquire the habit of not getting too close to women, since I was always afraid that they would soon leave me once again.

In the 1930s, we were a typical modern Central European Jewish family. My father had already completely assimilated Western European values and habits, even though he came from a family of distinguished rabbis. His ancestors included the wise Torah scholar Meshulam Rath, whom both our uncle the rabbi and also my brother Meshulam (Maximilian) had been named after. Before the Second World War, Rabbi Meshulam Rath, who was actually our father's cousin, lived in two small cities in Galicia and Bukovina, Chortkiv and Horoskov. He survived the war in Czernowitz, acting as a rabbi throughout. I remembered his daughter Surka from my childhood, she had visited us more than once in Vienna, and always brought a small gift for me when she came. In the summer of 1946, he and his family came to Palestine by train through Romania, Turkey, Syria, and Lebanon. Together with many of his Chassidic followers, wearing long black frock coats and broad-rimmed hats, I awaited my uncle's family at Rosh Hanikra, the border station between Lebanon and Palestine, excited to meet my relatives. I was the only man without any head covering in the crowd that had gathered to greet the respected rabbi upon his arrival in Eretz Israel. Although a long white beard filled up his small face, I immediately recognized the facial features of the Rath/Fried family. I accompanied my newfound uncle and his family on the short train journey to Haifa, their stop in Palestine.

While Rabbi Meshulam Rath was strictly Orthodox in terms of religion, his outlook on the world was progressive. He tried to adapt strict religious customs to modern realities. His pro-Zionist beliefs made him unwelcome within the ultraorthodox party Agudat Yisrael, which had a strong base in Poland at the time, and the party tried to block his rabbinical career. Nevertheless, in Jewish Palestine and later in Israel, he was often consulted for the answer to difficult Talmudic questions by Chief Rabbi Yitzhak Halevy Herzog, father of Israeli president Chaim Herzog. Rabbi Meshulam Rath's Halachic decisions have been collected in a large volume entitled *Kol Hamevaser* (The Voice of the Announcer). One of the rabbi's brothers, Moses Rath, who also left Kolomyia for Vienna during the First World War, wrote and published the first Hebrew-German textbook *Sfat Amenu* (The language of our people).

But Omama Frimtsche had the greater influence on our daily life in Vienna. It was she who taught us to observe the religious traditions. On Friday evenings, she lit the candles for Shabbat. Our father recited the kiddush, blessing the wine and the challah. And of course there was gefilte fish as an appetizer, and chicken soup with noodles. On Passover, my grandmother and our cook and housekeeper Mizzi, who was with us for many years, changed all of the dishes. The dishes and silverware for Passover were stored in the large sideboards in the pantry. Our everyday pots and pans were made kosher with boiling water. Our father strictly observed

Passover every year. As was custom in the Diaspora, we held two seders. Usually the whole Haggadah was read, telling the story of the Exodus of the children of Israel out of Egypt. As the youngest child, from the age of six I was responsible for singing the four questions—*ma-nishtana, haleilah hazeh, mikhol ha'lailot*— Why is this night different from all other nights? The second half of the seder, after the meal with two glasses of wine (or grape juice for the children), was less structured and usually dedicated to singing the traditional songs printed in the Haggadah.

On Friday evening and on the high holy days, we usually went to the Müllner temple on the corner of Grünentorgasse and Müllnergasse, which was burned down to the ground in 1938 on pogrom night. Rabbi Arthur Zacharias Schwarz presided over the congregation, the father-in-law of Teddy Kollek, who later became mayor of Jerusalem. The Müllner Temple was both Conservative and modern. On Friday evenings, the first part of Shabbat services, when the "Shabbat bride" is welcomed, was accompanied by an organ and a choir. The prayers were sung using the Ashkenazi pronunciation, unlike the Sephardic pronunciation that we use in modern spoken Hebrew. Omama Frimtsche, who was very pious, often prayed with my brother in the small *shil* (shul in her Yiddish dialect, a small house of prayer) on Stroheckgasse. She was so frum that she tied her house key to her arm with a handkerchief on Shabbat, so that all of her pockets remained empty. Who knows, otherwise she might have left some coins in her pocket and been tempted to go shopping. Of course, you are not supposed to carry anything on Shabbat.

Omama Frimtsche made sure our kitchen was strictly kosher. But outside of the house we often ate in regular coffee houses and restaurants, and we were also allowed to ride the tram on Shabbat. However, influenced by our grandmother, my brother Maxi had a year-long phase of being very observant, during which time he insisted on eating only kosher meat. When choosing a place for our *Sommerfrische*, the annual two-month summer vacation in the mountains, the most important criterion was whether and where we could buy kosher meat. I on the other hand was not worried about that at all and I often teased my brother, calling him "kosher Moishe."

From 1930 to '34 I went to a *Volksschule*, a public elementary school, on Grünentorgasse: the Schubert school, named after its best-known teacher, Franz Schubert. Since I was born in January, we had to ask the district board of education for permission for me to begin four months before my sixth birthday. Our class teacher during my four years of primary education was Marie Blesson. She worked with Pestalozzi methods and her patient and knowledgeable manner had a positive effect on all of the children she taught in those critical first years of schooling. She became a kind of mother ersatz for me. I was very surprised in 2006 to receive reports containing intimate details about my brother and myself from a radio journalist whose child had also gone to the Schubert school. She had found old questionnaires in the municipal archives in which our father and our class teacher Marie Blesson had charted our development for each of our four years at the school for the district board of education in Alsergrund. Initially, I was slightly appalled by the view these documents provided into my feelings and thoughts during my childhood years. Today, I hold them dear for two reasons. For one, they illustrate just how progressive Viennese elementary school education had been. Moreover, they show that many personality traits that I have always considered integral to my character were already present in my earliest childhood. For example, the questionnaires confirm that I have an "excellent memory." It also states that the child: "remembers what he has learned long-term, observes very closely, notices every detail, exhibits stamina, often contributes his own ideas, corrects his classmates, ... [and] is quick-witted." Marie Blesson saw in me a happy child, who however had a "hunger for love" and "reacted well to praise." On our home life after my mother's death she wrote:

"The child is quite spoiled by his grandmother, who, together with a 'Fräulein', has been in charge of his upbringing since the mother's death." Perhaps it was due to this grandmotherly indulgence that I was a fairly chubby child. To help me lose weight, two to three times per week the governess turned our bathtub into a hot and foul sulfur brew in which I had to stew for about half an hour—it had the desired effect.

Until the early 1930s, our family had no choice but to remain Polish citizens, since our parents were both born in the area of the Habsburg monarchy located in Polish Galicia. In the above-mentioned school questionnaire, for me, too, "Kolomea, Poland" was written in the column "national citizenship and right of domicile." Although my father had served in the Austro-Hungarian army in the First World War and had been stationed in Vienna, afterwards settling in the city, that did not make him eligible for Austrian citizenship in the First Republic. As a result, he had to pay very high school fees for us until we were able to become Austrian citizens in 1931.

I also remember the year 1931 for another reason. Every summer, we retreated for two months to Spital am Semmering, where our father rented a house near the train tracks. I loved counting the

With Omama Frimtsche (center) and governess in the Semmering mountains, 1930.

wagons of the freight trains that passed slowly through the mountains on their way from the Steiermark to Vienna and back, and I kept a tally of the longest trains. In the summer of 1931 our governess was Laura Korn. I was very fond of her, not least because she shared our late mother's first name. On the weekends, her friend Bruno Völkel often came to visit. Bruno was an avid hiker and together we would walk on Sundays to one of the nearby guest houses for a *Jause* or light meal. Even today, I can see Bruno clearly in my mind's eye with his frameless glasses—a rarity at the time—high hiking boots, short lederhosen, and long white or green knee socks.

On one of these Sundays, when my father had not joined us for the weekend, Bruno announced to my brother and me: "Today we will hike to Steinhaus for our *Jause*." The small village was about five kilometers away. This hike from Spital am Semmering to

Steinhaus made a huge impression on me. For the first time in my life, I walked from one place to another—and suddenly I understood the enormity of the freedom that human beings have: the freedom to stay or to go. Any time and any place. Weeks later, I was still excitedly telling my friends and relatives: "We walked from one place to another!" Up until then, I had known that you could ride from one place to another, and that to do so you were dependent on other people, or on some means of transportation: a train, a carriage, a car or a bus. Over the course of my life, I have enjoyed this freedom in full. As an adult, I have traveled thousands of kilometers alone in the car, free and self-directed.

Already as a child I was interested in politics. From the age of eight, I read the newspapers that father brought home: *Neue Freie Presse, Der Tag, Die Stunde,* and others. I can still see the headlines from January 1933: "Adolf Hitler—Chancellor of the German Reich." Even though I was supposed to be in bed by ten p.m. every day, I almost always listened to the French radio broadcaster Radio Strasbourg's 10:30 news in German, so I would know what "the West" was saying and what was really happening in the world and in Austria.

The civil war that erupted on February 12, 1934 is one of my more dramatic memories. Soon after school began, Marie Blesson sent her students home again, since there was neither electricity nor heat due to the general strike. That same morning, the Home Guard and the military were already marching down Porzellangasse towards Franz Josef Railway Terminal and Heiligenstadt with horse-drawn cannons. I will never forget how badly the *Gemeindebauten*, the social housing complexes, were damaged, for example the Karl Marx Hof. Like many Jewish families, who were not accepted as members

Schubertschule on Grünentorgasse, Vienna IX; Ari outer left.

of the conservative Christian Social Party, our family supported the Social Democrats. Widespread antisemitic propaganda claimed that Viennese Jews at the time were all from patrician families, but the opposite was true: small merchants, civil servants, tradespeople, and proletarians made up the largest segment of the Jewish population by far.

After completing my four years of elementary school in September 1934, I followed in Maxi's footsteps and started at Wasa Gymnasium, a humanist federal gymnasium, or university-track secondary school, on Wasagasse in the ninth district. By summer 1938, I had finished all four grades of the lower level and had four years of Latin and two years of Greek behind me. Only nine years and eight months old when I started, I was again the youngest student in my class, which did not cause me any concern. I was however bothered all the more by my first encounter with Austria's antisemitic school policy. I was placed into class 1B, the "Jew class," while 1A was the "Christian class." The formal reason given for this split, which existed for the first time in my year, was that all students went to the same religion class. The other—albeit unofficial—justification was that the "Christian class" could learn better without the often "impertinent" Jewish students. In fact, the split was the result of a directive issued on July 4, 1934 by Kurt von Schuschnigg, at the time Minister of Education. (Three weeks later, after the attempted Nazi putsch and the assassination of Engelbert Dollfuss on July 25, Schuschnigg became Federal Chancellor.) The directive stated that in all gymnasiums and teachers' colleges with enough students for more than one track, an A class for Catholics should be instated and a B class for all other students. De facto, it was only the Jewish students who ended up in the B class, the Wasa Gymnasium's few Protestant students were put into the "Christian class." This decree, which reveals much about everyday antisemitism in Austria before the Anschluss and the instatement of the National Socialists in government in March 1938, remains one of many topics repressed in Austrian society today. Even well-meaning Austrians with a liberal outlook are shocked to hear that there were already separate "Jew classes" four years before the Anschluss. Renate Mercsanits, one of the teachers at Wasa Gymnasium, has researched this episode of Austrian school history. Thanks to her, the relevant files and directives are now in the school's archives, open to anyone with an interest in the subject.

Since March 2006, a plaque in the stately main entrance of the school lists the names of all former Jewish students and teachers who were driven out in 1938. The name of our beloved German professor, Otto Spranger, is also on this plaque. He himself was not Jewish, but he refused to leave his Jewish wife and therefore had to resign. Spranger fled on skis over the Alps to Switzerland and from there to New York, where he was joined by his wife. After comprehensive training, he worked in the United States for many years as a psychotherapist. Meshulam and I met him again in New York in 1947. All three of us found it hard to believe that it had only been nine years since our paths had diverged under such sad and dramatic conditions. But our leitmotif was the wonderful feeling of having survived. Around twenty former "Wasagassler"—those survivors still able to travel—met to celebrate the unveiling of the plaque in March 2006. I had been given the difficult task of holding a speech in the name of all former Jewish students. In it, I compared us to tiny seedlings, transplanted from their beds into foreign soil.

We observed the attempted Nazi putsch in 1934 from afar, being, as always, on summer holidays with our governess, again on the Semmering at Villa Mary, which belonged to the Südbahn hotel. The assassination of Dollfuss along with the seeming likeability of the new Federal Chancellor, Kurt von Schuschnigg, led many Jewish families in Vienna to feel more loyal to their "fatherland."

On May 1, 1935, all of Vienna's middle school children, including the "Jew classes" had to attend a huge solidarity rally in the large stadium in the Prater. For weeks, every class practiced the new "Dollfuss song" and on the day the stadium was filled with the sound of thousands of voices: "Youth, close your ranks well / a dead man leads us / He gave his blood for Austria / a true German man / The murderer's bullet that hit him / awakened the People out of discord and sleep / We youth stand ready! / With Dollfuss in the new era!" Simultaneous demonstrations were held by the varying "corps" of

Austria's new corporative state—in lieu of the traditional Socialist Party May Day demonstrations, which had been banned in 1933.

On a bleak fall night in November 1935, our whole family gathered in the old classical building of Vienna South Station to say goodbye to Uncle Chaskel, Aunt Adele, Omama Frimtsche, and our cousins Mira and Lalla. They had decided to immigrate to Palestine, joined by Adele's brother. Even back then, the night trains "Remus" or "Romulus" went from Vienna to Rome via Bologna every evening at nine p.m., with through coaches to Venice and Trieste. It was a sad goodbye, as I did not know when or whether we would see each other again. At the time, Palestine seemed very far away and foreign to me. Furthermore, the atmosphere between my father and Uncle Chaskel was extremely tense—they parted in the middle of a serious fight, and they would never make up again. Chaskel had at first not wanted to take his mother with him to Palestine. My father was about to become engaged to Rita Liebermann, and although Omama Frimtsche knew Rita and got along well with her, my father preferred to found his new family without his former wife's mother.

Ten months after arriving in Tel Aviv, Uncle Chaskel took his own life on Erev Yom Kippur. (If I were not so happy-go-lucky, I would have to worry about myself; there have been many suicides on my mother's side of the family, spanning three generations. My cousin Mira was found dead in her Ramat Gan apartment in the early 1980s, some years later, her daughter Dina also took her own life.) After Chaskel's tragic end, our father organized Omama Frimtsche's immediate return to Vienna. He did not want her left to face her daughter-in-law Adele and the entire Friedberg family on her own. However Omama Frimtsche did not move back in with us in the fall of 1936, but into a room in the apartment of my grandmother on my father's side. Omama Malcia lived in a Biedermeier house on Kochgasse in the ninth district. There, the two spoiled us with wonderful tortes and other sweets.

In the meantime, there had been important changes to the family on Porzellangasse. After my mother's death, my father entered a close relationship with his clerk, Maria Hauer. I liked her, since she spoiled me and also often took me to soccer games at Prater Stadium. My father wanted to marry Maria, and she was more than willing to convert to Judaism for him. My cousin Surka had already convinced her father the rabbi, Uncle Meshulam Rath, to preside over the conversion and perform the wedding. But Maxi did not play along. He made such a fuss that it became impossible for Maria to marry into our family. My brother's absolute rejection found its apex in November 1934, when he refused to invite her to his bar mitzvah. Maxi did finally relent after dramatic scenes with Papa, but Maria chose not to come. In the summer of 1935, my father resigned himself to his fate and accepted that he would have to relinquish Maria if he did not want to completely ruin his relationship with his oldest son. Yet he still wanted to share his life with a woman. After his weekly visit to our summer abode—that year a house annexed to the Schloss hotel in Velden on Lake Worth—he went to Lake Millstatt for a week with friends from Café Viktoria near Schottentor. That circle included Maria and also Rita Liebermann. A few weeks after our summer vacation, Rita visited us on Porzellangasse for the first time. She and my father were alone in the living room for some time, and I spied on them through the keyhole of our bedroom door. Horrified, I saw them hugging and kissing. I realized at that moment, to my great regret, that it was over between Maria and my father. In November, after Omama Frimtsche had left for Palestine, there was a celebratory meal in the dining room—which was usually reserved for holidays, aside from our daily practice on the Bechstein grand piano. Uncle Jakob, Aunt Bassia, Dolly, Lore, and a few close friends of the family all sat around the large round festive table, raised their glasses, and drank *Brüderschaft* with Rita, sealing their friendship. That was the quasi-official engagement. *Brüderschaft* entails switching to the familiar address *"du,"* and everyone was reveling in their newfound intimacy. Only I was loathe to join; my heart still beat for Maria. I had been given the task of offering our guests petit fours on a silver tablet, and each time I asked quite naturally "What would you like?" using the familiar form of "you." But when it was Rita's turn, I did not want to use *"du,"* nor did I want to offend her by using the formal *"Sie."* I decided to address her in the third person instead: "What is one's preference here?" That broke the ice: everyone laughed, Rita hugged me, and from that moment on, we were all *per du.*

On March 6, 1936, our father married Rita (Henriette) Liebermann. She was 31 years old and, like our mother, came from Galicia, more exactly from Sambor (now Sambir), a small city about fifty kilometers northwest of Stryi. Rita became my second mother, she was kind and understanding. When we were in trouble with Papa, she stood up for us. The couple married with only the legally required witnesses present. My brother and I waited to congratulate the newlyweds at the Air France office on the Ring, from whence we left for the airport. On the very same day they flew, then an upscale means of traveling, to Genoa for the start of a trip through the Mediterranean. Father and Rita decided to forgo a visit to Egypt and instead stay for a few days in Palestine, in Haifa, where Rita's two-years-older sister Tamara, a staunch pioneer, had been living for over a year. They traveled a bit through the country with Tamara and also visited Omama Frimtsche. Palestine was more modern and interesting than they had expected, but they did not want to ever live there. They held fast to this opinion even after our good life collapsed with the Anschluss in March 1938. In March 1936, my father, who did occasionally donate to Zionist causes, refused to buy a piece of land in Tel Aviv as a symbolic sign of support, even though it was in the city center and the price was more than reasonable. Just a few years later, that would have turned out to have been an exceptionally good investment in our future.

Our parents brought back a Passover Haggadah from Palestine for my brother and I, in which Omama Frimtsche expressed the wish that her grandchildren Ari and Maxi might one day live in Eretz Israel. The inscription held little meaning for me. In general, I was still uninterested in Zionism. Alongside our piano lessons, we also had Hebrew lessons at home, but mostly just as preparation for our bar mitzvahs. At the time, nobody in our immediate family was considering leaving the country. Despite the many worrying events, our dreams and plans for the future all centered around Vienna. We felt like born-and-bred citizens of the city, even if Jews who had lived there longer and were more assimilated sometimes referred to us derogatorily as "Polish Jews." I was a devoted fan of FC Austria, not of the Jewish soccer team Hakoah, and Matthias Sindelar, the famous center-forward, was one of my revered heroes. In those days, I was more interested in the question of how I could continue to secretly play bridge with three of my schoolmates, one of whom, Eduard (Edi) Stern, was the son of the then European master in bridge, or in how to sneak into adult-rated movies, or in where we were going for our next summer vacation.

Shortly after returning from his honeymoon, my father bought a car—a used American-made model from Nash Motors. It was just an old black rattletrap and in fact pretty ugly, but I was very proud of it. Right from the start, I got along splendidly with our chauffeur, Alfred. Alfred was skinny and always in a good mood. With his thin mustache, glasses, and driving cap, for almost two years he was an important person in our lives. On the weekends and during summer vacation we took long car trips, getting to know many beautiful areas along the Danube and near Semmering. My brother and I usually sat on small stools in the well in front of the comfortable back seat. One of Alfred's most important tasks was to see that my brother and I, both chronic late risers, were on time for school at Wasa Gymnasium, less than a kilometer from our house. Of course we were mortified to be brought to school by car and with a driver, and told him to let us out on Türkenstrasse. Usually we snuck into our classes just before eight, but often we were late anyway, leading our math teacher, Josef Sabbath, who was later murdered in Theresienstadt, to comment sarcastically: *"Kommt Zeit, kommt Rath,"* a play on the German expression meaning "when the time comes, counsel (*Rat*) will come with it."

Just around this time, my father and Rita began thinking about moving from Porzellangasse to a beautiful villa in the northwest of the city, in the Cottage District in Döbling. Max graduated from the Elmayer Dance School in the fall of 1937, and I very much hoped that in a few years I too would attend that prestigious Viennese institution near the Hofburg.

But first, in December 1937, I celebrated my bar mitzvah. My best present was a week in Berlin during Christmas vacation to visit my cousins Dolly and Lore and my Uncle Jakob and Aunt Bassia.

I traveled via Prague and Dresden all alone on the night train, carrying an almost empty suitcase and wearing my oldest and smallest suit, since I was to buy everything I needed in Berlin. My father and uncle earned well from the rental income from the five houses they owned in Berlin, but because foreign exchange was restricted by the Nazis, no funds could be transferred to Austria. My parents therefore went on shopping trips to Germany three to four times a year. Now it was my turn. Dolly and Lore, at the time 27 and 23 years old, both stylish young women with many suitors, accompanied me to the enormous Tietz Department Store on my very first day. The first thing I bought myself was a small Tengo camera, which I used when no one was looking to take snapshots of the display cases with the Nazi newspaper *Der Stürmer*, the signs that read "Entry Forbidden to Jews," and the "Jew benches" scattered across the city. I wanted to prove to my physical education teacher Franz Stefan, known to be a Nazi even then, that these signs of active antisemitism in Hitler's Germany were not just Western atrocity propaganda, as was often claimed. I waited until I was back in Vienna to develop the film and proudly brought the photos to class. Professor Stefan looked at the images of Berlin and had to admit that they pictured reality.

On December 31, 1937, I celebrated my first New Year's Eve with my relatives in their large apartment on Meinekestrasse in the district of Charlottenburg. There was a lively dance party attended by many of Dolly and Lore's young friends. During the huge fireworks display at midnight, some of the young women hugged and kissed me in the dimly-lit dancing room. In retrospect, I can hardly believe how carefree the celebrations in Berlin were back then, even in the Jewish milieu, although Hitler had already been in power for five years and the catastrophe was at our doorstep.

Leaving Austria

In February 1938, the entire "Jew class" 4B, led by our PE teacher Franz Stefan, was included on a week-long ski trip in the High Tauern. I was a good skier at the time, and won a bronze medal for the lower level, making Professor Stefan very proud.

Already, swastika flags flew from many of the area's farmhouses. The shadows of future events were already looming. On February 12, Adolf Hitler invited Federal Chancellor Schuschnigg to Berchtesgaden. In the presence of Wehrmacht generals, he forced the Austrian chancellor to appoint Austrian Nazi leader Arthur Seyss-Inquart as Minister of the Interior and Security. Later, Seyss-Inquart was sentenced to death at the Nuremberg Trials for his crimes against humanity as Reich Commissioner in the Netherlands. On March 9, Chancellor Schuschnigg unexpectedly announced a referendum for Sunday March 13, planned to underline Austria's independence in the face of the threat of *Anschluss* or unification with Nazi Germany. On the same day, he rescinded the ban of the Social Democratic Party that had been instated four years earlier. The knowledge that the labor movement would be supporting Schuschnigg in his fight against the Anschluss and for Austria's independence allowed hopes to flare.

On Friday March 11, the struggle for power reached its peak. On the way to Wasa Gymnasium, on almost every corner Nazi functionaries in high boots and swastika armbands (already legal) faced off against supporters of the newly-legalized Socialist Party sporting their now legal triple-arrow insignia. At the student lodging on the corner of Porzellangasse and Grünentorgasse there had already been fist fights. Both sides were avid in their propaganda for and against the Anschluss. All of a sudden, members of the "Fatherland Front" Home Guard and of the former Social Democratic *Schutzbund* (protective force) had become allies, because the National Socialist saw these two former arch enemies as a common adversary. Very few people knew that during those very hours, Schuschnigg was being forced to bow to pressure from Hitler and had postponed the referendum indefinitely.

During the ten a.m. break, I suggested to my two best friends, Herbert Steiner and Pauli Singer, that we cut the rest of our classes and join the "Fatherland Front" in the city center to distribute leaflets against the Anschluss. I hadn't noticed that our class and Latin teacher Hans Pollak, one of very few Jewish teachers at Wasa Gymnasium, had been standing behind me the whole time and had heard everything. Without hesitation and to my horror, he decreed a harsh punishment: I was be locked in the small room in the library for the next two hours. And in fact, in my report cards for the semester and for my last year of school in Vienna, there is a note by Pollak that fills me with a certain pride: "Arnold Rath—two hours in the detention room for infraction of discipline." Herbert, Pauli, and I were forced to postpone our plans for two hours. We then went to the city center, picked up flyers from the "Fatherland Front" and distributed them to passersby. Shortly after six p.m., we hurried home. At six-thirty, a former trade union leader who had fled to Prague after the events of February 1934 was supposed to hold a speech on Radio Vienna in favor of an independent Austria. I sat with my brother, my step-uncle Josi Liebermann, and our housekeeper in the kids' room, waiting impatiently in front of the radio, but in place of the expected speech, only marches were playing. Around seven-thirty, Chancellor Schuschnigg came on the air. With a slightly faltering voice, he read out his forced resignation: "And so I take my leave from the Austrian people at this hour with a German word and heartfelt wish: God save Austria." Tears came to my eyes. Right after him, the newly-appointed Federal Chancellor Arthur Seyss-Inquart spoke. He called on his fellow countrymen to give a friendly welcome to the German troops, who marched into Austria that night. Soon after, for the first time, Radio Vienna played the Horst Wessel Song, the unofficial anthem of the Nazi party.

Not much later, my father managed to place a call from Berlin. Rita and he had been on one of their shopping trips, where they learned of the dramatic events. They had planned to return on Saturday so that they could vote in the plebiscite, but that had been impossible as the borders had been closed. As the last person in the family, I was allowed to talk to Papa for a short time. I proposed that they wait in Prague to see how the situation developed. But of course they came back at the first opportunity a few days later so that they could be with us, their children.

Saturday morning, Maxi and I went to visit our grandmothers in the Kochgasse. Huge swastika flags were flying from all public buildings, and also from many private houses and apartments. The stately building that housed the tobacco company Tabakregie, was covered in enormous banners, and Aida, our beloved pastry shop across the street from Porzellangasse 50, where I had so often gotten delicious leftover slices of torte for only a fraction of my allowance money, was no exception. We were particularly shocked that on that Saturday morning, all officers of the Vienna police force were already wearing swastika armbands. Very soon we saw young and old Jews kneeling in the streets, forced to scrub off election slogans against the Anschluss with a toothbrush, while the citizens of Vienna stood around and physically and verbally abused them.

On March 22, classes resumed. Our Jewish teachers did not return to school. Otto Spranger, our German teacher, entered the classroom and apologized for having to wear a swastika armband. The Board of Education of Vienna had declared the Wasa Gymnasium one of the "collection point schools" for Jewish students. In April, we were moved to Kalvarienberggasse in the seventeenth district, because the NSDAP wanted our large school building, conveniently located across from the Votive Church, for their party headquarters. Some interesting new additions swelled the ranks of the "Jew class." Jewish schoolchildren from other gymnasiums joined our group of 27 students "of Mosaic faith," because their schools had been made *judenrein* or cleansed of Jews. A few Christian students from "mixed marriages" also joined the class, as they were considered "half-Jews" under the Nuremberg Laws. For that reason, in June 1938, some Christian students also received their final report cards from Class 4B. On the fiftieth anniversary of the Anschluss, in March 1988, Counselor Gump, the former director of Wasa Gymnasium, grasped at this detail in an attempt to prove to me that there hadn't actually been separate "Jew classes." He had come to a lecture that I was giving in Vienna as a witness to that occasion, carrying two thick binders under his arm containing all report cards from 1938. Triumphantly, he presented the final evaluations to me. But the report cards from the first semester, when there had been only 27 students of Mosaic faith, were convincing proof of his error.

At home too there had been grave changes. Our faithful cook Mizzi, who had lived with us for many years like a member of the family, and Anni, the nursemaid for my little half-sister Henny, born in 1937, soon had to leave us: Christians could no longer be employed in a Jewish household. In their stead came Berta, a Jewish civil servant who had lost her job and now had to accustom herself to doing household work. Berta and I were often home alone, especially after our father was arrested in early May. Every evening I sat next to the radio, trying to tune into news from abroad. Berta sat next to me with her knitting and began to slowly stroke my thigh. After a while of this, she asked for a good-night kiss as well. I innocently brushed my lips on her cheek, but she insisted upon a French kiss. This scene repeated itself more and more often and one day, when she was sure she would be alone with me at home for a longer period of time, she beckoned me into her small servant's room. And so I lost my virginity at the age of thirteen-and-a-half. A real relationship began to develop between us, which lasted several weeks to my increasing enjoyment, until Berta left because she was able to emigrate. In retrospect, this formative experience seems like a story from *La Ronde* by Arthur Schnitzler. But I now also see it as early preparation for my life as an adult, one that made it easier for me to adapt to life in Palestine with a mixed group of girls and boys. I have often thought that my close relationships to the girls in our group was an ersatz for the lack of warmth and love from a mother and from my family.

Soon after the Anschluss, my father sat Maxi and I down for a serious conversation and explained that although we would have to change our plans for the future and would not be moving to the

Cottage, in general there was no reason for immediate worry. He reminded me that I had seen how it had been in Berlin that winter, how life went on without significant restrictions although the Nazis had been in power there since 1933. Nobody had an inkling that the dramatic meeting of deep-seated Austrian antisemitism and political German National Socialism would hasten and greatly intensify the persecution of the Jews.

In the very first days of the Anschluss, it became clear that the Jewish population of Vienna would be facing extreme changes. Only very few Jewish families fled immediately, like our friends the Goldbergers, who paid a large amount to cross the Czech border by car in the confusion of the first days. Even fewer of these refugees were able, like the Goldbergers, to later flee to America. During those early days, not far from our apartment, Maxi was made to join a *Reibpartie*, a "rubbing match," as it was generally called when Jews were forced to scrub the streets. Luckily, our blonde nursemaid Anni, who was still with us at the time, was able to quickly free him. A few days later, when our driver Alfred wanted to pick up the car as usual to bring our father to his office on Stubenring, the young man from the garage across the street stopped him and demanded the car key. "The car belongs to us" he said emphatically, as Alfred recounted afterwards. Like thousands of other Viennese residents who unscrupulously emptied out the apartments of their Jewish neighbors, stealing furniture and valuables, the man working at the garage wanted, on his own initiative, to requisition our car for himself. But the formal "Aryanization" of Jewish businesses, which was conducted systematically, put an end to his plans. SA Sturmführer Boris Zeilinger, who in the meantime had been instated as Nazi commissioner for the paper wholesaler Fried & Rath, immediately noticed that a Nash car was listed in the inventory. Without delay, he revoked the illegal expropriation and in the following weeks, Mr. Zeilinger drove by our home each day himself to pick up our father and drive with him to the warehouse. Alfred was employed in the office and for Maxi and I, our life of ease in 1930s Vienna had come to an end.

Even if my parents had no thoughts of leaving the country and my brother and I had been indifferent to the Zionist project up to that point, under the circumstances, we now began to take an interest. Instinctively, we only wanted to move to a country from which we would never again be forced out. At that time, the term "Palestine" was synonymous with Zionism, and the Palestine Office on Marc Aurel Strasse was the main hub of Zionist immigration. All at once, the words Omama Frimtsche had written two years earlier acquired a very different sound. Her fervent wish that Maxi and I might one day live in Eretz Israel suddenly began to take the shape of a real plan for the future. Our shock at the Austrian population's incredible enthusiasm for Hitler and the "new era" had destroyed any foundation for continuing to live in Vienna.

The first practical step in this new stage of our lives was to join the Zionist youth movement Makkabi Hatzair (Young Maccabees). Earlier, acquaintances had tried to recruit me for the revisionist youth movement Betar (named after a stronghold in Palestine), which conducted its marching exercises in a club across from the Heimat movie theater on Porzellangasse. But I was put off by the military style—their blue and brown uniforms and epaulets—even if it was in Zionist form. Unlike us, our father took a long time getting used to the Zionist idea. One day, Maxi came home with an illustrated brochure for Mikveh Israel, the well-known agricultural school near Tel Aviv. He wanted to apply to study there in order to gain an entry permit for Palestine. Papa was silent as he looked through the pamphlet. Then, with tears in his eyes, he said: "My son will not be transporting manure." He had no way of knowing that his younger son would later spend five years working in a cowshed.

At the beginning of May, the police arrested three thousand Jewish businessmen, including my father. At six-thirty in the morning there was a loud knocking on the door to our apartment: "Police! Open up!" The kids' bedroom was across from the entry to our apartment. My brother and I jumped up in our nightshirts and looked fearfully through the peephole in the front door. Two men in civilian clothes were standing in the hallway. Carefully, we opened the door only as wide as the chain allowed. To our horror, they said that they wanted to take our father with them. We ran into Papa and Rita's bedroom at the back of the apartment and told him he had to get dressed right away because the police were there to pick him up. My father remained incredibly calm and collected. He quietly got dressed, signed a few blank checks for Rita, assured us that he would soon be back, said good-bye, and left with the two policemen. I would not see him again until December 1946 in New York.

The very next day, Rita and Maxi went looking for my father. They found him in a school on Karajangasse in the twentieth district. The arrested men had been brought there because the jails were completely overfilled. They could see him at the window from the street. When I went myself one day later, the school was empty. Later, the Gestapo turned the building into a collection point for transports to Auschwitz and Theresienstadt. Word went around that it was possible to get news about the fate of the prisoners at the Gestapo headquarters in Hotel Metropol. When the wives of those arrested were told with typical German correctness that their husbands were all in Dachau, everyone at first thought that it could not possibly be true. But some weeks later, the proof was lying in our mailbox in the form of a small blue letter. My father had sent us a sign of life on July 16, 1938. He did not write a single personal message on the few numbered lines, but simply authorized Rita to send in a declaration of property in his name "within the prescribed time limit." The Gestapo had ordered all Jews to provide such lists, we were no longer allowed to own property. As soon as our father was arrested, SA Sturmführer Boris Zeilinger, whom I have already mentioned, took over both the paper wholesaler Fried & Rath as well as our houses in Berlin.

Rita did everything she could to get our father released from Dachau, and later from Buchenwald, and she made arrangements for the entire family to leave the country. Distant relatives in the United States had promised us an affidavit. We also had acquired permission to enter Cuba, so that we could wait there for the American quota for Polish immigrants to open. Maxi and I had children's permits for a Kindertransport to England, but we were both adamant that we would immigrate only to Palestine. Paradoxically, we were probably only able to make this choice because our father was imprisoned in Dachau. Otherwise he would have surely insisted that we wait and flee together as a family. But from Dachau, my father signed permission for his two underage sons to leave for Palestine, certified by a notary public. German law and order were paramount, even in the concentration camps.

We then began the process of jumping through hoops trying to acquire valid German passports. All requests went through the district police headquarter in charge, and had to be accompanied by various official certificates. For each of these, you had to wait on a separate line at a different office: the Revenue Office, the Reich Emigration Tax Office, The Public Health Department, the District and Municipal Boards of Education, etc. To simplify this complicated bureaucratic process, in August an "Office for Jewish Emigration" was opened in Rothschild Palace on Prinz Eugen Strasse, across from the Belvedere. If you got in line in the evening, the next morning you could be processed and receive a valid passport stamped with a red "J" for "Jew." The Germans had added this stamp at the request of the Swiss authorities, who wanted to be able to easily spot Jewish immigrants. My shrewd brother, who would only turn seventeen in November 1938, had in the meantime acquired identification as a Zionist functionary of Keren Kayemet, the Jewish National Fund. This allowed us to skip the long lines for the Emigration Office. The office was an ingenious invention: a long row of tables had been set up in a large hall. At each one sat a civil servant from each of the various municipal offices, who certified our exit visas, stamping them as if on an assembly line. At the end of this procedure, we had to present our German passport and all of our papers for a final certification by an SS officer. That officer was none other than Adolf Eichmann, whose first responsibility consisted of getting as many Jews out of Vienna and the "Eastern March" as quickly as possible. To fulfill this task, Eichmann even cooperated with Ehud Überall, a key functionary at the Palestine Office on Marc Aurel Strasse. Together, they organized illegal ships to transport people down the Donau and across the Black Sea to Palestine. Ehud Überall, a close friend of Teddy Kollek and one of David Ben-Gurion's coworkers, became well-known in 1948 under his Hebrew name Avriel as the first Israeli Ambassador to Prague.

Before that, with the approval of the Soviet Union, he had organized the transport of weapons from Czechoslovakia to Jewish Palestine. As a result of the expedited emigration of Austrian Jews organized by Eichmann, out of all countries under Nazi occupation, Austria had the largest percentage of Jews who survived the Shoah. Of the 195,000 Jews living in Austria in March 1938—180,000 in Vienna alone or ten percent of the capital's residents—130,000 got out in time, even in 1940 after the start of the Second World War. One-third or 65,000 died in the camps.

Maxi was able to procure a Youth Aliyah Certificate for Palestine, where he would join a group from Vienna on Kibbutz Gvat near Haifa. I was one of the first group of fifty Jewish children from Vienna, Graz, Linz, and Wiener Neustadt to be chosen from over one thousand candidates for emigration. In September, as part of a multi-step selection process, I was sent with two hundred children for four weeks to a preparatory seminar in a school on Schiffamtsgasse in the 2nd district. It was a difficult group to be in, for we were in bitter competition. We all knew that only one in four participants would be chosen to go to Palestine. Sinai Ucko, a teacher from the Ahava School near Haifa and Aron Menczer, a leader of the Jewish youth movement Gordoniah in Vienna, made the selection. Menczer was popular with all of the children, who were very attached to him. He received permission from the Gestapo to accompany the first group to Trieste, with the condition that he return immediately to his children in the Gordoniah. Menczer kept his promise and returned to Vienna. Later, he was even allowed one time to accompany a group of young people all the way to Palestine, where in the meantime his brother was living. Nevertheless, he returned again to his children. In 1942, he was deported to Theresienstadt and was in the end murdered in Auschwitz together with a group of Jewish orphans from Poland. Aron Menczer was the Austrian Janusz Korczak.

I have very clear memories of the last part of the preparatory seminar. We had to write an essay explaining why we wanted to go to Palestine, to Eretz Israel. I did not decline to mention that I already had good chances of getting a children's visa to England and that my family was waiting for an affidavit from America, but that I was determined to immigrate only to Palestine, the country from which I could not be driven out again. The next day I was called in to see Aron Menczer and Sinai Ucko. Accusingly they asked me: "With such good chances of leaving Nazi Vienna, why are you claiming a spot on a boat to Palestine at the cost of children who have no other option to get out of here?" I answered in a firm voice: "That's my truth. Do you want me to lie in my essay? I'm going from here to Palestine, whether you take me with you or not." Perhaps they were won over by my determination, perhaps they felt sorry for me because my father was in a concentration camp. Whatever the reason, I was one of the fifty lucky ones who were later chosen for the journey.

I have already told the story what happened on October 31, 1938, the day I barely escaped arrest and deportation to forced labor. The next day, I turned my back on Vienna for many years to come. On the way to the train at Vienna South Terminal, we made a stop on Kochgasse to say goodbye to both of our grandmothers. Omama Frimtsche gave us food for the journey. She was overjoyed to know that her grandsons were now leaving for Palestine after all.

The Ahava Youth Home

The long nighttime journey to Trieste was difficult and sad. Although we were relieved to have gotten out of Nazi Vienna, many of us must have suspected that we had perhaps just seen our parents and relatives for the last time. I stood for a long time at the window with tears in my eyes, staring into the night and holding the hand of Eva Weiner, the only one of our Beserl Park clique who had been able to flee with me to Palestine at the time. Fearfully, we rode towards our uncertain future.

In Trieste, we boarded the *MS Galilea*, an Italian passenger ship that carried almost only Jewish immigrants from Austria. We had our first shock even before the ship left the dock. From the moment we boarded, all fifty of us were regarded as a collective and we were all treated the same, no matter our background. First, Mrs. Stoessel, who had accompanied us from Vienna, collected any money our parents had given us for the trip. We even had to relinquish the prepaid international reply envelopes that we had packed just in case we needed them, supposedly so that they could be fairly distributed. To add insult to injury, they even took away the candies that many of us had received as going away presents. The only thing I was allowed to keep was the aluminum pot of apricot jam and the honey cake that Omama Frimtsche had given me for the journey.

Soon however, the mood on the ship improved. One of the

boys in our group played the accordion; we sat on the deck, sang the Hebrew songs we had just learned and danced the hora. I spent a lot of time with my brother Maxi, who had arrived in Trieste a day before us, to help the many hundreds of immigrants traveling to Haifa with us with formalities. The meals in the rather elegant dining hall and the friendly service of the Italian waiter reminded me of visits to hotels and restaurants during our annual summer vacations. We repressed the thought that these were our last days in the lap of luxury. Soon we would land in the completely unknown and foreign country of Palestine.

Among the many immigrants on board was a certain Mrs. Menczel from Linz, who was traveling with bulldogs that she bred as watchdogs. Later she would become a well-known dog breeder in Palestine, even though for many years she barely spoke Hebrew. I also remember seeking out the company of girls on the boat. That was fairly precocious for the times. I think it was due to the fact that I had had to leave my home and family from one day to the next, and I was looking for warmth and intimacy.

From aboard the *Galilea*, I wrote a goodbye letter to my Beserl Park friends: "But despite everything, I can't imagine that it's really true now, that I won't see you all ever again (at least not most of you), that a new life is really about to begin for me and that with every minute I'm moving further away from my old life and so from everything that I truly loved. But there's one thing that gives us strength: knowing that we're traveling to Eretz and that we can do something for our people. You were all so nice and so dear ... I'm writing in the smoking room, there's a Wagner concert on now. It's also sunset. It is indescribable."

Shortly before our arrival in Haifa on November 8, the ship's bulletin reported that the German Legation secretary at the Paris embassy, Ernst Eduard vom Rath, had been shot by the Jewish refugee Herschel Grynszpan. Grynszpan killed him in protest of the *Polenaktion*, the Nazi deportation of all 15,000 Jews of Polish descent who had been living in Germany to the Polish border. These people waited for weeks outdoors under miserable conditions because the Polish government did not allow them to enter. Among them were Grynszpan's parents and siblings. His desperate act was used by the Nazi leadership as justification for the Pogrom Night on November 9, 1938, in which almost all of the synagogues in Germany and Austria were burned down or otherwise destroyed. With hitherto unknown brutality, Hitler's minions persecuted and murdered Jewish citizens and demolished their property. The broken shards of glass that covered so many streets across the Reich glittered in the light, giving these pogroms the harmless sounding nickname "Kristallnacht." Afterwards, in a perverse reversal of culpability, the National Socialists sentenced the Jewish population to a collective fine of one billion reichsmarks for the damage.

I immediately worried that Grynszpan's attack would have disastrous consequences for my father, who was still imprisoned in the concentration camp and who unfortunately had the same last name as the murdered diplomat. Eight years later, when I met up with my parents again, my father told me what had happened at the time. As revenge that he, a Jew, still lived to carry the name Rath, the SS guards beat him and put him in solitary confinement. The torture resulted in severe spinal injuries that would later leave him unable to move without a wheelchair for much of his life.

During my first post-war visit to Vienna in October 1948, I learned that the Müllner Temple, where I had celebrated my bar mitzvah in December 1937, had been completely destroyed on November 9. Our rabbi, Zacharias Schwarz, Teddy Kollek's stepfather, was beaten, his skull fractured. Teddy Kollek managed to take Schwarz with him from Vienna to Palestine in the spring of 1939, but he only lived for a few more months. He is buried on the Mount of Olives in Jerusalem.

On the afternoon of November 8, 1938, a Tuesday, we drew up to the harbor in the pouring rain. Four weeks later, my brother and I made a solemn promise to speak and write only Hebrew with one another from that moment on—a pretty radical decision, since at the time we knew only the rudimentary Hebrew that we had learned in preparation for our bar mitzvahs. But we wanted to symbolically distance ourselves from our childhood in Vienna, and from the German/Austrian culture. To this day, Hebrew remains our shared language. Only at social occasions where people are present who don't understand Hebrew do we sometimes speak German or English with one another.

We also changed our first names. Even in assimilated families, back then Jewish children were traditionally given a Hebrew or Jewish name in addition to their German name, although these names were not officially registered on the child's birth certificate. Since neither of our grandfathers were alive when we were born, my brother was named after our paternal grandfather, Meshulam. The name has been in our family for generations and goes back to an ancestor who was considered a great Torah scholar more than two hundred years ago. I have a fairly Germanic first name in my birth certificate: "Arnold." But for almost all of my life, I have been called "Ari." Perhaps it was short for both Arnold and my Jewish name, Aron Leib, after our maternal grandfather. Leib is Yiddish for Lion, and in Hebrew, lion is "aryeh." The least common denominator of these three names, Arnold, Aron, and Arjeh, was Ari. After arriving in Palestine, I first received the official name Aharon, which is entered in my British identity card. When I had to renew my Israeli passport in the 1950s, I changed this to Ari. It was a good decision. The short name Ari has often quickly broken down barriers to foreigners and also made dealing with important politicians much easier for me.

At the time, family names were also made more Hebrew when immigrants arrived in Palestine. But Meshulam and I wanted to keep our last name, and were able to do so with a little luck. We simply transcribed our name as רט with only "resh" and "tet" and even David Ben-Gurion recognized it as a Hebrew name—a derivative of the word *retet* or trembling with joy.

We too experienced such joy at our arrival in the Holy Land, but it lasted only a short time. Meshulam and I had to separate. Since he was already seventeen years old, the director of the Youth Aliyah assigned him to live at Kibbutz Gvat. A group of young boys and girls his age from Vienna were already there, twenty kilometers east of Haifa. Parting was hard for us. We had often fought during our childhood in Vienna, but our shared fate and the journey on the ship had brought us closer. We had of course known when we left that we would be living in different places in Palestine, but now the separation seemed unbearable.

Meshulam was very unhappy in Gvat. He did not know anyone and the physical labor was difficult for him. In December 1938, on Chanukah, he tried to run away for the first time. He managed to get to Haifa, and we spent a couple of days together at the house of distant relatives. The director of the Youth Aliyah in Jerusalem and his madrich or counselor in Gvat, Lolik, were able to find out where he was staying. They talked to my brother and managed to convince him to go back to the kibbutz. But soon he ran away again and tried to get permission to live in student accommodations in Kiryat Motzkin. His best friend from Vienna lived there, Erich/Eli Preminger, who was studying at the Technion in Haifa. Additionally, Kiryat Motzkin was not far from my new home in Kiryat Bialik, and we would have been able to see each other more often. In his loneliness, he longed to be together with me. But when he tried to register at the student accommodations, the official knew right away who he was. Meshulam had to return to Gvat and learn to live there.

After parting from Meshulam at the Haifa harbor, I waited with my group for transportation to our new home in a suburb of the city. Finally, three grey buses with metal grills for windows pulled up. As we soon learned, this had to do with the Jewish-Arab battles that raged from 1936 to 1939 and were played down by the British, who called them "riots" or in Hebrew *me'ora'ot* (episodes). One result of these battles was that the British Mandate government had decreed that Jewish and Arab buses must look alike, to prevent attacks from both sides. The barred windows were a measure that had been taken against hand grenades.

We got in, but we did not leave, because we were waiting for the small armored British police car that would escort us. The girls sat in the bus wearing their best clothes, and we boys in our best suits, with white shirts and ties. We all thought of the song that Aron Menczer had taught us: "A people travels homewards to the land of their ancestors, following the blue-and-white banners. Homeless for thousands of years, we are traveling home."

The path to our new home led from the harbor through the

Arab city to the south and then through Arab suburbs—a dangerous journey at the time. In our preparatory classes in Vienna, our teachers had stressed the heroic and idealistic life of the Jewish pioneers in Palestine. I had no idea that parts of the country were in fact battlegrounds. In the 1920s, there had already been violence by Arabs in the mandate region against both Jewish settlers and the British authorities. When—a result of increasing antisemitism in Europe and the rise of Hitler—Jewish immigration to Palestine rose from 175,000 immigrants in 1931 to 460,000 in 1939, tensions escalated, peaking, as stated above, in the years between 1936 and 1939.

After over an hour, we arrived at the Ahava Youth Home in Kiryat Bialik. The home had been founded in Berlin in 1922, when the Jewish Community set up an orphanage for the children of victims of the war and of pogroms. The building still stands today at Auguststrasse 14-16, an inconspicuous plaque memorializes its founder and director, Beate Berger, and the house mother, Hanni Ullmann. It is one of very few unrenovated buildings in a now upscale Berlin neighborhood full of fashion boutiques and galleries, sometimes it is used as a venue for art exhibitions. In 1934, the Ahava School moved its entire inventory, including the children and teachers, from Berlin to Palestine, where they could take in German Youth Aliyah candidates. Even in Jewish Palestine, Beate Berger insisted on her German title, *Oberschwester* or senior nurse.

Taking in 51 children from Austria was not easy for the German youth or the teachers, because of both linguistic and social differences. Nobody understood what we wanted when we asked for a *Jause*, and it was days before we received a meager afternoon snack at four p.m. The German teens looked down on us Austrians, since most of the Viennese Jews were originally from poor areas of

Eastern Europe, from Galicia and Bukovina, from Lemberg (now Lviv), Cracow, and Czernowitz. The teachers repeatedly intervened to fight these prejudices, but they were deep-seated in the children. In retrospect, it's hardly surprising; almost none of the children had immigrated to Palestine of their own free will. For many of them, making aliyah was the only chance they had to survive, only rarely had the children been raised as Zionists by their parents.

We had no acclimatization period. Since there was an epidemic of scarlet fever in the main house when we arrived, we were housed in rented one-family homes meant for parents with two to three children and now occupied by twelve boys and girls. Every day, we had to do five hours of hard physical labor: we chopped wood, cleaned our houses, and worked in the kitchen, the vegetable garden, and the cow shed. Afternoons, we had four hours of lessons in subjects like Hebrew, the Torah, Jewish history, Palestinian history and geography, and agriculture.

Shortly after our arrival, we were all given to a thorough physical examination. I was shocked when the doctor diagnosed a constriction of the chest. "You will have to go to orthopedic gymnastics twice weekly" she prescribed. And for many months, I went in the afternoon to my training. The exercise and the hard work soon took care of the problem.

My first day of work at Ahava has been burned into my memory. Our caretaker Perez Urieli came into our room in the morning and said: "Ari, you don't have to wear good clothes today, but you should have tight underwear on." Then off we marched. In the courtyard of the Ahava school stood a large wooden barrel on wheels, which we pulled up to our house. Then Perez said: "So my dear Ari, this is the septic tank and you need to empty it." He put a bucket on a rope into my hand and gave me an encouraging look. I was deeply shocked. But Perez was in no way trying to harass me. The work was unappetizing, but necessary—otherwise all of the latrines would overflow because of the overcrowding at the accommodations. Looking back, I think of this episode as my "baptism by sewage." After that, everything else was child's play, the odor of cow manure took on a pleasant fragrance.

Perez Urieli's original name had been Franz Hainebach. He had studied pedagogy and had already worked as a madrich in group homes for Jewish youth in Germany. Often *madrich*, or *madricha* in the feminine form, is rendered as 'teacher', 'educator' or 'counselor', but these are insufficient translations, literally the word means something more like guide or pathfinder. A madrich accompanies his students on their way, he teaches them but he also acts as a personal guardian and counselor. Peter Urieli's experience and encyclopedic learning soon made him a father figure for us parentless children.

The educational and cultural values at Ahava shaped me for life. Ahava means love in English, hence the educational concept of the institution is already present in its choice of name. In the early 1920s, educational reform was en vogue in Berlin, and there were many different approaches that put the welfare of the child at the center and tried out new, less authoritarian methods of teaching and raising children. Physical violence against children was absolutely taboo. The support and education of body, intellect, and soul were all treated equally.

During Shavuot (the Feast of Weeks around fifty days after Passover), we all gathered in the small auditorium in front of the dining hall to take part in debates on philosophical and religious subjects. For this "open court," as it was called, kids took on the roles of prosecution, defense, and judge, and each one had to take a position on the question at hand—an original way to awaken the interest of young people for difficult topics. Scholars such as Martin Buber and Ernst Simon came and discussed with us the meaning of Plato's *Republic* or of *Aleinu leshabeach la-adon hakol* (it is our duty to praise the Lord of all things) the concluding prayer that is spoken at least three times a day. It gives thanks to the Lord that he "did not make us like the nations of other lands" and praises Adonai, before whom we "bend our knees and bow down." Even as a fifteen-year-old I had problems with the text of this prayer, which also hopes to see "the glory of Your strength, to remove all idols from the earth and to completely cut off all false gods to repair the world, Your holy empire." The superior power ascribed to Adonai is incompatible with the centrality of tolerance in my worldview. And the use of the Hebrew word "goyim" for all countries still bothers me today, since it has become a derogatory word for people who aren't Jewish.

In the best tradition of our German-trained teachers, music played a large role in our education. Twice a week we had choir practice with the then well-known musicologist Bernd Bergel, who taught us classical choral works alongside the obligatory Hebrew songs. He was the nephew of the German Jewish writer Sami Gronemann and also wrote his own compositions. Perez Urieli also organized regular classical music evenings on his old gramophone, with a crank that had to be turned after each record. In the summer, at the end of the school year, we put on an opera with the help of Bernd Bergel and Perez Urieli. Perez wrote satirical texts about our life at Ahava, set to popular arias from Carmen, Aida, or The Magic Flute.

For example, to the melody of the "Chorus of the Street Boys" in Carmen we sang: "Imdu na, hassissma: lo nasus mipo" (Stand fast, our watchword is: We stand our ground.)

Although Perez Urieli and our house mother Hadassah Chavkin, one of the few madrichot who came from Poland, lovingly and empathetically tried to comfort us, we suffered greatly from homesickness. Our group of 51 boys and girls from Austria were split into three groups by age. I just made it into the group of fourteen-year-olds. After eight years as the Benjamin of the class in both the Schubert school and Wasa Gymnasium in Vienna, I was used to being the youngest. My position may have even given me an advantage; I had to compete with the older kids and prove that I was their equal to earn a place among them. I also became friends with the somewhat older girls in our group.

Perez chose the name *choter* (offshoot) for our group, to symbolize renewal. In the bible it is written: "And a shoot shall spring forth from the stem of Jesse." One of the boys who could draw well painted an old, sawed-off stump from which a young, green branch grew. For three years, the picture hung in our dining room as a symbol of the Choter Group.

Each group lived in one wing of the two-story Ahava house. Four children shared a sixteen-square-meter room, girls and boys separately. For our personal property like clothes and books we had to make due with a fifty-by-fifty centimeter cube-shaped box. We were together day and night, there wasn't a corner where we could go to be alone. Especially during puberty, this often led to tensions. To this day I remember my discomfort at using the common showers. Full of curiosity, the boys in my group compared the progress of each other's physical development. Whoever had the largest penis or the most pubic hair was admired, the rest of us were teased mercilessly.

At one end of the six-room hallway was our common shower room, at the other was a large common room/dining hall. There we ate breakfast and dinner together and met up in our free time to play board games and cards. Once a week, Perez Urieli held a group meeting where we discussed conflicts and concerns, as well as the political situation in Palestine and, after September 1939, the course of the war. As soon as the war began, Perez hung a large map of Europe on the wall, on which we worriedly followed the movement of the front. The meeting room was also used in the evenings, where we darned socks to musical accompaniment.

In October 1939, almost one year after arriving at Ahava, Perez tasked me, together with some others, with preparing an exhibition on the accomplishments of our first Ahava year. We collected photos and made posters that illustrated clearly how much our lives had changed in only twelve months. As a motto, Perez choose a quote by Josef Chaim Brenner, a writer in the Zionist labor movement who had been murdered in his home near Jaffa during the first Arab revolt against the Jewish immigration. It read: "The freedom of humankind is more precious than anything, and freedom lies in work." In retrospect, I'm appalled by the similarity to the infamous Nazi saying "Arbeit macht frei"—Work sets you free—that hung over the gate to Auschwitz.

Perez's attempts to hold what he called "soul talks" with me were met with little reciprocity, especially after a grave disappointment one evening. As one of the last children, I was scheduled to go to Perez's small bookshelf-lined apartment after dinner for our talk. Despite my reservations, I told him about my difficulties with my rival Shraga Weinreb, a religious boy from our group. Shraga was four month older than me and physically more developed. In our old age we became friends, but at the time he tormented me with his strength. He often made snide comments and was always showing off in front of the girls. When I asked Perez for advice, he didn't reply for a long time. Exhausted, he had fallen asleep in his leather armchair. I quietly tiptoed out the door and went back to my room with my sadness. From then on, I kept my feelings to myself and tried to solve my problems on my own.

Whoever travels to Israel today cannot imagine the austerity of life in Palestine back then. *Anavah*, modesty or humility, was a necessity, demanded by our living conditions. In time, it became stylized as a virtue. It has long since deferred to an alarming greed for money. Despite modern cities like Tel Aviv and Haifa, and the establishment of numerous kibbutzim, the country was still very poor and underdeveloped. The difference to central Europe, where we had grown up, could hardly have been more stark. Small dusty roads led through squalid suburbs, where workers still lived in huts made of tin and wood. Small, new Jewish settlements bordered Arab and Bedouin villages. The British took little interest in modernizing agriculture or building industry. Enormous areas of land were still not reclaimed, large plots of future farmland had to be laboriously freed from rocks. While most of the new arrivals met these challenges with an iron will, some became ill, contracting jaundice or malaria.

At the time there was a large textile factory named "Ata" founded by a Czech man in a suburb of Haifa. It provided clothing for the entire country. For that reason, almost everyone wore khaki. Those who had not brought furnishings with them from the old world received a few spartan pieces of furniture to set up house. As a rule, food was also in short supply, a shortage that we felt acutely in Ahava. During the week, our breakfast was bread and margarine, on Shabbat each of us received one slice of challah. A one hundred-gram package of butter was divided into ten portions, we saved these for the crowning finale of our breakfast. We ate many vegetables, and eggplant played a leading role. With it we made dishes that tasted like chopped liver or breaded schnitzel. There were almost no sweets at all, except an occasional small piece of halva. Our snack was bread with diluted marmalade and watery hot chocolate. Once in a while we would break into the pantry at night to get to the prunes, dried apricots, and halva.

The only exception to this scarcity were my occasional trips by bicycle to Kiryat Haim, a workers' suburb of Haifa, to visit the Eisenstein family, distant relatives of Omama Frimtsche. Every few weeks they would invite me to tea and cake, which we ate in the dining room under a large portrait of Theodor Herzl. People had so little back then, nobody bothered to lock their homes. They trusted their neighbors, but they also didn't have anything to steal.

In the spring of 1939, our group grew with the arrival of Ilse and Jehuda Epstein, siblings from Breslau. A few months earlier, they had immigrated with their parents through what was known as a "capitalist certificate," which meant that they had to show that they owned one thousand British-Palestinian pounds, a large sum in those days. Mother Epstein, a tall, elegant, good-looking lady, opened a perfume store on Ben Jehuda street in Tel Aviv. But Father Epstein, a lawyer, was unable to work in his profession since he did not speak English or Hebrew, and also had to first pass the difficult exam to join the Palestinian bar association. Although with few exceptions the members of our group came from Austria, the Epsteins had chosen to send their children to us in the Ahava rather than to a Hebrew middle school in Tel Aviv. One of the reasons may have been that they knew Rabbi Sinai Ucko, also from Breslau, who was our teacher for bible studies and Jewish history.

At her arrival, Ilse was given the Hebrew name Alizah, the joyful one. Almost at first sight I fell in love with the beautiful girl with the haunting blue-gray eyes. Although Alizah was one and a half years older than me, she became the first love of my life. We spent every moment of our free time together; we must have had a premonition that we would not have much more time. My joy about this first love was often overshadowed by dark clouds of worry. Together we read Goethe's *The Sufferings of Young Werther* and quietly hummed Chopin's "Funeral March" when we were both assigned to dishwashing duty. In the spring of 1940, our fears were confirmed. From the beginning, Alizah's parents had looked warily upon our love, now they brought Alizah back to Tel Aviv, shortly before her seventeenth birthday.

◆

Ten months after we arrived in Palestine, World War II broke out. Our links to Europe became more and more tenuous. Our family was incredibly lucky, and by July 1939, my closest relatives had all managed to immigrate to Cuba, where they waited for the Polish immigration quota for the United States to open, since they had been born in the Polish part of the Austro-Hungarian monarchy. My second mother Rita and my two-and-a-half-year-old half-sister Henny were the last to arrive in Havana, on a ship from Bremen. Earlier, I had learned that my father had already reached Cuba at the beginning of that year. He had been released from Buchenwald concentration camp under the condition that he relinquish all of his assets and leave Germany within 48 hours. In the fall of 1941, my parents and my sister received permission to enter New York City.

Since I had already acquired the habit of reading the daily paper when I was in second grade, I was very glad that the Ahava school subscribed to the Swiss *Weltwoche*, an important source of news. I was able to decipher the labor movement's Hebrew daily, *Davar*, but it published little news from abroad. Because of Switzerland's neutrality, the *Weltwoche* even came fairly regularly during the war, albeit with a delay of several weeks. Only those who signed up were able to study the Choter group's precious copy of the paper on Shabbat or in the evening. I was one of the few who read the paper in full each time, to keep up with the course of the war and other political developments.

One of the few letters that my brother and I received during the war was a goodbye letter that Omama Frimtsche had sent to Palestine from Stryi in June of 1940. She wrote that she had become old and weak, and she could tell that her life would soon come to an end. She was overjoyed that we were both now living in Eretz Israel, and she left us her house on Kraszewskiego Street 1. As a Polish Jew, her residency permit for Austria had been rescinded in early 1939, and she had no choice but to move back to her birthplace in Galicia. She died there in June 1940, under Soviet occupation. In 2008, I visited Stryi and searched in vain for her grave.

A few weeks after receiving Omama Frimtsche's letter, in the summer of 1940, we were directly affected by the repercussions of World War II for the first time. Today, the extent to which Palestine was involved in the war is largely forgotten. In 1940, Italy declared war against France and Great Britain. In June, July, and August of that year, Italian and German aircraft launched their first attacks against the British Mandate in Palestine. The port of Haifa and the British oil refinery in the Bay of Haifa—recently completed in 1939—were key strategic targets. On September 9, the Italian air force attacked Tel Aviv from a base on Rhodes. One hundred twenty people died in the bombings and over ninety were wounded. A residential area on Pinsker Street in the city center, between Allenby Street and Dizengoff Square, was hit particularly hard.

I was alarmed by the news because Aunt Adele, my mother's sister-in-law, and her two daughters lived in a house on Yarkon Street, parallel to the Tel Aviv Beach Promenade. Aside from my brother, Adele and her daughters were my only close relatives in Palestine. I therefore asked Moses Calvary, our art teacher in Ahava, for a three-day vacation so that I could go to Tel Aviv and check whether they were alright. I hitchhiked the first part of the journey from Kiryat Bialik to Tel Aviv, and got a lift in a large Arab truck that was driving from Iraq via Jordan to the Mediterranean and from there on to Egypt. Although the two drivers insisted that I sit between them, I chose to sit next to the door. After only a few minutes, the two made their first advances, putting a hand on my naked thigh. Horrified, I jumped out at the next crossing and took the bus the rest of the way.

In the early afternoon, I arrived at Aunt Adele's house, which was, to my great relief, wholly unscathed. My cousins were spending the afternoon at the beach with friends. Instead of asking about me or my brother, my aunt embroiled me in a torturous discussion over a cup of tea. "Do you actually know how your mother died?" she asked. I answered that it was only one year later that I had learned about her death at all, and therefore I knew very little. With relish, Adele gave me the details of the suicide and also intimated that my father had been having an affair with his clerk. She did not mention my mother's grave illness at all. I heard all of this for the first time and felt like the ground beneath my feet was slipping away. But that only spurred Aunt Adele further. Shaken to the core, I took my leave as soon as possible.

On that same afternoon, I had planned a visit to the Epstein family so that I could see Alizah again. To make the futility of our relationship clear to me, Alizah's parents had also invited some of her suitors for the afternoon, including her future fiancé. Right away, I understood that I had no chance of a future with her. In my despair, I tried—as a fifteen year old—to enlist in the British military through the Jewish Agency. Naturally, they sent me away again. The pharmacist also put a quick end to my nascent thoughts of suicide by refusing to sell Veronal to a minor without a prescription. Crestfallen, I returned to Haifa.

Moses Calvary was waiting for me at Ahava to hear how my trip to Tel Aviv had gone. I told him about the conversation with my aunt, and how I had no memories of my own of my mother. Calvary had also lost his parents at a young age and so understood what it meant to me. He had been helped at the time by Julia Neumann, the wife of Erich Neumann, a famous psychoanalyst and former student of Carl Jung. Both were typical Yekkes, or German Jews; before 1933 they had lived and conducted research in Berlin. Now they were fighting for their livelihood in Palestine. Erich Neumann had a psychotherapeutic practice and tried to augment his meager income with lectures about Depth Psychology. A circle of intellectuals interested in Jung's theoretical psychology had grown around the Neumann's house on Gordon Street. Julia Neumann specialized in chiromancy, the analysis of the form of the hands and the lines on the palm. Calvary was certain that she could tell me something about my mother.

A few weeks later I sat next to Julia Neumann, bent over an ink print of my right hand. She said that there was musical talent in my family, not me, but a close relative. In fact, my brother Meshulam was a talented piano virtuoso and had a particular knack for improvisation. She characterized my father as quick-tempered and argumentative, but urged me not to be too critical in my judgment of him. My mother in contrast had been very patient, obliging, and charitable. Relatives had also described her similarly. Julia Neumann said my character was much more like my mother's than my father's. I left her practice relieved and comforted. When I said goodbye, she promised to keep the print in case I ever needed advice again. In June 1946, she made a new handprint and compared it to the old one. This time, she said that I had a great talent for social interaction. She even departed from her usual conventions and made a prediction about my future: "Soon, whole new worlds will open up to you." I saw Julia Neumann for the last time in 1978, when I had some business in the Egyptian Embassy and stopped by her practice while I was waiting. Again, she compared the old prints to a new one, and told me something that I had already known for quite some time: I had a talent for writing.

In the spring of 1941, we lived through the nightly bombings of the German Luftwaffe, who were stationed in Damascus, then under the control of Vichy-France. Field Marshall Rommel's troops were already in Marsa Matruh, on the western border of Egypt. The British administration had made plans to evacuate Palestine to the

Galilee mountains if necessary, should Rommel's Africa Corp succeed in conquering Egypt.

The Haganah, the underground army of the Yishuv—the Jewish community in Palestine, with a population of 50,000 at the time—was determined that should this happen; they would fight alone against the German troops at Mount Carmel to the south of Haifa. You can still see large overgrown cement blocks in the narrow ravines of Mount Carmel, planned as building blocks for a fortress. Meanwhile, the British had developed an effective deterrence to air attacks by the Luftwaffe. They hung nets between balloons that were anchored to the ground and flew at a height of four thousand meters. This forced the enemy aircraft to fly higher, impairing their accuracy.

Many bombs also fell on the fields surrounding the Ahava school. For a few weeks we were even evacuated to a religious children's home ten kilometers east of Haifa. When we fled, we hiked with our backpacks the whole way, passing Arab villages and fields until we reached Kfar Hassidim, the village of the pious.

In late May and early June 1941, whole regiments of Allied troops marched behind our school; mostly from the ANZAC Corps, made up of soldiers from Australia and New Zealand. In the evenings we brought coffee and cake to the friendly soldiers, to bolster them before they left for the front. From Haifa they went north toward Lebanon and Syria, both of which supported the Vichy regime. Since other laws applied during wartime, the British authorities released 43 Haganah officers so that they could support the Allies in this campaign. One of the freed officers was Moshe Dayan, who would later become one of the most important military strategists and politicians in the state of Israel. Dayan knew the terrain in South Lebanon and led the Allied reconnaissance troops on the road to

Beirut. On a hill twenty kilometers north of the Palestinian-Lebanese border, when he was scouting a bridge with his binoculars, he was shot by a French sniper. Dayan was badly injured and lost his right eye. For forty years, until his death in the fall of 1981, Dayan's black eye patch was his hallmark, recognized around the world.

In the summer of 1941, Lebanon and Syria were captured by the Allied troops, after which the situation in Israel became slightly calmer. But it would still be half a year until Rommel's Africa Corps began its retreat from northern Africa after the Battle of El Alamein.

The Young Kibbutznik

By early September 1941, I had finished my schooling at Ahava in under three years and was considered an adult, although I was not yet seventeen. Wanting to contribute to our country and our community, I and thirty other members of our Choter group had already formed a new smaller group in the spring, in which we prepared for our lives in our own kibbutz.

At Ahava, we had enjoyed a traditional religious education, including study of Tanakh—the five books of the Torah plus the Prophets. We had also been taught Jewish history. We kept Shabbat and the Jewish Holidays faithfully. Many of us had been strongly influenced by this education. But most of the kibbutz settlements were secular because of their socialist ideology. I hoped to found a liberal kibbutz in the tradition of our shared upbringing in Ahava, where secular and religious members could live together.

In early 1940, four boys and two girls from Italy joined our group. They came from respected Jewish Italian families and had relatively good connections to the Italian authorities. Hence, even six months after war broke out they had been able to immigrate to the British Mandate of Palestine. Their families were well-known in Italy at the time: the siblings Channah and Jehuda Morpurgo, Nurit Ravenna, Baruch "Chichio" Sermonetta, Schaul Ventura, and Schmuel Pontecorvo, the only secular member of the group. I quickly became friends with them, but I still wanted to live together with the pious members of our group from Vienna. We received support for our unusual idea from Berl Katznelson, the leading ideologist of the Workers' Party, Mapai, who believed that religion should not play a role in party politics. Unlike many other Jewish leftists, he also believed in nurturing Jewish values. Jewish holidays should be celebrated, but imbued with secular content. For example, for our Passover seder the kibbutzim made their own Haggadahs that celebrated not only the liberation of Israel's children from Egypt, but also the beginning of Spring. Berl Katznelson, co-founder of the Ahdut Avoda in the 1920s, of Histradut (the general federation of trade unions), and later of the Mapai party, had had a decisive influence on the political landscape of Jewish Palestine. I can see the small man with the large mustache before my inner eye, wearing wrinkled khaki-colored clothes and radiating incredible charisma, with piercing, fiery eyes and a kind smile. Katznelson was also editor-in-chief of the labor newspaper *Davar*. When he heard about our group, he proposed that we go to Beit Yehoshua, a fairly unknown kibbutz 25 kilometers north of Tel Aviv. Two years earlier, it had been founded by members of a youth movement from Galicia called "Akiva." Beit Yehoshua lay at the edges of the swamps in Wadi Falik, an area populated by Bedouins and the site of occasional armed incidents.

As a result of his proposal, the representatives of Beit Yehoshua, Rina und Witzek, visited us a few times, painting pictures in brilliant colors of our wonderful and harmonious future life with them on the kibbutz. But our Italians were greatly influenced by Bertl Eckert, the ideologist of another, older, Italian group, Hapoel HaMizrachi, the Zionist religious labor movement. Eckert had been co-founder of the first kibbutz of the religious kibbutz movement, HaKibbutz HaDati (the observant kibbutz). He convinced them that true religious life was only possible in a wholly observant kibbutz, in which all members prayed daily and they could fulfill all of their religious duties. It was hard to resist the six-and-a-half-foot tall, charismatic man and his powerful rhetoric. We discussed the question late into the night, in small groups and one-on-one. A downright ideological conflict flared up about the importance of tolerance for our group: religious dogma and liberal beliefs clashed fiercely.

By the beginning of summer, the fate of our group had been decided: we would go our separate ways. Eight of our pious members joined the religious kibbutz Sde Eliyahu in Beit Shean Valley, seven wanted to take completely different paths. In the end, only fifteen members of my original group remained with whom I moved to Beit Yehoshua. They were my comrades and my companions, but they were not intimate friends.

Before leaving for good, we took one last group trip with Perez Urieli in August 1941, this time to Jerusalem, where we learned a great deal about the unique city. We were allowed to go to the Wailing Wall—at the time accessible only via one narrow alley—only under the protection of the British police. For security reasons, the British authorities also forbade our excursion to Hebron to visit the holy sites of the graves of the patriarchs and matriarchs. At the end of this week, which had brought us closer together, we said good-bye with tears in our eyes and went our separate ways.

The failure of my original plan to found a kibbutz for religious and non-religious people alike was one of the formative experiences of my political youth. I never got over my bitter disappointment at failing to create for us a shared community, and as a result I kept my distance from religious organizations for the rest of my life. And just as Berl Katznelson had predicted, the religious Mizrachi party went on to use their political influence to prevent liberal initiatives such as ours. Later, Mizrachi merged with another party to form the National Religious Party, which became the political home of the settlers in the occupied territories.

◆

I never really settled in to life at Beit Yehoshua. Their promise that we would find a pleasant new home and be given thorough preparation for kibbutz life turned out to be empty when we arrived in September 1941. Our accommodations were six round bell tents, each shared by two or three members of our group. We had to pitch the tents ourselves on the hard loam soil, using strong ropes to bind the tall center pole to pegs that we rammed into the earth as deeply as we could. But in late fall and in the winter, windy storms often blew the tents away anyway. We pitched them again and again, often in the middle of the night in pouring rain. Our mattresses were burlap sacks filled with straw and for light we used petroleum lamps. In spring and summer we sweat in the badly-ventilated tents; in fall and winter we froze terribly.

At work, we were horribly exploited. There was no more talk of the tasks we had been promised in rotating agricultural areas. For months we toiled as wage laborers in the orange grove belonging to the local large landowner, where, for example, we used heavy pickaxes to dig irrigation ditches around each tree. For this work we had fierce competition from the experienced Yemenite workers from a nearby village. If we were lucky, we earned half of a British-Palestinian pound per day. That made up ten to twelve pounds per day that we contributed to the kibbutz, but of course we never saw a "grush" of that money, as one-hundredth of a pound was called.

Our other "skilled labor" consisted of cleaning out the large mule stalls in Tel Mond, run by Italian prisoners of war. With shovels we loaded manure onto high trucks and then, after driving over half an hour to the area's orange groves, unloaded it again. In this way the plantation owner got his fertilizer almost for free, or for the pittance that he paid Beit Yehoshua for us. We filled and emptied three to four large trucks a day, with no time left for a break. Our meager lunch—bread with marmalade, sour cream and oranges—we ate on the drive back and forth, seated on top of mule manure.

Rina and Witzek had promised a liberal Jewish lifestyle but in reality, Beit Yehoshua kibbutz seemed like a religious sect. Its members zealously followed the group's religious leader, Joel Dreiblatt, a heavyset, bald, unappetizing man without an iota of spiritual inspiration. Dreiblatt was their incontestable authority, he did not have to work and was revered by all like a Hasidic rabbi.

Our situation was miserable, it had to change. In September 1942, I went to Tel Aviv to look for Berl Katznelson in the *Davar* office and tell him about our problems. On Rosh Hashanah, he visited us to see the situation for himself. We sat together in one of the small round tents and deliberated. Katznelson understood right away why we did not want to stay there. Shortly after, he arranged for our group to go to the Ramat David kibbutz near Nahalal in the Jezreel Valley. I alone stayed on at Beit Yehoshua for almost six months, since the kibbutz had asked me to work for a while in the cow barn. I was not unhappy about this request, since I had my doubts about whether our group from Ahava would get along with the sabras from the Gordoniah youth movement in Ramat David.

"Sabra" was the term for those who had been born in Israel, as well as for the cactus fruit which is sweet on the inside but prickly on the outside. For us, immigrants who had been socialized in Europe, their often rude tone was difficult to bear. Furthermore, in the meantime I had become closer with Bronka, the director of the cow stall. She was eight years older than I, and consoled me for the difficulties in Beit Yehoshua.

Nevertheless, after repeated urging from my *chaverim*, I said goodbye to Bronka in early 1943 and joined my group at Ramat David. Those months were also the time of decisive World War II battles—El-Alamein in North Africa and Stalingrad in the Soviet Union—turning points in the war in which Hitler, with his unwavering delusions of grandeur, sacrificed one million soldiers. In my small round tent on the kibbutz, I had put up a map of Europe and North Africa and followed the movement on the front using pins and thick red thread. I listened to the news every evening on my small radio: BBC from London and news from the Wehrmacht headquarters in Belgrade.

In the fall of 1943, we joined together with around forty young people who had managed to immigrate from Czechoslovakia via Denmark and Italy in 1940, after the start of the war. Together, we wanted to finally found our own kibbutz. But before we could do so, the kibbutz association sent us to Neve Eitan in Beit Shean Valley, where there were acute labor shortages at the time.

Even though I had been living in large groups the entire time since arriving in Palestine, I still often felt alone. Without being conscious of the fact, since I had fled Vienna and been separated from my family, I lacked someone whom I could trust, a soulmate, a good friend with whom I could share my daily life. That changed when I met Avri Zuk. He was in the Czechoslovakian group, but he did not join us in Neve Eitan until the spring of 1944, because he had been recuperating from a bad injury.

Almost from the very first day we met in Kibbutz Neve Eitan, a unique friendship bound me to Avri. He was a good-looking young man with dark hair and piercing brown eyes, women were always swarming around him. Not only did he possess a wonderful sense of humor, but also a rare wisdom about life and the world. People who did not know him sometimes misunderstood his sarcastic remarks, which were usually just how he expressed his wise attitude towards life. Our family constellations were similar. He was also the youngest in a family with two sons and one daughter. Avri was the only one of them to survive the Shoah.

He had fallen off a driving truck while volunteering as a fighter for the Palmach, the commando unit of the Haganah, and had broken his hip. He lay in a hospital in Tiberias for months, where the Czech girls visited him every week. When he finally arrived at Neve Eitan, he was the only one accorded any measure of comfort: he was allowed to live in a wooden hut. Because of the accident, Avri was no longer able to do hard physical labor. He compensated by soon becoming one of the best bookkeepers and office managers that the kibbutz movement has ever had.

Our decades-long friendship was founded on mutual trust and knew no secrets. To this day I am very close to his family; his wife Jaffa, whom he married young, his sons Assaf and Yuval, his daughter Tami and his grandchildren. When Avri went with his family to visit his birthplace Žilina, eighty kilometers northeast of Bratislava, about which he had often told stories, it was no question but that I would join them. Our one deep rift did not last long and we remained friends until his death in 2006.

Kibbutz Hamadia, 1949. Photo: Moshe Cohen.

◆

In September 1945, our group moved again. This time, the kibbutz movement functionaries sent us to Hamadia in the Jordan Valley. The Jewish National Fonds, whose main task was to buy land for Jewish settlements from Arab "effendis," had bought a 300 hectare (740 acre) plot in the area and given it to a group of young people in the fall of 1942. These initial settlers of Hamadia were almost all sabras from middle-class families. They had attended the first Hebrew high school in Tel Aviv and most certainly could have continued their studies at the Hebrew University in Jerusalem, but because of the war they longed to contribute to the Jewish community.

The name Hamadia already reveals its location at the center of old Arabic territory. "Hamdi" was the name of a village founded by vassals of Sultan Hamid. The founder of the kibbutz built upon this name and called it "Hamadia," even though the official channels had already chosen the name "Hermonim." On a clear day, you can see Mount Hermon in Syrian Golan from the hills of Hamadia. Because we had rejected the official name, years later the functionaries tried to give the kibbutz a new Hebrew name that referred to the fact that two roads cross there, one of which leads over a Roman bridge: "Netive haEmek" (the way to the valley). But for those of us who lived in the kibbutz, a new name was out of the question. To protest, I went to Jerusalem with two friends. We met with success because we had thought of a fitting Hebrew interpretation of "Hamadia": "hamad ya"—pleasing to God.

Near the kibbutz was a Bedouin village called Bavati. Its populace worked the fields, long small strips of land that bordered on the land we had newly acquired. These fields were irrigated by open troughs that we and the Bedouins could access at certain hours of the day. Repeatedly there were disputes, and sometimes fist fights, because the Bedouins blocked the flow of water to our fields. At the time, we never questioned that the land that had been bought by the Jewish National Funds for a large sum of money was our rightful property. Although we belonged to the socialist youth and kibbutz movement, we never wasted a minute's thought on the fact that we had appropriated the land of the poor fellahin.

When we arrived, Hamadia consisted of a few tents and wooden huts, but there were also already four cement houses and a water tower. One of the most well-known photos of the founding days of Hamadia is a picture of Michael Zilzer (Elizur) leading mule-drawn carts laden with barrels of drinking water up the hill. Like many others, he later left the kibbutz, embarking on a diplomatic career which he began as the first embassy secretary in Great Britain. He was later ambassador to Austria and then Australia.

At least there was something of a preexisting structure when we arrived at Hamadia. Avri and I would have preferred creating something new of our own, but we had been unable to prevail over the functionaries' decision. For us, it was a real sacrifice; having to give up forming our own kibbutz for political reasons.

The fate of our group was closely tied to the political developments of the labor movement. In 1944, the Mapai party split, marking a decisive turning point for the labor movement. The split was caused by a change in David Ben-Gurion's policy. When the first reports of the extermination of the Jews in Europe became public in 1942, Ben-Gurion and Chaim Weizmann called a large Zionist Conference in the Hotel Biltmore in New York City, where the "Biltmore Program" was adopted. Ben-Gurion and Weizmann defended their right to found an independent Jewish Commonwealth after the end of the war. They wanted the freedom to take in those who would hopefully survive, and not be at the mercy of restrictive British policy. This called for a fundamental change in the goals of the Workers' Party, since until that point, the so-called state solution was more common in the nationalist, revisionist camp. This group, following the ideas of Vladimir Jabotinsky, who had already died by then, did not hold much truck with the idea of building up the country by founding kibbutzim and developing the country's agriculture. Their slogan was: "In blood and fire Judea fell—in blood and fire Judea shall rise!" Now, Ben-Gurion was also calling for a "Jewish Commonwealth" within the British Commonwealth. We assumed we would one day be an independent part of the great British Empire.

Ben-Gurion returned to Palestine in 1942. At Kfar Vitkin Moshav (a moshav is a type of cooperative farmers' village), the Mapai party organized its first large conference, with the future of

Palestine after the war on the agenda. I did not want to miss the opportunity to be present at such an important decision and drove a horse-drawn cart from Beit Yehoshua to Kfar Vitkin, where the heated debates glued me to my seat. The left-wing faction and activist groups championed the opinion that it would be a mistake to vote for the foundation of a Jewish state directly after the end of the war, because the work of Jewish settlement had only just begun. If a Jewish state was founded now, it would mean dividing the land, and they did not want to set borders before it was more densely settled. There were also heated discussions on the question of whether and to which extent alliances should be made with the Soviet Union. Looking back on this discussion, it is important to not forget the course of the war at the time: in 1942, the Stalingrad winter, the turning point of the war, had not yet taken place. We saw Russia's enormous efforts to defeat Hitler in battle, which were indirectly contributing to the rescue of the European Jews. In Jewish Palestine, not least for this reason, sympathies for the Soviet Union ran high, something also expressed in the many Russian songs we sang in Hebrew translation. Most of the Workers' Party, which was on Ben-Gurion's side, endorsed socialist values, but warned against getting too close to the Soviet Union and underlined the importance of Jewish values. Already in Kfar Vitkin there was a vote that intimated the party's split, which finally came about in 1944 in Jerusalem, when I was already living in Neve Eitan.

In Hamadia too, the turmoil in the Workers' Party led to a split among kibbutz members. Our group had been sent there by the directors of the kibbutz movement in order to create a clear majority for Mapai supporters. Shortly before going, I had attended a six-week seminar, organized by Berl Katznelson and run by the Haifa labor movement, that had made a deep impression on me—personally and politically. The goal of the seminar at Beit Ruthenberg in Carmel was to convince labor movement youth to remain true to the Mapai party and not join the left-wing faction of the Ahdut Avoda party. Each day, we listened for four to five hours to lectures about the goals and history of the Jewish labor movement. Many of the speakers were among the greats of Yishuv: Ben-Gurion, Salman Shasar (later to become Israel's third president), Moshe Shertok (Sharett), and Berl Katznelson. The seminar convinced me that the socialist-Zionist movement was on the right path and so I took up Berl Katznelson's proposal to found a "young guard" within the party. At that opportunity, I got to know Moshe Dayan. Since the battles in Lebanon three years earlier, where he had lost his eye, he had completely retreated from public appearances. Now he was chosen to join the board of the young guard. I was asked to discuss his stage appearance with him. Immediately, I was charmed by his charisma, his self-irony, and his intelligence. "What do they want from me?" he asked, "Do they need a symbolic hero on stage?"

Already during that Haifa seminar, they had tried to recruit me for the youth movement, but I was willing to participate only when the united youth movement, Tnua Me'uchedet, was founded in 1945. Since I had the reputation as a troublemaker in Hamadia, the kibbutz agreed to send me away for a while as a delegate. That was the quasi beginning of my public political career.

Political Baby Steps

On a late Saturday afternoon in the fall of 1945, during the break of a kibbutz movement conference in Tel Aviv, which I was attending as a delegate of Hamadia, a handsome kibbutznik came roaring in on a motorcycle. He descended and walked up to the chairman, Levi Shkolnik—later, as Israel's Prime Minister, known under the name Levi Eshkol: "We have a majority of 51 percent!" he called out jubilantly. The 22-year-old man in the blue shirt and with masses of black hair was Shimon Perski—today better known as President Shimon Peres—a comrade from Kibbutz Alumot near Tiberias. He had been elected Secretary of the labor youth movement HaNoar HaOved, and was pleased by his victory.

My first meeting with the ambitious party functionary Peres was followed by many joint activities in Israel's labor movement. In January 1949, he founded Moadon Hatzerim (the Youngsters Club, which I also joined). Peres hoped that the members of this club would take on leading positions in Israel's new state in the future—and in fact many key Israeli politicians stemmed from the kibbutz movement. We had particularly close contact in the summer and fall of 1965, when I was working for David Ben-Gurion, since Peres was at the time Secretary of the Rafi party, for which Ben-Gurion was running. There is no question that Peres possessed great political talent, which was however greatly impaired by his penchant for

With Shimon Peres in the 1980s.

scheming. I was witness to his notorious inability to accept criticism after he lost the election in the summer of 1981. At the time I wrote in the *Jerusalem Post* that Yitzhak Navon should step down from the presidency and join the leadership of the Labor Party. Peres never forgave me for making that suggestion. He has avoided me for over thirty years, although we share many political views.

At any rate, back in the fall of 1945, I was tasked with founding a new local chapter of the united youth movement in Haifa. I became the madrich for newly-acquired members. Whenever there was an important political meeting in Haifa, I was allowed to sit in and listen.

In the following year, fierce debates erupted. I attended one key meeting of the Mapai party central committee where, in front of four hundred delegates, a fight broke out over the question of which strategy to adopt in our fight against the policies of the British Mandate government. The great hopes which the Zionist labor movement had pinned on the surprise electoral victory of the Labour Party in Great Britain in July 1945 had been dashed. Clement Attlee and Ernest Bevin prevented Jewish immigration to Palestine with the same elan as Winston Churchill before them. Ships full of illegal immigrants were stopped by the powerful British naval fleet, and their passengers, almost without exception survivors of the death camps, were deported to Atlit near Haifa or to Cyprus.

The Jewish population of Palestine was looking for a suitable response to this state of affairs. In one camp were the members of Irgun (Etzel), the national military organization that was a de facto right-wing underground army, and the even more extreme Stern group, who attacked and ruthlessly murdered British soldiers and officers. Then there were the activists, including Ben-Gurion, and finally the minimalists who followed Pinchas Lubianiker. In the end, the conference resulted in a compromise: It was okay to fight the British, but only in order to defend the immigration of Holocaust survivors from Europe.

In the summer of 1946, there was a series of clashes between the Yishuv and the British Mandate. The "Night of the Bridges," June 16 to 17, 1946, when Palmach units, with the support of the right-wing underground, blew up eleven bridges in the areas bordering Lebanon, Syria, and Jordan, was followed by "Black Sabbath" on June 29, 1946, when British soldiers raided kibbutzim, searching for illegal weapons and secret weapons production sites. Thousands of young Jewish fighters were arrested and brought to prison camps in Rafiach or Latrun, where they were interrogated. Naturally, I was worried about my kibbutz. Ignoring the curfew, I made my way to the train station in the Arab section of Haifa in the southern part of the city near the port. When soldiers stopped me and controlled my papers, I showed my British identity card and said that I worked for the railway. In the end, I finally managed to board a train going towards Jezreel valley and Damascus. The conductor slowed the train for me as I'd requested near Hamadia, so that I could jump off and go by foot over the fields to my kibbutz. Once there, I learned that Hamadia had not been raided.

The violence escalated on July 22, 1946, when members of the Etzel group bombed the south wing of the King David Hotel, seat of the administrative headquarters of the British Mandate government. On July 30, the British hung a four-day curfew over Tel Aviv. Even baking bread was forbidden. Numerous activists were arrested and jailed.

My group in Haifa was also actively engaged in the fight against the British. To find out how the British would react, we decided to openly ignore the curfew. We went from house to house, recruiting young men for our action. Often their wives and mothers did not want to let them go, but in the end around three thousand men gathered in the center of Haifa. Our destination was the port, where we wanted to prevent the deportation of illegal immigrants. A scene unrolled before my eyes that seemed like it was straight out of Sergei Eisenstein's famous film *Battleship Potemkin*. We marched through Alozorov Street and then turned into Herzl Street. At a key strategic point, the British had positioned themselves with water cannons to block our path to the main street. But instead of water, they sprayed petroleum into the crowd, an extremely dangerous move because of the threat of fire. We tried to get out of the way down a side street, but eight or ten British soldiers blocked our path. After an officer had issued three warnings—"Stop, or we'll shoot!"—the British began to fire. One young woman died right next to me and two other comrades were shot. Everybody tried to get to safety. A few hours later, the British lifted the curfew, but we had been unable to stop the deportation of illegal refugees to Cyprus.

A few weeks later, there was another action. Under the command of two officers, Yitzhak Rabin and Haim Bar-Lev, both later General Chiefs of Staff in the Israeli military, a Palmach battalion raided a detention camp in Atlit, freeing a few hundred immigrants whom they brought by truck to Kibbutz Beit Oren on Mount Carmel. From there, the freed prisoners were to be allocated to varying kibbutzim southeast of Haifa. To confound the British soldiers, I went with a few hundred activists up to Mount Carmel. We walked several kilometers to Beit Oren, mingled with the illegal immigrants, and handed them our British identity cards. The British soldiers were unable to make heads or tails of the chaos. Luckily, they did not start shooting at civilians.

I was certain that the right-wing underground assassinations would make absolutely no difference to the policy of the British Mandate government. The British were able to convince the Yishuv leadership that refraining from underground actions would help to calm the situation. One of the less pleasant chapters in the annals of Yishuv is known as "The Season"—that period during which members of the Haganah delivered members of Etzel and the Stern group into the hands of the British.

In the youth movement, we continued our protest with more moderate actions. At night, for example, we tore placards calling for extremist actions off the walls as soon as the radicals posted them. Now and again, we also got into fist fights with right-wing nationalist Irgun supporters. I still carry a souvenir of those days, a scar on my right eyebrow from one supporter's brass knuckles.

In those days, as an active member of Haganah, you almost automatically also became a member of the underground defense army of the Jewish population. My group had been recruited as early as 1939, six months after our arrival in Palestine. In the beginning it was too militaristic for my taste, but I could not keep up my rejection for long. At fifteen, we were solemnly sworn in by a Commander and vowed to defend the lives of the Jewish population in Palestine no matter the circumstances. This was followed by practical military training in the kibbutz. In Beit Yehoshua, we had target practice at night using smuggled Polish guns. Even as teenagers we went on patrol, since our kibbutz was situated in an Arab area. With very few exceptions, every Jew living in Palestine back then felt that it was their duty to take an active part in the struggle for liberation. Most Jews supported the Haganah. Their members came from the wider labor movement, but also from the middle-classes and from the cities. We were all registered and listed and we had access to weapons, but we did not wear uniforms. Only the Palmach units (the shock troops) were fully mobilized and wore khaki uniforms. Some Haganah supporters also worked for the Jewish auxiliary police, which had been founded by the British. Since the Haganah permeated all strata of the Yishuv, when the military of the newly-founded state of Israel was named, David Ben-Gurion insisted on making this continuity clear. To this day, the military carries the name "Zeva Haganah le-Yisrael" or Israel Defense Force. The right-wing underground movement was integrated into the Haganah in 1948.

At the time, I did not give a single thought to pacifist ideology. There was nothing I wished for more than to live in a Jewish state of our own, and I hoped that a peaceful division of the land between Arabs and Jews would be possible. Apart from the Brit Shalom movement, which tried to make peace with the Arabs, there were very few pacifists in Palestine back then. The aforementioned peace group was founded by professors from the Hebrew University of Jerusalem, including Martin Buber and the school's first rector, Judah Leon Magnes.

In 1946, Yom Kippur, the Day of Atonement, fell on October 5. Traditionally this highest of all Jewish holidays, dedicated to repentance and reflection, is spent in prayer and fasting. That year, head rabbi Yitzhak Halevy Herzog, father of the future president of the country, gave special license to all so that we could prepare for military action. The Jewish administration headed by Ben-Gurion was already aware that one possible solution to the Arab-Jewish conflict was the division of the country. For that reason they were eager to set up Jewish settlements in southern Palestine so that it too could be claimed for the Jewish state.

Members of the youth movement were therefore sent to support a group of young people who wanted to found a kibbutz near Be'er Sheva. One of their core members was Jakov Sharett, son of the de-facto foreign minister, Moshe Sharett. I volunteered for this action. Right after breaking the fast, one hundred and twenty of us left in a convoy of at least two dozen trucks, driving from Rehovot, a nineteenth-century city thirty kilometers south of Tel Aviv, to the Negev desert. After about three hours, the convoy stopped in a large field eight kilometers west of the city of Be'er Sheva. We all got out and immediately began to empty the trucks. Within a few hours we had built three or four wooden huts out of prefabricated wooden walls. For defense, we built a palisade trench and put

Kibbutz Hatzerim, 1946. Courtesy Kibbutz Hatzerim.

up a watchtower. We had to get roofs up on them before daybreak, because the British Mandate respected traditional Ottoman rules, which stipulated that if a house had been erected without permission, it could no longer be torn down once it had a roof. The settlement that we erected that night grew to become Kibbutz Hatzerim, to this day a large and well-to-do kibbutz, adjacent to which the Israeli military built a large airbase in the 1960s.

This action was one-of-a-kind and should not be confused with the "wall and tower" settlements erected mostly in the Beit Shean Valley in the late 1930s during a period of Arab uprisings. Our 1946 action is remembered in Israel to this day. A moving song has even been written about it, about the eleven flowers that suddenly bloomed in the Negev Desert.

♦

I usually spent my weekends on the kibbutz. Since I only came home once a week, I didn't even have my own bed in Hamadia. I was given a room sometimes here and sometimes there, my few possessions wandered with me. In Haifa, I lived over the trade union restaurant in a six-square-meter room (65 square feet) that fit only a bed and opened to the garbage dumpsters. I was very glad when the union bought and renovated the Carmelia Court Hotel and I was able to stay there for a few months—changing rooms every couple of days until the hotel was completely finished. Our youth movement group soon grew and I moved in together with the other three madrichim in a 16-square-meter room.

Not long after, the change took place that Julia Neumann had seen in my palm lines a few months earlier: I was about to travel to a new world.

Youth Movement Delegate

In the fall of 1946, the kibbutz movement functionaries chose me as delegate to the US-American Zionist youth movement Habonim ("the builders") to recruit young American Jews for life on a kibbutz in Palestine. The challenge was to convince them to leave their families and give up their comfortable lives in America in favor of a spartan lifestyle in Palestine. Our mission, entitled "Land and Labor for Palestine," also entailed the recruitment of discharged Jewish soldiers and sailors as volunteers on Haganah ships used to smuggle illegal immigrants into Palestine. A first group of kibbutz members had already been sent to America in 1938 and '39, and had been unable to return to Palestine when war broke out. By now they were too old for this mission, younger people were needed to mobilize American teenagers. I was 21, supported the cause, and thought it sounded like an adventure. There was only one problem: I did not speak English. The organizers were unconcerned, they were sure I would learn fast.

Finally, after over eight years of separation, I would see my family again in New York. My brother Meshulam was also staying there at the time; he still wore the uniform of the Jewish Brigade of the British Navy. In November 1946, I applied for a visitor's visa to the United States, to the surprise of the American consul, who called my attention to the fact that the quota for Austrian-born immigrants was not yet full. "You would have no problem getting an immigrant visa" he said to me. But I had no intention of availing myself of American hospitality. I was certain that I would be returning to Palestine. The consul was very surprised; at that time many people, even religious Jews, were trying to get visas for the United States—often unsuccessfully because they had no relatives in the New World. He had apparently taken an interest in me nonetheless, and asked how I planned to travel to America in light of the continuing international longshoremen's strike.

The only passenger ship traveling between the Middle East and America was the *Marine Carp*, an American merchant marine vessel that had been a troop transporter during the war. Its route went from Alexandria to Haifa via Beirut, where it continued on to Istanbul, Piraeus, and New York. The very next day, it was due to sail. "Can you be at the American shipping agency office at Haifa Port ready to depart at eight in the morning?" He would put me on the *Marine Carp* stand-by list. I said yes without hesitation. I knew how difficult it would be to organize crossing because of the quota regulations. Of the nine hundred passengers that the *Marine Carp* took on board at its various ports, there were only thirty slots for Palestine: fifteen Jews and fifteen Arabs. If I didn't get a spot now, I would probably have to wait months for the next opportunity.

The twenty hours that remained until departure were incredibly hectic. In order to get everything done in time, I spent fourteen pounds—a month's wages—to hire a driver, who brought me first to Tel Aviv, where I received final instructions from the kibbutz movement. Then we drove to Haifa so I could pack up some things from my shared room, and finally to Hamadia to say good-bye to my friends. When I arrived at the kibbutz in the evening, they were

*Family reunion in NYC, 1947.
From left: Rita, Ari, Henny, Meshulam, father.*

celebrating the completion of a new cow barn. I was greeted boisterously, and I passed around bottles of banana liquor, eggnog, and cherry brandy that I had brought for them. But I did not take part in the celebrations, since I had to be at Haifa Port early the next morning. That evening, I saw two of my friends, Shike Baharav and Menachem Rotkopf, for the last time. They both fell in battle in 1948 on Mount Gilboa, on the border between Israel and what is now the West Bank.

The *Marine Carp* did not offer much in the way of comfort. It had large areas for sleeping and a few big common areas, including a reading room in which I spent hours each day. I had brought a German-English dictionary with me and a pile of old issues of the *Palestine Post*, which I now tried to decipher to learn English. One of the passengers on board was Sarah Bavli, who later wrote an Israeli etiquette book and trained diplomats in deportment. We had many discussions in which she prepared me for life in the New World.

I remember one thing in particular about that trip: the delicious and abundant food. Since no open packaging was allowed back into the refrigerator, huge amounts of food were thrown away—bread, butter, eggs, cheese, and ham. In the Greek port of Piraeus, a whole fleet of small boats were already waiting for our ship to cart the garbage away. I was shocked, having become so used to the austerity of life in Palestine. Nobody there ever threw away food.

I spent my last night of the trip on deck in freezing temperatures because I wanted at all costs to be among the first to spy the Statue of Liberty. The price I paid was a bad flu, which I brought with me to New York when I landed on December 8, 1946. To my surprise, the ship sailed almost directly into the city, docking at Pier 84, which led directly to West 42nd Street in Manhattan. I had of course seen pictures of the New York skyline before, but now the skyscrapers rose before me in the morning haze.

Hundreds of people were waiting behind a rope in the arrivals hall. Suddenly, a ten-year-old girl broke away from the group and ran toward me—it was my sister Henny. She only knew me from photos; when we separated in 1938 she had not yet been two years old. But she had recognized me even wearing the rather absurd hat that I had bought on our stopover in Piraeus for my arrival in New York. Then I also spotted my father, Rita, and Meshulam. I had last seen my father in May 1938, when the Gestapo officers arrested him early in the morning. To my relief, his horrible experience in German concentration camps and the hardship of fleeing Austria had not left any visible traces.

After everything that had happened, we instinctively no longer wanted to speak German with one another, and never again did we use that language when we were among ourselves. But since my English was rudimentary and my parents did not understand Hebrew, we had to invent an improvised Yiddish, which we had at least heard in Omama Frimtsche's times. Soon, we switched to English.

My father was not nearly as wealthy as he had been in his Vienna days, but he had managed to build up a paper wholesaling business again in New York, also exporting to Cuba and the Dominican Republic. The five of us lived in my parents' three-room apartment in a typical brownstone on the corner of 93rd Street and Central Park West. Elegant twenty-story buildings abutted the simple homes of the middle classes. Aside from the pink-flowered tableware, which my parents had been able to save, nothing was left to remind us of our apartment in Vienna. Meshulam and I slept on sofas in the living room. There was not much room for five people, but for a short time, we enjoyed the fact that we had finally been reunited. Together we visited the Metropolitan Opera and went to the theater.

Nevertheless, I noticed that there was tension between my father and Rita, which had in fact begun right after their honeymoon in 1936. That first crisis was surely partly due to my father's volatile temper, but also to the different social classes to which Rita's family and the Rath family belonged. While Rita's family had lived on what was known as "matzah island" in Vienna's twentieth district, in a petit bourgeois milieu, my family had lived in the upscale ninth district. Rita's family tried to ingratiate themselves with my father, the wealthy businessman, but all her life Rita helped to support her family of origin, the Liebermanns. Her older sister Dora, cursed with one cross-eye and one half-blind eye, became a particular object of my father's hatred because she was always trying to meddle in our family's affairs, especially after the birth of my sister Henny.

After the Anschluss, both the Rath and the Liebermann families immigrated to Cuba, where the animosities continued. My uncle Jakob, who had managed the brothers' joint property in Berlin, had been able to sell one of their houses and smuggle some money out of Germany for the immigration to Havana, despite the Nazi's strict regulations on money transfers. In Cuba, the two brothers invested in a boardinghouse when it became known that the *St. Louis* would be arriving at port in late May 1939 with over nine hundred German immigrants on board. However this "ship of fools" as it came to be called, never arrived at its planned destination, because the Cuban government made a deal with the Nazis and refused to recognize the refugees' visas. Despite many attempts at intervention, American President Franklin D. Roosevelt also refused to accept the refugees, substantiating the Nazi propaganda claim that no country in the world wanted to take in Jews. The *St. Louis* was forced to turn around, finally docking back in Antwerpen. Although it was possible in the end to distribute the refugees to different countries, after war broke out many of them landed back in the claws of the Germans. Only around half of the passengers survived the war.

For my family, Cuba's refusal to let the *St. Louis* land resulted in financial ruin. There were no guests for the boarding house. Later, my father complained that the Liebermann family had ridiculed him at the time. The shadow of Havana hung over the relationship between the two families in New York as well, and the closer Rita's contact to her family, the more strain she put on her marriage. There was one episode a few weeks before my brother's departure that seems particularly symptomatic to me. One Friday evening, I came home with a bouquet of flowers that I wanted to give to Rita for

Shabbat. My father made such a fuss about this gesture that I became determined to move out as soon as possible.

In 1955, when my father could no longer walk and became confined to a wheelchair—a delayed effect of his mistreatment in Buchenwald—their relationship finally ended. On a visit to see Meshulam and me in Israel, Rita left my disabled father for good; he went back to the United States alone.

◆

In December 1946, the first thing I did was to recuperate from the flu. That gave me the opportunity to search through the telephone book for my old friends from Vienna, for example the Goldberger girls from Beserl Park, whose flight via Czechoslovakia to New York I have already recounted. The Manhattan telephone book alone had more than two dozen pages of Goldbergers. Whenever a listing had the addition "insurance agent," I called the number and was in fact able to find the family. In America, "Titti" had given up her nickname, since it was suddenly rather lewd, and now went exclusively by "Jane." The Goldbergers had settled in well and we soon had a happy reunion.

Shortly after the war, peculiar reunions and coincidences were the order of the day. In the fall of 1947, I was visiting Jane and her mother in their comfortable house on 242nd street in Riverdale, north of Manhattan, when to my surprise I ran into an elegant, gray-haired woman whom I recognized immediately: Margit Weiner, the mother of Eva who had immigrated to Palestine with me in November 1938. Margit and "Kuckie" Goldberger, Jane's mother, had been close friends since their childhoods. In late 1940, Margit Weiner, a widow, managed to flee via Siberia to Shanghai, where she spent the war under Japanese occupation. Just a few days before our reunion she had arrived in New York after weeks spent crossing the Pacific Ocean. She wanted to spend a few months with her childhood friend before going on to Palestine to stay with Eva and her granddaughter, who had been born in the meantime. Eva, who now went by Chava, had married our agriculture teacher from Ahava, Zvi Savir, in the fall of 1945. When Margit Weiner arrived in Haifa in the spring of 1948, intense fighting raged across the country. She needed a bulletproof car to get to her daughter in the suburb of Kiryat Bialik. Her son-in-law Zvi she met only once, he fell in June 1948 in battles near the Latrun police fort.

On Saturday afternoons, my parents and I sometimes patronized the nostalgic meeting place of former Austrians, the café La Coupole on West 72nd Street. There they served Sacher and Linzer tortes, the quality of the coffee was well above the American average, and one could read the refugee paper, *Der Aufbau*. The efforts of the owners, Viennese immigrants themselves, to create a coffeehouse atmosphere were unmistakable, but it remained no more than a failed attempt to capture what had been lost.

On December 15, 1946, my high fever finally abated and I could return to the most important task at hand: namely, improving my primitive English so that I could begin my work in the Habonim youth movement. My sister Henny never missed an opportunity to make fun of my mistakes, for example when I attempted to pass on greetings to relatives of my friends in Palestine. Back then, a phone call from Palestine to New York was unthinkable, and letters took weeks to arrive. When these people thanked me for at least bringing a sign of life from their family members in Palestine, I would answer self-assuredly "never mind," instead of "you're welcome."

Henny was pleased as punch to speak better English than her much older brother, but after a few days, she took pity on me and began to correct my mistakes. She enjoyed her role as teacher.

In the days before Christmas and the New Year, Christmas trees and Hanukkah menorahs stood side by side as storefront decoration or in the lobbies of elegant residences, as if it were the most normal thing in the world. That would have been unthinkable in 1930s Vienna.

My plan had been to continue improving my English the way I had on my journey: by reading the daily paper. But since my father took the *New York Times* with him every morning to his office on Cedar Street, I had to buy my own paper. On the corner of 93rd Street and Columbus Avenue, an older New York Jew had a newsstand in a green wooden hut. When I came for the fourth time at ten a.m. and asked for the *New York Times*, the heavyset, unshaven man with tortoiseshell glasses and a wool cap spat out at me in contempt: "Greenhorn!" he said with a Yiddish accent, "For you the *Daily Mirror* and the *News* are not good enough? You should have the *New York Times?*" Clearly he thought it was presumptuous of me, with my bad English, to think I could read such a highbrow newspaper.

Every day, with the help of an English-German dictionary, I translated numerous articles from the *New York Times*, which always reported in-depth on events in Palestine. The British military's attempts to capture illegal Jewish immigrants on the high seas, bring them to Haifa, and then deport them to camps in Cyprus, were being followed closely by many American readers.

I celebrated my first New Year's Eve in New York with family and some of my parents' friends from Vienna in a large restaurant on Broadway and 86th Street. For my 22nd birthday on January 6, 1947, we took the train down to Washington, D.C. to see the capital. And then my reprieve was over. When we returned to New York, I began my work for the youth movement. I had already made many phone calls to the General Secretariat of the Habonim on Union Square, site of many American trade union offices and also the offices of the varying Zionist labor movement associations. The Habonim rented rooms for their headquarters from the Poale Zion party, the "workers of Zion."

After a long subway ride from 96th to 14th street, I stepped into the elevator and went up to the Habonim offices on the twelfth floor. My jitters before my first meeting with my new boss subsided when the secretary greeted me warmly and in fluent Hebrew. Surrounded by posters with large photos of Jewish Palestine, I soon felt at home.

In the conference room, the three leading members of the Habonim Secretariat were expecting me. Arthur (Artie) Gorenstein, Murray Weingarten, and Leon Jick were all around my age. All three had served in the American military and were now studying on GI bill scholarships. Artie Gorenstein was studying history at Columbia University, Leon Jick was enrolled in a Jewish Studies program at the Reform Union Hebrew College, and Murray Weingarten was studying education at Yeshiva University. All three later taught at renowned universities in the United States or in Israel. Together with me, they were starting a new training phase in Zionist education that had already been coordinated with the kibbutz movement in Palestine: young *shlichim* (emissaries) from Palestine were to set up new branches of the Zionist youth movement together with American *madrichim*.

Artie Gorenstein, a good-looking, brown-haired young man with piercing blue eyes and a deep bass voice, was the General

Secretary, the *masker*. He was director of Habonim for all of the United States and Canada. Murray Weingarten was the intellect of the kibbutz movement, and developed the concept for the educational program. He spoke Hebrew well and was able to help me when my English was insufficient. Leon Jick, the third person in the group, was also a handsome, somewhat heavyset man with an impressive ring of hair around his head. He was responsible for the New York region.

We got along splendidly from the start. Until recently, they had been working with the much older *shlichim* from Jewish Palestine who had gotten stuck in America when war broke out in September 1939 and who had not been able to return to Palestine until summer 1946. They were clearly happy to now be working with somebody their own age from Eretz Israel. We talked in depth about my new tasks. Together with Leon Jick, I would manage the Habonim branches in the New York region. It was a challenging duty, but there were no objections. In a baptism by fire, two weeks later I was to hold my first lecture in English.

To hasten my language progress, Weingarten introduced me to his fiancée, Evie Cohen, who also worked for the New York Habonim office and wanted to improve her Hebrew. In 1948, the young couple was part of the first American Habonim group to immigrate to Palestine after the war. For three months, Evie and I met twice weekly, speaking with one another in English and Hebrew, reading texts in both languages, and correcting one another. We both made great strides. Without a doubt this method of learning was a big part of the reason that my English soon became fairly fluent. Since I have a visual memory, I had no trouble with English's difficult, non-phonetic spelling. When my friends from Habonim were unsure about how to spell something—orthography is not an American strongpoint—they soon said: "Ask Ari."

At the end of January 1947, the time had come. The local Habonim group was expecting me at the Jewish Cultural Center in Forest Hills, Queens for my first lecture on life on a kibbutz and the current political situation. Since visitors from Palestine were extremely rare at the time, my lecture had been widely advertised. When I arrived in front of the two-story building at the Forest Hill Station, everything was covered in knee-deep snow—a novel experience after eight years in Palestine. Jay Bushinsky, the sixteen-year-old leader of the local chapter, was waiting for me in front of the Jewish Center. He seemed very excited, and I soon understood why. The small auditorium on the top floor of the building was full to the last seat; more than sixty people, youth and adults, had come to hear me speak. I had little trouble with the section of my talk about the current political situation in Palestine—after all, I read the *New York Times* every day. But without Jay's help, my descriptions of life on a kibbutz would have been a complete disaster. Nevertheless, the audience applauded and we set up a new date with the group to continue the discussion more deeply. As embarrassing as the memory of that evening is for me today, for my language skills it represented a breakthrough. Having been thrown in the deep end and come out safely, I was in high spirits and ended my lecture by teaching the audience the song *Semer Semer Lach* (A Song, a Song for You), which had been written on the occasion of the founding of the eleven settlements in the south of Palestine. Jay Bushinsky, whom I now see regularly, moved with his young family to Palestine ten years after that meeting, working with me for a while at the *Jerusalem Post* and later becoming the first CNN correspondent for Israel.

It did not take long for me to develop a certain skill at my new job. Leon Jick and I shared a small, spartanly furnished office on Broadway, north of Union Square. Despite the lack of space and thanks to a clear division of labor, we worked extremely well together. Leon concentrated on historical issues, while I focused on Palestine and current events. Together we were responsible for seven Habonim chapters in Brooklyn, Queens, and the Bronx, but strangely we had no chapter in Manhattan. Walking one day on Riverside Drive along the Hudson in the spring of 1947, one day I noticed a "For Rent" sign on the entrance to a small house that looked a little like a pavilion and was decorated with Chinese ornaments. Leon Jick and I grabbed the opportunity; we rented the house and, with the help of two dozen volunteers, renovated it within two weeks. We even put in a small garden. I stood out in this work because of my practical experience on the kibbutz. Shortly before Passover 1947, we inaugurated the first chapter of Habonim in Manhattan.

A key element of our Zionist education program was planning and running the Habonim summer camps, Camp Kvutzah. Cities in which Habonim was active rented plots of land with tent sites, kitchens, huts, and bathrooms. Often there was a lake nearby. The idea was for campers to model communal living, as a way of practicing life on a kibbutz in Palestine. The director of the Camp Kvutzah division was Rose Breslau, sister of Dave Breslau, one of the founders of Habonim in the United States in 1935. The small energetic woman ruled her unit with unquestioned authority. She alone decided who would manage the summer camps and who would be sent as *madrichim*.

In late May 1947, there was an interesting topic on the agenda of the weekly meeting of the Habonim Secretariat. The Poale Zion Association of Ottawa asked for our support with building a new camp, with the help of the developer Sam Shubinsky. This camp was planned as the beginning of regular activities in Canada's capitol. Shubinsky had promised to build the necessary camp infrastructure with his *chaverim* and his company. Since everyone with experience already had work to do, Artie Gorenstein made me director of this summer camp. It was the first time that a *shaliach* (representative) from Eretz Israel had been given such an important duty. In the weeks that followed, Rose Breslau and her team thoroughly prepared me for this job. I also needed to extend my visa at the American immigration office in New York. Without any problems, a visa for another six months was stamped into my "British Passport for Palestine." Neither was it a problem to travel to Canada with this passport, and my friends in Habonim were pleased that all formalities had been taken care of. Two months later, it would turn out that we had been gravely mistaken.

My family was of course very proud of me and of the many duties that I had been entrusted with, but they were also sad that I would be away from them all summer. On the last Sunday in June, two experienced Habonim *madrichim* and I left for Ottawa. Hilda from Baltimore and Leibel from Philadelphia were to be my assistants. Early in the morning we boarded the first Greyhound bus of the day; ten hours later, we arrived in Ottawa. There, Sam Shubinsky, his son David, and four more *chaverim* were waiting. We were driven to the Shubinsky's spacious house in elegant limousines. As director of the camp, I drove with the Shubinskys while father and son filled me in on the state of preparations. All evening, friends of the family and members of the Poale Zion Organization stopped by to meet us and wish us luck. Two seventeen-year-old girls from Habonim in Toronto also arrived to join our Camp Kvutzah group. The mood was almost euphoric. At last there would be a Zionist youth movement in Ottawa too. This had not been possible earlier in part because Canadian Jews were at the time not nearly as assimilated as American Jews. Many had their roots in traditional Eastern European families, and Yiddish culture played a large role in their lives.

The next morning, a large convoy left for the site. I drove in front in Sam Shubinsky's jeep, behind us drove five trucks fully laden with tents and equipment. One entire truck was needed just for the enormous tent that would be used to house the dining hall. The end of the convoy was taken up by a dozen smaller vehicles carrying construction workers and smaller tools. We felt like we were about to found a small kibbutz in Canada.

The property was near Gatineau Park, around forty kilometers from Ottawa in the bordering French-Canadian province of Quebec. There were a few scattered farms in the area, populated by French-speaking farmers who watched our progress with a mixture of curiosity and suspicion. There was one somewhat threatening moment when, around noon, we hoisted the Union Jack and the Zionist flag bearing the Star of David on a high mast. Some of the young farmers even began to whistle in protest. On the spur of the moment, I went over to the next farm to explain to the neighbors who we were and what we were doing: "I'm not British, I come from Palestine." No sooner had I said the word "Palestine," the atmosphere changed completely. The Franco-Canadians applauded in approval and called out: "Beat them!" When I then said that I myself worked the land on a kind of farm their enthusiasm knew no bounds. To prove I was telling the truth, I borrowed a scythe from one of the workers and mowed a few square meters of grass, much to their astonishment. From then on, we were sure of their support. We bought milk, butter, eggs, cheese, and vegetables from them, and knew that we could count on them in an emergency. The whole scene reminded me of my work in October 1946 after Yom Kippur, when we built a new settlement in the Negev desert against the will of the British.

The effect of the outcome of this adventure on the young Habonim members was unbelievable. As soon as we had put up the first of the twelve sleeping tents, we danced around the tent singing. The next day, daily life began. A few of the sixty campers' mothers took turns in the kitchen. Each tent was given the name of a kibbutz; the most popular was of course the "Hamadia" tent. Unlike the Hakhshara camps that provided agricultural training, the main purpose of our camp was to strengthen community spirit and give the young people an idea of what Zionism was about.

The time flew by. Before taking down the tents six weeks later, we put on a huge good-bye party with singing and dancing. Hundreds of the campers' family members came and together we celebrated the success of the Habonim summer camp. Our neighbors celebrated with us of course, and wished us success in driving the British out of Palestine as soon as possible.

From Ottawa, I went for a few days to the Laurentian Mountains to the summer camp of the Montreal Habonim group. There I conducted a seminar on the political struggle of the Jewish community in Palestine and the efforts of the Jewish Agency against the British administration. My listeners knew very little about the Yishuv policy on Jewish Holocaust survivors, whom the British refused to let enter Palestine. At the time, the United Nations Special Committee on Palestine was investigating the situation in Europe and in Palestine.

From Montreal, I continued on to the summer camp of the

Toronto Habonim group, which traditionally took place near Hamilton in Ontario, before returning by bus to New York in late August 1947. I had no trouble passing the Canadian border on the bridge over Niagara Falls. Exactly in the middle of the long bridge, we crossed into American territory. Not expecting any trouble, I showed the American border police my British-Palestinian passport with the extension of the visa for the US. To my surprise, policeman ordered me in a harsh tone to exit the bus immediately with my luggage, because my visa had expired. Distressed, I showed them my extension. "That's only valid as long as you're on American soil," they explained briskly. "The minute you left the country, this document became invalid." Nobody had warned me about this beforehand. To renew my American visa, they said, I would have to go to the same consulate that had given me the original visa—in Jerusalem. In the meantime, the bus had gone on without me to New York. I stayed back alone with my luggage on a narrow strip on the wide bridge—in no-man's-land between Canada and the United States. The border guard told me to go to a small hut on the bridge. There, he emptied the entire contents of my luggage onto a large table. He was particularly interested in the Zionist brochures of the Habonim and in my correspondence with the Habonim Secretariat, which contained many—transliterated—Hebrew words. In those days, young men from Palestine were often suspected of connections to the Jewish underground. For two hours, the border guard interrogated me and I slowly began to realize that I was not in the best of situations. Without a valid American visa, I was not allowed to return to the United States, neither was it possible for me to re-enter Canada. At least I had been allowed to call my friends from the Habonim in Toronto, who immediately did everything in their power to help me. Through contact to a lawyer who was a member of Poale Zion, an interim solution was finally found: I would be allowed to return to Toronto under the condition that I report to the police every other day. It took almost a month until the Jewish Agency was able to make an arrangement with the American immigration authorities. Finally, after putting down the enormous sum of five hundred dollars for bail, I was given a transit visa and was able to travel to New York.

Despite this calamity, I have only the best memories of that September in Toronto in 1947. Although I was only there on sufferance, I drove through the city with a megaphone, calling on people to come to a demonstration of solidarity with the passengers of the *Exodus 1947*. The British immigration authorities had refused to let the ship land in Palestine. On September 8, it finally docked in Hamburg, which at the time was under British occupation, where all 4500 passengers, mostly Holocaust survivors, were interned in camps. The public outrage at this treatment was tremendous.

In October 1947, I finally arrived back in New York. My transit visa made it exceedingly clear that this trip could not last much longer. To extend my visa, I had to always have a valid passenger ticket for a ship back to Palestine on my person. Only because of the resourcefulness of the Jewish Agency did I manage to stay one entire year longer.

In November 1947, I decided to expand my work for the Habonim to include the greater New York area. In Newark, Jersey City, and Passaic, New Jersey, more than a dozen boys and girls aged fifteen to sixteen had gotten in touch to say that they wanted to found a Habonim chapter. One of these activists was Hannah Lutzky from Passaic, whose parents gave us use of their living room in their typical American wooden house every Friday evening. Hannah was a good-looking and very bright girl. She seemed more mature than many of the other girls, and was one of the top students in her high school class. From the beginning, she took on the organization of our meetings, which were soon attended by thirty people.

In rain and snow, from early December 1947 I took the bus to Passaic every Friday afternoon to the Lutzkys' home to sing Hebrew songs and talk about founding a Jewish state. One of our main topics of conversation was of course current political events and the meaning of the November 29, 1947 United Nations resolution to partition Palestine into a Jewish and an Arab state. We followed the violence closely that had begun on November 30, when Arab units attacked Jerusalem and the fighting quickly spread to the entire country. After our political discussions, we stayed for a long time, sharing a pot luck dinner. There was soup, salad, gefilte fish, roast chicken, brownies, tea, and coffee—a traditional Shabbat spread which we ate from plastic dishes.

On one of these Friday evening in early 1948, there was a big surprise waiting for me in the Lutzky family home. That evening, Golda Myerson, who took on the name Meir after the founding of Israel, and her 23-year-old son Menachem had come as guests. Golda und Hannah's mother enjoyed a close friendship that went back to their time together at a teacher training school in Milwaukee. Golda's father had fled the pogroms and gone to America in 1903. In 1906, he brought his family to join him. Golda Myerson had however been living in Palestine since 1921. During her short trip to the United States, she was collecting donations for badly-needed equipment for the Haganah, the Israeli underground army. In under two weeks she had managed to collect fifty million dollars, a sum that would today be valued at around half a billion dollars. At that time, Golda was acting director of the political department of the Jewish Agency and had become well-known in the summer of 1946, when she took over leadership of the Yishuv. The British authorities had arrested her boss, Moshe Sharett, along with almost the entire leadership. Ben-Gurion was able to flee to France before he was caught. Because Golda Meir was an American citizen, the British could not arrest her. She had come to America accompanying her son Menachem, a talented musician who was coming to New York to continue his cello studies at the famous Julliard musical conservatory. After Golda returned to Jerusalem, Menachem began to visit the Lutzky's regularly, and it was not long before the dream of the two schoolmates from Milwaukee came true: their children, Hannah and Menachem, got married.

Obsessed by the idea that her son should become a famous cellist, Golda organized lessons for him from a famous professor in Zagreb. This change of countries was a trial for the young marriage, especially since Hannah was already pregnant. When complications arose in her pregnancy, Hannah insisted on returning to Tel Aviv. This brought the fury of her ambitious mother-in-law upon her, and soon after their arrival in Tel Aviv, her marriage to Menachem ended. Not long after, Hannah gave birth to their child, a girl with Down's Syndrome whom she named Meira.

To this day I am horrified about the way in which the "mother of Israel" handled this situation. Until her death, Golda Meir ignored her granddaughter. Through my friendship with Hannah Lutzky, I knew how much both of them were hurt by this rejection. Not until Meira Meir published an obituary for her grandmother in December 1978 did the scandal become public. My feelings about Golda Meir were and are ambivalent, not least because of this intransigent behavior. And her politics in the 1970s did more to strengthen than to disapprove my appraisal of her.

In November 1947, it became clear that the Land and Labor for Palestine mission was beginning to have an effect on people's private lives as well. My brother for example married Florie Rogoff, the secretary of Ralph Goldman, the project's director. My old friend Ralph still lives in Jerusalem today and despite his 95 years goes every day to his office at the "Joint," the old Jewish American relief organization. After the honeymoon, Meshulam returned to Palestine with his American wife, where the two moved into Kibbutz Hulata on Lake Hula—which had not yet been drained—north of the Sea of Galilee. Hulata is below the Golan Heights near the Syrian border and in shooting range of the Lebanese border. Right after Israel was founded, it was the site of heavy fighting. Syrian and Lebanese artillery bombed the kibbutz, triggering shell shock in Meshulam. His hair went completely white and he had to go to Haifa for a few weeks to recuperate.

New Duties, New Paths

Nineteen-forty-seven was a decisive year for the fate of the Jewish people. In Palestine, the struggles around illegal immigration and against the British Mandate government escalated. Not even the elite parachute division, whose soldiers were known among the Jewish population as *"kalaniyot"* (red anemones) due to their red berets, were able to solve the problems. In the spring of 1947, British foreign minister Ernest Bevin decided to bring the Palestine problem before the United Nations. In 1920, the League of Nations had given Great Britain the mandate to administer Palestine and Transjordan. Since the League of Nations disbanded at the start of World War II, the problem was now under the jurisdiction of the United Nations, which had been founded after the war.

Although Great Britain did not agree, in the United States, Europe, and South America it was general consensus that after the Holocaust, immigration to Palestine should be expanded to include more survivors. In 1946, the Anglo-American Committee of the American and British governments wrote a report recommending the immediate immigration of 100,000 survivors to Palestine. But Foreign Minister Bevin rejected the proposal, even though it had been co-written by his Labour Party comrade, Richard Crossman. At the time, this rejection was considered a catastrophe for everyone who was waiting for an immigration visa to Palestine. In retrospect, it also greatly accelerated the foundation of the State of Israel.

By the spring of 1947, the British government had clearly lost control over the situation in Palestine, and demanded a special meeting of the UN General Assembly. Before this meeting, it needed to be decided who would represent the Jewish people, since there was neither a country nor a government. Four groups claimed this right, and presented their motions in the four corners of a rather small room at United Nations Headquarters. The first was the Jewish Agency for Palestine, headed by David Ben-Gurion and the chairman of the World Zionist Organization, Chaim Weizmann. Second was the ultra-orthodox party Agudat Yisrael, which had been founded in the early twentieth century in Berlin and attracted large numbers of Polish Jews. Their rabid anti-Zionist ideology before the war had prevented many young Polish Jews from immigrating to Palestine, which could have saved them from the Holocaust. Agudat Yisrael believed that the idea of a Jewish state was blasphemy. Redemption from the Jewish Diaspora was in their view only possible with the coming of the Messiah; it was a decision that rested in God's hands alone. The third group was Peter Bergson's nationalist American League for a Free Palestine. Ideologically, it was heavily influenced by Zionist revisionist Vladimir Jabotinsky and was close to the revisionist Jewish underground. The final group was Lessing Rosenwald's American Council for Judaism, headquartered in Chicago, which believed that the only future for Judaism lay in complete assimilation. All four parties claimed the right to represent the Jewish people, in the end, the Jewish Agency was chosen.

It goes without saying that I wanted to be there in person for this historical decision. Because I only had to be present at my youth groups in the afternoon and evening, I found an opportunity to attend. I knew Sy Kennen, a member of the Jewish Agency in New York and later a founder of the American Israel Public Affairs Committee (AIPAC). He was responsible for the Jewish Agency's press table for international journalists and I offered to volunteer. A few days later, we learned that the UN General Secretariat had named the Jewish Agency for Palestine as the official representative of the Jewish people for the Special Committee meeting. I was determined to get access to that meeting. With the help of Dan Pinnes, correspondent for the labor newspaper *Davar*, I was able to get a press pass as his assistant, valid until the fall of 1948. The large UN building that stands today had not yet been built. The General Assembly met in Flushing Meadows in an enormous auditorium that had once been part of the World's Fair. The Ad Hoc Political Committee in turn met at Lake Success, also in Queens. The most important operative decision of the General Assembly that April was to create the United Nations Special Committee on Palestine (UNSCOP), which had until the fall to present its resolution to the fall meeting of the UN. Late that summer, UNSCOP presented its proposal to divide the country into a Jewish and an Arab nation, with Jerusalem as an international enclave.

I remember the dramatic discussions on the partition plan in the Political Committee in the fall of 1947. I was deeply moved by the talk by Czechoslovakian Foreign Minister Jan Masaryk, son of the founder of the Czech nation, Tomáš G. Masaryk. He said with conviction: "I am not an expert on pipelines. But I do know one pipeline: the one that carries the blood that flows through the entirety of Jewish history." One day in the large lobby in Flushing Meadows, I noticed that all of the representatives of the Eastern European nations were huddling around Andrei Gromyko, then

USSR representative for the UN Security Council. I had become friendly with Ján Papánek, the Czech delegate, and right away asked him what they had been discussing. His sensational answer was: "The Eastern Bloc countries have decided to support the partition of Palestine and the foundation of a Jewish state." "Can I report that?" I responded. "You can quote me," Papánek said. Dan Pinnes was elated that I had managed to get such important news for *Davar* and express-telegraphed it to Tel Aviv—it was my first scoop, long before I became a journalist.

The vote on the partition plan took place on November 29, 1947. With 33 yays, 13 nays, and 10 abstentions, the UN General Assembly voted for the foundation of a Jewish state on an area comprising almost 55 percent of the British Mandate of Palestine. The Arabs were to have 43 percent of the country and Jerusalem was to stand under international control.

◆

That fall, I had also begun to work together with Teddy Kollek, who would go on to gain fame as mayor of Jerusalem from 1967, and with whom I have enjoyed a lifelong friendship. In 1935, at the age of 24, Kollek had moved to Palestine from Vienna as a member of the Zionist-Socialist youth movement *Blau-Weiss* (Blue-White). He was one of the founders of Kibbutz Ein Gev on the eastern shore of the Sea of Galilee and also worked in the Political Department of the Jewish Agency.

Many of David Ben-Gurion's closest colleagues were from Vienna, perhaps, I believe, because they were more elegant and more diplomatic than the German Yekkes, who were often intractable. Teddy Kollek played a leading role in this circle. Ben-Gurion

With Teddy Kollek, 1995.

had sent him to New York because he suspected that sooner or later there would be fighting against the Arabs. He was proven to have been right. Only one day after the United Nations vote, bloody battles began in Palestine.

For the Jewish population to be able to defend itself, it needed weapons. Ben-Gurion had chosen Teddy Kollek for a key top-secret mission to acquire them. I knew Kollek slightly from the kibbutz movement, and he asked me to work with him soon after his arrival in New York. Kollek was staying in a suite at Hotel Fourteen, where we also held our clandestine meetings. Soon, I became part of the inner circle. As my first important duty, I was to meet a middleman and hear his offer for thousands of bazooka grenades. These were needed for antitank defense. It was agreed that I enter the lobby of the Hotel Alpin on Times Square holding the *New York Times* in my hand so that he would know who I was. I was approached by a man wearing a light-colored suit and a straw hat, who offered me 40,000 bazookas for a price of one million dollars. To show that he was serious, he gave us two samples a few days later.

The day after receiving the weapons, two Haganah armament experts and I drove the two grenades in my father's Buick to a quiet site outside of the city—a risky venture. In the rearview mirror I noticed that a policeman was following us, making signs for us to pull over. I drove to the side of the road and rolled down the side window. "Excuse me, Sir," he said shrilly and somewhat annoyed, "You just lost two cardboard rolls out of your trunk." He told me to drive back and pick them up. At last, we reached a secluded forest, where the experts fired the grenades. They worked, and the delivery was arranged.

Anyone who has ever worked with Teddy Kollek knows what it means when he gives you an assignment: you are accountable from the beginning to the very end, including dealing with whatever problems may arise. That meant that after having acquired the weapons, I was not by any means relieved of my duties. Next, I had to take charge of shipping them to Palestine. In a rented warehouse in Brooklyn, I spent a few weeks with a couple of friends, packing the grenades into boxes and disguising them as canned goods. Then I expedited the boxes to the Brooklyn port, where they were loaded onto a Soviet ship called *Russia*. To this day my heart races when I think of the chutzpah it took to drive the weapons through New York in a borrowed delivery van multiple times a day.

In early 1948, one of the Haganah's special envoys came to New York: Yaakov Yanai, a close friend of Moshe Dayan. In the rooms of the Zionist Archives, around forty envoys from Palestine met with Foreign Minister Moshe Sharett. Yanai reported on the desolate situation regarding the Jewish population's military capacity, and urged us to intensify our efforts to buy weapons. I wanted to return to Palestine immediately to join the fight, but Sharett indignantly rejected my request: "Your work in New York is just as important as fighting on the frontlines," he said. For that reason, I was not in our homeland at the founding of the nation on May 14, 1948, but celebrated with thousands of Jews in Times Square, dancing the hora around the triangular *New York Times* building. But our joy was short-lived. On the very next morning, five Arab armies marched into Israel and the Egyptian Air Force bombed Tel Aviv.

To give Teddy Kollek and his twenty or so workers the feeling that we belonged to the Israeli army's troops, Defense Minister David Ben-Gurion arranged for us to be sworn in as officers of the Israel Defense Force in late May, 1948. On a Saturday evening, we met in the garden of an elegant villa in Mount Vernon, north of New York City, where Colonel Ephraim Ben-Arzi accepted our oath of allegiance to the State of Israel and its army. The villa was put at our disposal by Abe Feinberg, a wealthy American businessman and an advocate for Zionism. At the ceremony, two actors from the Habima theater, which was making a guest appearance in New York, gave a reading. In Israel, all of that was meaningless, the measure had simply been taken to appease us so that we remained in America.

◆

In September 1948, the meeting of the United Nations General Assembly was moved from New York to Paris because of the upcoming presidential elections in the United States. Naturally, I also went. Teddy Kollek gave me a personal letter of introduction to

Asher (Arthur) Ben-Natan, the Mossad representative to Europe and later Israel's first ambassador to Germany. Ben-Natan had been born in Vienna and was the spitting image of the actor Curt Jürgens. He had an attic office on Avenue de Wagram, where the Jewish Agency and the first Israeli diplomatic mission were housed. He gave me the order to go from Marseilles to Israel in two weeks' time as commander of a ship carrying nine hundred half-legal immigrants. I also wanted to go to Vienna, to visit my mother's grave. Ben-Natan was not only not opposed; he immediately gave me a second mission. On the way to Austria, I was to find a certain Russian Jew in a displaced persons camp between Augsburg and Salzburg. The man was in possession of a suitcase belonging to a friend of his who had died; this bag could only be handed over to an official representative of the State of Israel. Inside were allegedly Red Army patents that could greatly increase the efficacy of our mortar shells. Ben-Natan supplied me with documents that established my identity as an official representative of the Jewish people, as well as authorization to receive the suitcase. Once in Vienna, I did in fact manage to track down this man and I gave my authorization to an Israeli friend. While I was not present for the transfer of the patents, I was able to do my part to make sure they reached their final destination.

I arrived in Vienna almost ten years to the day after fleeing the country. During my train journey, I had a typical Austrian experience. As always, I had more than enough reading material with me, including an issue of the *Herald Tribune*. When the train stopped in Salzburg, most passengers debarked and I stayed back in my compartment alone. Two Austrian couples looked in and asked in English whether the other seats were free. I nodded silently and disappeared again behind my newspaper. The women were clearly sisters. One of them had immigrated to America with her husband and was visiting, the other lived in Vienna and had come with her husband to meet her sister in Salzburg. The four of them chatted away. The Viennese woman complained about how much they suffered under the Russian occupiers. "And now," she whined, "all the Jews are returning too and want their old apartments back." Then she grumbled about the transit camp in the Rothschild Hospital, where Jewish refugees and survivors were waiting to continue on to Palestine. I had difficulty remaining calm, but I bit my tongue.

When we rode into Linz, our passports were controlled. Shortly after, we would leave the American zone and enter into the Soviet zone. An American petty officer looked at my passport, an identity card from the British Mandate for Palestine, stamped with a Star of Zion, the signum of the provisional Israeli government. The officer was very friendly, but warned me: "You're going to run into difficulties at the border with this passport. The Russians here only accept Soviet or American passports. Travelers with British passports are usually only allowed to travel into the Soviet zone from the British zone in the south." Traveling back to Salzburg and then to Graz would have been a detour of at least one-and-a-half to two days and I therefore decided to take the risk. And in fact, the Soviet border soldier on the bridge over the Ems escorted me from the train and brought me to his supervisor, who understood a little German and English. I showed him my passport with the Star of David and said: "Israel, Israel, nyet Britanski." His face lit up and he answered: "Israel ochin harasho—very good." He gave me a quick hug, asked for my pardon, and accompanied me back to my compartment personally. My traveling companions were astounded. The Viennese couple had traveled the route many times before and had sometimes seem people taken out of the train, but never had they seen someone come back in. Now they wanted to know how I had managed. I answered nonchalantly: "I'm not British, I'm from Israel." Up until that point, we had been conversing in English. Now I added: "We can speak in German, I was born in Vienna and am going to visit my mother's grave." There was a dead silence as they realized that I may have been listening to their previous conversation. Immediately, the attempted to relativize their statements. They had absolutely nothing against Jews in general, there were always some people interested only in their own gain, etc. It was, in a nutshell, revolting.

A few hours later, we arrived in Vienna. The city looked like, no, *was*, the backdrop of the famous film *The Third Man*, starring Orson Welles. A few huts stood in a desolate area, the rest of the entire neighborhood around the Westbahnhof Station had been reduced to rubble. Following the advice of the Austrian resistance, the Red Army had attacked Vienna mostly from the west. The Wehrmacht had bitterly defended the center of the city, readily accepting widespread destruction in turn.

Ben-Natan had naturally also written me letters of introduction to his contacts in Vienna. Hence I was able to find sleeping quarters near the Votive Church—and my old *Gymnasium*. There, in a handsome four-room apartment in an old patrician house, lived a certain Herr Teichholz, he too a Holocaust survivor. He provided housing for people who were organizing transit to Israel for illegal immigrants. After picking up the keys, I went out onto the evening streets. First, I retraced my old walk home from school: Wasa Gymnasium, Liechtensteinstrasse, Porzellangasse. For me, Vienna had become a ghost town. None of the Jewish stores were still there. I read new, unknown names and felt like I was walking through a cemetery.

The next day, I went to our house on Porzellangasse 50, where the son of Mr. Wraneschitz, the caretaker, was still living. He recognized me immediately and took me to see our old apartment on the first floor, now occupied by a family that had been bombed out of their home. The new residents literally fell to their knees, begging me to at least leave them one room to live in if I was moving back into the apartment. "I have no plans at all to do so. I'm here for sentimental reasons, I just want to see my childhood apartment," I explained to the distraught woman in an attempt to calm her down. I had mixed feelings entering the apartment. Rita and my father had done major renovations in 1936 for their wedding; the marble fireplace was still there and the patterned wallpaper, now grungy, was still clinging to the walls. I was surprised by the extent to which I felt like a stranger there.

I asked the caretaker's son after the Pech family, who had lived below us on the mezzanine floor. I had been good friends with Walter Pech, who proved his upright honesty by the way he dealt with a valuable present that I had received for my bar mitzvah in December 1937. It was a Steyr bicycle, and had been my pride and joy. Walter also liked it. Directly after the Anschluss, he was among those parading around in the brown Hitler Youth uniform; he no longer knew me on the street. A few days later, he rang the bell, came in, and explained to me that, as a Jew, I was no longer allowed to ride a bicycle. It was to be confiscated on the spot. However, he made me a deal: Since a bicycle unit was going to be founded in his Hitler Youth mob, he would appropriate my bicycle for himself. Officially, word would be that he had confiscated my bike, but he promised to return it when I left the country. What could I have done? My beloved bicycle thus became part of the Hitler Youth Bike

Unit. Occasionally, Walter parked the bicycle in the hallway of our apartment, where a rope winch was used to hang it from the ceiling. That way, at least I could see it. Walter kept his word. When I told him about my plans to flee the country in October 1938, he returned the bicycle and I had it shipped to Haifa. For ten years it served me well, and gave me precious freedom. Probably it was the only bicycle in Jewish Palestine that had also served the Hitler Youth.

Now the caretaker's son told me that Walter had fallen in the war. Nevertheless, I wanted to visit his mother. Mrs. Pech recognized me immediately: "It's Ari," she said, started to cry, and hugged me. My unexpected visit had most certainly rekindled memories of her son. Possibly she also thought: "The Jew boy survived it all and my Walter fell." But it was probably important to her to spend a few hours with me. I had to look at photos of Walter with his horses in the Cavalry, Walter on the Russian front, and Walter in Normandy, where he had fallen in 1944. A few months before my visit, his parents had visited his grave for the first time, which was in one of the enormous military cemeteries in France. But we also talked about the good times during our childhood. When I said good-bye to Maria Pech, I wasn't thinking about a Wehrmacht soldier who had died in the war, but was empathizing with a mother who had lost her only son.

On November 9, 1948, there was a memorial in the auditorium of the Musical Society for the tenth anniversary of Pogrom Night, and I was an honorary guest. Cardinal Theodor Innitzer spoke at the occasion, the same man who had offered a warm public welcome to Hitler in 1938, and ordered his bishops to support the new regime. Chancellor Leopold Figl, who had been interned in Dachau concentration camp himself under the Nazis, called upon the Jews of

Vienna who had survived the war abroad to return and take part in rebuilding post-war Austria. Israel's first Consul to Austria, Daniel Kurt Lewin, who spoke perfect German, replied with a quivering voice: "For us, all of Europe is one big cemetery. We can no longer live here. We will erect the State of Israel."

The actions of multiple Austrian governments after the war suggest that Figl's appeal was no more than lip service. During the post war years, the SPÖ (Social Democratic Party of Austria) and the ÖVP (Austrian People's Party) regularly expressed antisemitic sentiments in public. Often cited are the words of SPÖ Minister of the Interior Oskar Helmer at a meeting of the Austrian Cabinet of Ministers on November 9, 1948. Helmer, on the question of how much restitution should be paid for stolen Jewish property and when, declared: "Everywhere I look I see only signs of Jewish expansion ... The Nazis too lost everything in 1945 ... I am in favor of dragging this thing out for as long as possible." Even back then, I was conscious of the fact that the Austrian people rarely regretted their participation in Nazi crimes. Although two-thirds of Austrian Jews survived the Holocaust, the number of Jews who returned to Austria was minimal. It would be forty years before Austrian fascism was explored in any depth, after the Kurt Waldheim affair.

Just as I was preparing to leave the auditorium, I noticed two women and a man at the exit. One of the women looked familiar. It turned out to be our former pediatrician, Dr. Sala Weitz. She, too, recognized me and, happy to see me, invited me to accompany them to a café.

To this day I am adamant that anyone who did not live through the Holocaust themselves has no right to make moral judgments about survivors. We know from so many testimonies that people often had to act in immoral ways in order to survive the torment. Nevertheless, my reunion with Sala Weitz was unendurable. She told me how horrible her experience in the pediatric hospital in the 2nd district had been, where she had been able to hire her sister and brother-in-law as assistants. In 1942, every two weeks she had to put together child transports to Auschwitz. She wrote up lists, got the children ready... Just listening I began to feel sickened, but that wasn't all. In the very next breath she complained about Vienna now being full of Polish Jews doing business on the black market. "They're rekindling the whole *rishes*," she said, using the Yiddish word for wickedness, by which she meant antisemitic ressentiments. I got up and left the café.

A few days later, I traveled from Vienna to Marseilles, to fulfill Asher Ben-Natan's next mission. The *Caserta* was already anchored at port—an old Italian freighter which was to bring over nine hundred immigrants to Israel. Most of the passengers were survivors from Poland and Romania. Our common language was Yiddish, which I had taught myself in New York in order to read the three important Yiddish daily papers published there at the time. The *Caserta* was furnished in the typical manner of immigrant ships: the passengers slept in three-tiered bunks in the converted cargo hold. The ship sailed under an Italian captain; my job as "commander" was to care for the passengers. This gave me the privilege of my own cabin next to the skipper's cabin, which I turned over to three pregnant women after we set sail. They belonged to a British chapter of the Habonim Youth and were traveling to Israel to found a kibbutz in the north, near the Syrian border.

Soon after leaving Marseilles we ran into a terrible storm. Many of the passengers suffered from seasickness, and armed with a large bottle of valerian and sugar cubes given me by the captain, I went for hours up and down past the bunks in the sleeping quarters, attempting to calm my groaning patients. When the number of seasick passengers did not lessen, the captain and I decided to allow the passengers to rest for 24 hours in the Strait of Messina. It was a difficult decision, our supplies were scarce. For two days, we survived on emergency rations: rock-hard zwieback and tea. After the storm subsided, young Sicilians came with their boats and sold us oranges, which were better than any medicine. Thus equipped, we continued our journey, and three days later, to our great relief, Mount Carmel appeared on the horizon.

I called all passengers on deck, which was quickly overcrowded, and held my first address in Yiddish: *"Der groyse tog iz gekumen. Mir werden gleikh sayn in Eretz Yisroel, in unzer eygene medine."* (The big day has come. Soon we will be in the land of Israel, in our own country.) Spontaneously, everyone began singing Hatikvah, "the hope," which had been the hymn of the Zionist movement and was now the national anthem of the young state of Israel.

My second arrival in Haifa, met by blue-and-white flags, Jewish police, and Israeli government agents, filled me with pride and great joy. Ten years had passed since I arrived in Palestine in November 1938, and could only be driven to the Ahava school in an armored car, under the protection of the British harbor police. Now, I took care of the formalities for transferring the care of the *Caserta*'s nine hundred passengers to officers of the Jewish Agency and the Israeli authorities. The simple fact of the formerly non-existent name "Ministry of the Interior of the Israeli Government" filled me with such juvenile exuberance that I was even able to patiently bear the bureaucracy of the inexperienced Israeli officials.

Early in the afternoon, I boarded a bus to Kibbutz Hamadia. Tall eucalyptus trees flanked the narrow road and the straw was glistening on the newly-mown fields in the late afternoon sun. When we reached the "capital" of Jezreel Valley, Afula, I could feel my home approaching. My friends, whom I had not seen for two years, greeted my warmly. Nevertheless, I took the bus to Tel Aviv the very next morning to report to the military. Back then, the journey took over four hours and there were not always seats on the overcrowded buses.

In the Defense Ministry, I went to Yosef Yisraeli, a department head I knew well from the kibbutz movement; he was responsible for the circa thousand kibbutzniks who served in the military. I showed him the Israel Defense Forces officer's ID that I had received from General Efraim Ben-Arzi at the swearing-in ceremony in New York in late May 1948. Yisraeli laughed heartily and said: "You can frame your ID as a souvenir. It has no practical value here. But if your kibbutz agrees, you can enlist right now and become a soldier." I would have loved to have done just that, but Hamadia's secretariat had another opinion. Twenty of our members were already doing military service, and the kibbutz needed able-bodied men for its own defense—the dangerous border to Jordan was only a stone's throw from our fields. Although I served in the military's reserves until 1980 and fought on the front during the wars of 1967 and 1973, I still feel the stigma of never having served as a soldier. In the last two years of my military career, I was deployed as a press officer, accompanying groups of foreign journalists to the Golan and the Suez Canal.

After the excitement of my missions in Europe and the failure of my military ambitions, a fairly calm life awaited me in Hamadia. Since I was one of few members of the kibbutz able to milk cows, I

Ari milking at the kibbutz, ca. 1949.

was assigned to work in the barn. It is hard to imagine a starker contrast to New York and Europe. Sixty dairy cows lived in our barn. They needed to be milked three times a day at intervals that were as regular as possible in order to fulfill our daily quota of twenty-seven to thirty liters per day—internationally, a high average. Each of us had to milk twelve to thirteen cows each shift. Every morning we got up at three-thirty a.m. and milked and fed the cows and cleaned the stalls for two hours. We repeated this procedure at 11:30 a.m. and at 5:30 p.m. The milking hours were scattered across the day, which meant forgoing a social life, to my great annoyance. I managed to convince the cow barn team to change the rhythm and move the first shift to midnight. That way, we could participate in evening activities on the kibbutz. I had brought LPs from America as well as a modern record player, and had been given permission to keep them as private property as an exception. Regularly, I organized concert evenings after dinner. On other evenings we had discussions about the political situation and the future of the kibbutz movement. I have loved being with children my entire life, and I got along well with them. Therefore, I took regular shifts helping out at the nursery on Shabbat. Many of the children from those days are now grandparents themselves and have become good friends. Every once in a while, we had visitors from abroad; I looked after them and tried to explain kibbutz life to them.

In that period, I got to know a young woman with whom I had a close relationship for many years. She was five years younger than me and went by the biblical name Tziporah, her friends called her Tzipke. She was thin and wore her thick blond hair in a braid—the very picture of an Israeli-born sabra. In 1949, Tziporah had come to live with us at Hamadia with a group of sixteen war-weary demobilized soldiers. I knew some of them from three years earlier, having mentored them in the youth movement. They had lost their baby fat, now their faces mirrored the experience of war. All of them were relieved that they had come out the other side. After the first parliamentary elections in January 1949, we hoped that the (separate) ceasefire agreements with Egypt, Jordan, Syria, and Lebanon would lead us on the path to peace.

The kibbutz secretariat decided that I should be the *madrich* of this group. We met after work each day and twice weekly I gave a lecture on current political events. Tziporah stood out for me on the very first meeting; she seemed particularly vulnerable and sensitive alongside her more rugged *chaverim*. Although—or maybe because—we came from completely different worlds, we got along very well. We fell in love and became a couple in the spring of 1949. Tziporah's world had consisted of her life with her parents in Kiryat Haim, a working-class suburb of Haifa, the youth movement, and her experiences in the military. I was taken with her humility, her non-judgmental openness to other people, and her incorruptible sense of fairness. I also got along well with her family. The Polskis came from the Polish-Russian border area and had immigrated to Palestine in the 1920s. Tziporah's father was a technician at the Rutenberg Company, Palestine's first electric utility. We often visited them in their small modest home in Kiryat Haim, where they still cooked on a petroleum stove.

In May 1949, I introduced Tziporah to my parents and Henny when they visited me in Hamadia on their first visit to Israel. She got along particularly well with my brother Meshulam and his wife Flori. After the birth of my niece Orit in December 1949, we often went to visit them in Hulata. Tziporah loved taking care of the baby and knitted her first pair of shoes.

Although we got along well, we never applied for a family tent, in which we could have lived together. I had difficulties committing to the relationship with Tziporah, as wonderful as her character was. She in turn did not make any demands, and so our relationship ended after eight years, against her will.

◆

In the spring of 1951, the leading members of the united youth movement came to Hamadia and asked the kibbutz to release me for two years to take on the post of General Secretary. I was not exactly enthusiastic; I had only been back for two and a half years and I did not want to leave. But the kibbutz movement made an offer we could hardly refuse in the event that I, and the Hamadia leadership, agreed. There was an acute shortage of labor at the time, and we tried very hard to recruit new members. If I took on the job, the organization promised to send sixty boys and girls who had just finished their training in the Nachal brigade to the kibbutz. (The Nachal, the Fighting Pioneer Youth, is an IDF infantry corps that exists to this day in which soldiers are given not only military, but also agricultural training.) For Hamadia and its then ninety members, the addition of so many highly-qualified young people represented an incredibly important reinforcement.

And so I moved to Tel Aviv for two-and-a-half years to become General Secretary of the youth movement. At the time, the movement comprised around nine thousand members distributed across the country. There were five offices in Tel Aviv. One of my tasks was the recruitment and training of *madrichim*, who in turn prepared young people in their home towns for life on a kibbutz. One of the perks of the job was a jeep, which I used to visit offices across the country, and to visit our members in new kibbutzim. Without it, I never could have covered 200,000 kilometers per year.

At least once a week I drove to Jerusalem, not exactly a safe trip at the time. In 1952-3 there were multiple attacks by Palestinian Fedayeen fighters from Gaza and the West Bank. Especially after nightfall, there were times when one could only drive from Ramla to Jerusalem in guarded convoys of eight to ten cars. The last stretch of the way was considered particularly risky: the so-called Jerusalem corridor, where there were often attacks. I remember one episode in particular. One day, I was waiting for enough cars to gather to form a convoy, when suddenly Chief of General Staff Moshe Dayan came speeding up. He refused to accept the security measures, insisted on passing immediately, and drove alone into the danger zone. Shortly afterwards, we had enough vehicles for a convoy and also continued our journey. A few kilometers later, we found Dayan's car empty on the side of the road—he himself was huddling with his driver in a roadside ditch. The hothead's relief when we showed up was clearly visible. Together, we continued on to Jerusalem.

My colleagues and I, Elisha Shemer in particular, organized training seminars for the *madrichim*. We also organized a large conference each year, in which we tried to lay out the advantages of social democracy over communism for the young people. The Iron Curtain had already fallen over Europe.

One event from those years stands out particularly clearly in my memory. In the summer of 1952, we celebrated the seventh anniversary of the united youth movement in the square in front of the Habima theater in Tel Aviv. For this event, I had been able to win over then Foreign Minister and later Prime Minister Moshe Sharett as the main speaker. He railed against the leftist socialist Mapam party, which held close ties to the Soviet Union even though one of their leading members, Mordechai Oren, had been arrested and tortured by the communist secret service.

At the time, the international public was carefully watching the show trial against Rudolf Slánský, General Secretary of the Czechoslovakian Communist party. He had been charged with high treason and industrial espionage. He had also been charged with supporting Israel by supplying weapons in the 1948 war, although it had been with the Kremlin's consent. The Soviet Union—which did not even attempt to disguise its antisemitism—was the driving force behind the trial. On December 3, 1952, Slánský was hung from the gallows.

Four years later, I listened for three hours one Friday evening as Mordechai Orens, a key witness in that trial, told the story of what had happened to him as a delegate to the 1952 World Peace Council in East Berlin. On his way back to Vienna, he had been taken out of the train in Prague and held for months and tortured in a special prison. In the end, he broke under the coercion and testified against Slánský. Orens' moving report cemented my belief that Soviet communism was inhumane.

During the week, I lived in a commune in Jaffa, which had been incorporated into Tel Aviv in 1950. We rented an old turn-of-the-century house also inhabited by the Greek consul and his Palestinian wife, as well as a few Arab families, with whom we got along well. Unlike the Youth Movement General Secretaries before me, who had had their own rooms in Tel Aviv, I insisted on living communally, a "kibbutz in town" as I once explained our living situation to my Greek neighbor, who had expressed surprise at twelve young women and men sharing an apartment—and often also housing guests. I wanted to send a signal to our *madrichim*. After all, we insisted that they also live communally, and not with their parents.

During that period, youth groups were encouraged to support existing kibbutzim. But there was one particularly talented group from Tel Aviv who I supported in founding their own kibbutz. The young people were all sabras, and as a Nahal group they had set up an outpost directly on the border to the Gaza Strip. In October 1953, they founded Kibbutz Nahal Oz. Not long after, Roy Rothberg, one of their leading members, was shot near the border while leading a herd of sheep to pasture. I was very upset by his death. He had been an exceptional *madrich*, whom I had valued greatly for his conscientiousness and his friendly manner with the young people in his care. Moshe Dayan gave a controversial eulogy, whose key sentences were often cited for many years to come: "What can we say against their terrible hatred of us? For eight years now, they have sat in the refugee camps of Gaza, and have watched how, before their very eyes, we have turned their land and villages, where they and their forefathers previously dwelled, into our home. ... Let us not fear to look squarely at the hatred that consumes and fills the lives of hundreds of Arabs who live around us. Let us not drop our gaze, lest our arms be weakened. That is the fate of our generation. This is our choice—to be ready and armed, tough and hard—or else the sword shall fall from our hands and our lives will be cut short." To this day, Nahal Oz has repeatedly been a target of Qassam rockets.

♦

In 1953 I returned to Hamadia, and the following year I became Secretary of the kibbutz. It was a volunteer position that included a huge amount of extra work. In exchange, I received half a day free each week, which I used to first found, and then edit and write for the kibbutz newspaper, *Ma Nishma* (What's Up?). The kibbutz Secretary is a kind of factotum, responsible for everything from helping people with personal problems to acting as building contractor. Having so many responsibilities sapped my energy, especially since the practical work went along with endless committee meetings. I also did hard physical labor, tending our carrot and sugar beet fields. After a plow dug up the sugar beets, we harvested them by hand, throwing them onto a wagon that held seven to eight tons. We also had fish ponds on Hamadia, which are there to this day, and we were the first kibbutz to grow cotton. The chicken coops and the cow and sheep barns were all abandoned in the 1960s. At that time, the kibbutz decided to replace agricultural with industrial production. Since then, Hamadia has run a large door factory, founded by Itzik Kessari. (In the early days of the kibbutz, individual initiative was encouraged. Each member should have the opportunity to develop their full potential.) Like my friend Avri, Itzik Kessari was from Žilina in Slovakia. He was also an extremely talented craftsman. He had survived the Nazi period in a forced labor camp, where he had built furniture and equipment for the Wehrmacht. He came to us together with his group Yitzerah (Creation) in 1949. Together with one of the founding members of Hamadia, Avremel Israeli, a *chaver* who was originally from Vienna, Kessari first set up a carpentry shop because of the many new immigrants in the nearby town of Beit She'an—a direct consequence of the 1948 war.

In the 1940s, Beit She'an, which had been founded in biblical times, was an Arab city. Most inhabitants did not relocate to Nazareth as advised by the Jewish district mayor Elisha Sultz, and so, after battles with the Israeli military, were forced to flee over the Jordan to Transjordan, where they still live today. After 1949, many Jewish settlers from Rumania and Morocco established homes there. The city grew quickly, and window frames and doors from Hamadia's factory were in high demand. As part of the 1952 Reparations Agreement, we received furniture manufacturing machinery from Germany. Today, Hamadia is also known for its plastics factory, Inbal, which started by making sailboats and playground equipment and later manufactured switchboxes for Siemens. Many of the workers commuted from Beit She'an. In the past decades, life in Hamadia has completely transformed.

Today, the kibbutz has around 120 members, but, as in many other kibbutzim, the centrality of community has faded. Socialist ideas no longer play much if any role. I have followed these changes closely and with concern. First, there was the computerized itemization and billing of every tomato consumed in the dining hall, the next phase was to get rid of the dining hall entirely. Today, the idea of communal living has been absurdly reduced to paying individual salaries to kibbutz members, as per usual in a capitalist economy. Moreover, Hamadia, like other kibbutzim, has also become active in the housing sector. Apartments are rented to outsiders, and land zoned for building is sold or leased. However this has not made Hamadia as wealthy as other settlements closer to the water, where there has been a boom in land prices. Even if I am not happy with these tendencies, my friends have told me that building new villas and residential buildings guarantees the continued existence of the kibbutz. Some children and grandchildren of the early kibbutz members have returned to Hamadia, which boasts a kindergarten, elementary school, and a special needs school, and has become central to the region.

◆

My experiences in America and Europe enriched my life on the kibbutz. Often, the Labor Unity party and kibbutz movement asked me to accompany visitors on trips to Israel, showing them the progress of our young nation. In 1944, the year Labor Unity split from Mapam, I had become an active member of the party.

In 1956, four months before the Suez Crisis, I received a call from the director of the international division of Labor Unity: "Ari, in Tampere in Finland the IUCY (International Union of Socialist Youth) will be holding its annual congress. You have been chosen as delegate for the Israeli Socialist Youth. Your flight and all other costs will be covered of course." This was a great honor, because the party could only afford to send one single delegate. The kibbutz gave its consent and so I flew to Helsinki at the beginning of June. Enthralled by the long days and short nights, I continued on by train to Tampere. I still see myself, all alone, a one-man-delegation among many larger contingents. I sat during the day in the pouring rain in a small tent above which I had hoisted the Israeli flag. That got people curious, and I spoke with many of them about life in Israel. As a side event to the summer congress, the IUCY office also held its annual conference. I became friends with the conference chair, Nath Pai from India, with whom I engaged in passionate discussions about how the IUSY could support the rise of Europe's social democratic parties. After Stalin's death in 1953, the fundamental difference between socialism and communism had become a burning issue.

In no time at all, I became a part of the inner circle and therefore continued my journey, traveling with Nath Pai and our Scandinavian colleagues to Bommersvik, the traditional meeting place of Sweden's Socialist Youth. Bommersvik lies on a lake thirty kilometers outside of Stockholm. The seminar was attended by a great number of prominent socialists, many of whom later went on to play a key role in Scandinavian politics. My working group was on the organization of leisure time in affluent societies. We assumed that the working day would be reduced to five or six hours in the automated society of the future. A very naïve idea in retrospect!

I was particularly impressed by one young Swede who already held a high-level job at the Ministry of Education and whose contributions to the discussion were always well-formulated and to the point. I had the chance to get to know him better since we wrote the group's final statement together. It was not yet clear where his path would lead him, but it was obvious that he had a great career ahead of him. His name was Olof Palme. We ran into one another often over the years, for example when Palme managed the office of Prime Minister Tage Erlander or when I was covering Ben-Gurion's

Scandinavian trip for the *Jerusalem Post* in 1962. I also met with Palme in 1963 in Jerusalem, during Erlander's visit to Israel. After the official program I invited him late in the evening to Fink's Bar, an international hotspot at the time. Immediately we were once again embroiled in a heated discussion. The Palestinian leader Yasser Arafat had founded the Palestinian Liberation Organization (PLO) in 1962, and Sweden had been one of the first governments in Europe to support this step. Their support met with massive rejection in Israel. I too was convinced at the time that the PLO was a terrorist organization and should not be recognized, which would only lend them credibility. Olof Palme held a diametrically opposed view: only the political recognition of the PLO would make a peace agreement between Israel and the Palestinians possible. It would be another thirty years until, among other events, the Oslo Accords would prove that Olof Palme's assessment had been correct.

In 1969, Palme took over Tage Erlander's office as Prime Minister of Sweden. I met him for the last time in 1985 at the International Press Institute conference in Stockholm. He hosted a welcome dinner at Operakällaren, a fine dining restaurant near the Stockholm Opera, and we reminisced about Bommersvik. A group of participants were keen to organize a follow-up meeting. I sat down at Palme's table and told him about our proposal; he was enthusiastic about the idea and offered to host the meeting. We never got the opportunity; Palme was assassinated on February 28, 1986 on his way home from the movies in a case that has not been solved to this day. Not long ago, I met Palme's son Joachim in Vienna at a conference at the Bruno Kreisky Forum, where we discussed the future of social democracy.

♦

In the summer of 1956, before leaving Scandinavia, I made plans to stop over in London. I wanted to get to know the British in their own country; up until then, I had only ever made their acquaintance as soldiers or police of the British Mandate government. My contact was Edi Tanner, a distant cousin on my mother's side. He was ten years younger than I and his family ran a small hotel in Golders Green, a neighborhood where many religious Jews still live today. Edi spent much of his free time exploring Jewish issues and had founded a discussion group in which he and his friends met regularly on Saturdays to talk about Israel and current political events. In the summer of 1956, they were focusing on Israel's security. Ben-Gurion had already spoken publicly about security problems in June, and during the summer the situation had escalated. There had been repeated attacks by Fedayeen who entered Israel from the West Bank and attacked villages and vehicles, answered by retaliatory strikes by the Israeli army. Many civilians and soldiers had already died. Tanner hoped I could offer first-hand information and analyses. Up until then, his group had been heavily influenced by Jochanan Moses, a brave young Yekke and El-Al pilot who was very critical of Ben-Gurion's policies.

Two days after my arrival, I went with Tanner to the house of Maurice Gewirzman, where the Saturday discussions took place. To my surprise, our host greeted me warmly in Hebrew and told me that he had attended Tel Aviv's first high school together with Moshe Sharett before coming to London to study in the early 1920s. He had never lost touch with people in Palestine/Israel. Gewirzman had become wealthy trading in electronics, making him able to not only buy a large amount of property in Palestine, but also financially support the development of the Haganah. He also belonged to the investment group that in 1949 built the Sharon, Israel's first large luxury hotel on what was then the completely undeveloped beachfront of Herzliya, north of Tel Aviv.

Around 25 young people came to my lecture. I noticed a very good-looking young woman with blue-green eyes when she offered me a tray of canapés. "You seem to feel at home here," I said to her. "That's because I am at home," she answered, introducing herself as Dorothy Gewirzman. I also learned that she was about to become the sister-in-law of Yochanan Moses, her younger sister Marilyn had recently become engaged. There was a discussion after my lecture and then most attendees left. Those of us remaining—Edi Tanner, Dorothy, her best friend Josephine and her fiancé, the Israeli diamond dealer Willy Nagel, a Belgian friend of theirs, and I—drove to Chelsea to the Blue Angel nightclub. Much to Edi's dismay, Dorothy and I talked together almost the entire evening and she proposed to take me on a tour of London in her father's car the next day.

Sunday morning, Dorothy pulled up to my student hostel in a black Morris. We spent a wonderful day together, we got along as if we had already known each other for ages. Late in the evening I brought her home, my plane was due to fly the next day. "It would be so nice if we could spend one more day together," Dorothy said, articulating my own thoughts. I decided on the spot to extend my stay through Monday, even though Tziporah was already waiting for me in Paris. I sent a telegram to the Israeli embassy in Paris and said that I would be arriving on Tuesday.

I remember very well how difficult it was for us to say goodbye that Monday evening. We didn't even promise each other to stay in touch. I didn't believe I had a realistic chance with her—she was a

London girl from a wealthy family and I was a destitute kibbutznik. The next day I met Tziporah in Paris, where we spent three days before continuing on to Vienna. We stopped over in Salzburg, by chance on Erev Yom Kippur, and I went to the synagogue there. After a few days in Vienna we journeyed to Italy, where we saw the art treasures in Florence, Rome, and Naples, finally leaving by ship from Genoa to Haifa. I have only vague memories of this trip, since I was plagued by the knowledge of my inner betrayal. I kept thinking about Dorothy and was increasingly irked by Tziporah's introverted personality, which did not fit well with me extroverted interests. In all of my relationships with women, not only intimate emotional understanding, but also lively intellectual exchange has always been of utmost importance to me. I value education, curiosity, worldliness, and quick repartee. It was also important to me that my partner speak English; increasingly I moved in an English-speaking world in my professional life, especially after starting at the *Jerusalem Post* in 1958. Sooner or later, that much had become clear to me, my relationship with Tziporah would come to an end.

In late September, we returned to Hamadia. New apartments had been built over the summer for long-time members of the kibbutz. The new rooms had fourteen instead of twelve square meters, and also a small balcony. What is more, each room connected to a two-square-meter bathroom with shower and toilet—an unbelievable luxury at the time and one that was not reserved for one person alone, but had to be shared. Our friends had interpreted our long European vacation as a honeymoon before the fact, and assumed that Tziporah and I would move in to one of these luxury accommodations. But I decided to stay in my old room. Soon after, I broke up with Tziporah.

Tensions in the Middle East continued to escalate. Not only was there no end to the skirmishes on the border to the West Bank, the Suez Crisis was also nearing its apex. After an officers' putsch against King Farouk in July 1952, Gamal Abdel Nasser came to power in Egypt. He wanted to bring progress to the underdeveloped country. After trying without success to get Western support for the construction of the Asswan Dam, Nasser developed an Anti-Western stance. In the summer of 1956, he nationalized the Suez Canal, which had been built and operated by a British and French-owned company. Nationalization closed the passage between the Persian Gulf and the Mediterranean to Israeli ships, as well as to international ships that traded with Israel, a situation that could not be borne for long. Covert negotiations took place between Israel, France, and England, and military action against Egypt was agreed upon. Within one hundred hours, the Israeli army, under the commando of Moshe Dayan, occupied the Sinai peninsula. In Israel, the mood was euphoric over the quick victory. Ben-Gurion held a speech in the Knesset extolling a "third Israeli Empire." But after an ultimatum by the Soviet Union and the United States, the Israeli troops had no choice but to retreat. Israel was to keep the Gaza Strip only, until March 1957.

Some of my friends from the kibbutz, including Avri, went to the front. I was aggravated that my reserve battalion had not been mobilized, but that didn't stop me from going to the site of the action as soon as possible. As soon as the fighting was over, I drove with eight friends from the kibbutz in an open delivery truck to El Arish in the northern Sinai. We wanted to visit St. Catherine's Monastery, a Greek Orthodox monastery at the foot of Mount Sinai known for its icons, as well as for the skulls of its former monks in its crypt. It is said to be the site where Moses received the ten commandments. The area was closed to civilians, since so many people wanted to visit the Sinai peninsula. Whenever we were stopped we just said: "We're on the way to the new Nahal outpost on Tiran Island," and they waved us through. We reached the monastery, stayed the night as guests of the friendly monks, and the next morning at daybreak, we climbed Mount Sinai. Before leaving, we signed our names in the monastery's guest book. When I went back in 1967, only thirty more guests had signed the book. On our way back home, we ran into UN troops who had already been called in to act as a puffer between the Egyptian and the Israeli militaries. After the retreat of the Israeli army, the UN took over control of Sinai.

In early 1957, I also went to Gaza to see for myself the situation in the Palestinian refugee camps. Many former inhabitants of Jaffa lived there. They had fled to Gaza in the 1948 war, usually by sea to keep the overland routes open for the Egyptian military. The camps were divided into separate areas for different families and clans, who had settled in such groups in Jaffa as well. The conditions under which these people still had to live nine years after fleeing were horrifying: large families shared very little space while the original inhabitants of Gaza lived in comfortable two- to three-story houses. I spoke to many Palestinians who had felt more secure during the few months under Israeli military administration than they did now under Egyptian administration. They worried that the Americans would not keep their promise to put Gaza under an international mandate and would instead give it back to the Egyptians. In fact, the Egyptian military did later return and executed many Palestinians suspected of collaborating with the Israeli military.

Although in retrospect I put great value on my education at Ahava, my understanding of education had been shaped in the main by my European background and included earning not only a Matura [Austrian secondary-school leaving certificate], but also an academic university degree. After the end of the Suez Crisis, there were good chances of a few years of calm and peace, but first I had to convince the leadership of Kibbutz Hamadia that it made sense to allow me to study. It proved no easy task to convince my friend Avri, Kibbutz Secretary at the time, that if I did go to university it did not necessarily mean that I would leave the kibbutz. In general, there was a lot of skepticism about university studies. For one thing, studying demanded stamina, furthermore, there was a real danger that after academic training I would have absolutely no more interest in physically demanding agricultural labor. I was deeply offended by this mistrust: "Give me a chance to prove you wrong," I demanded rashly, until they finally gave in. As the first member of the kibbutz to study, I was given a two-year leave under the condition that I finance my studies myself.

And so I moved to Jerusalem to start my courses in economics and history in the fall semester. I was sure that the university had been waiting for a student like me. This turned out to be far from true, I didn't even have a Matura certificate. First, they said, I would have to wait one year for a spot and I could take the Matura exams while I waited. Finally, I managed to enroll on a provisional basis. I had three months to prepare for the exams. Day and night I sat alone with a mountain of books and papers. From October, I also attended courses in history and economics, and at the end of November I passed my Matura exams.

Dorothy also reentered my life. After meeting in London we had sporadically sent one another postcards. During Passover 1957 I met her, at my sister Henny's initiative, on Montefiori Street in Tel Aviv; she was in Israel for ten days for her sister Marilyn's wedding. My memories of that chaotic week are turbulent, since my father was also visiting from Europe. He was supposed to have been staying with me in Hamadia, but he found it so uncomfortable there that I put him up in Hotel Sharon in Herzliya, where the Gewirzman family was also staying. All week I commuted, hitchhiking, from Hamadia, where I had been called back for the hay harvest, to Herzliya, where a romance was developing between Dorothy and me. She left as planned, but promised to return in a few months to fulfill one of her father's wishes and learn Hebrew. Dorothy came to Jerusalem shortly after I started studying at university. She lived with relatives and visited an ulpan, a public Hebrew school, for six months.

One day in May 1958, I was sitting with Dorothy in a café on Ben Yehuda Street. Her language course was over and we had to discuss our future. I didn't know what to do and mumbled: "We should get married." Dorothy was thrilled: "That means that we're engaged now. Please buy me a small ring."A wheel was set in motion that I could no longer stop. We told my brother the news and soon after my future bride returned to London. She was preparing our fall wedding from there, and getting ready for a life in Israel. Around two weeks after she had gone back, I received a long letter from her father. Although Maurice Gewirzman liked me, he was worried about how I would be able to support a family as a kibbutznik and a student. He proposed that I continue my studies at the London School of Economics; Dorothy and I could live at his house. I thanked him from my heart but refused his offer; I wanted to stay in Israel. Two weeks later Dorothy wrote how happy she was that I had turned the offer down—my future father-in-law had just been testing me. He was afraid that my interest in Dorothy had been given a boost by his wealth. Now there were no more barriers to the wedding, which was to take place on November 4, 1958.

I do not want to hide the fact that my feelings about my future were mixed. How *would* I support us both?

Journalist at the *Jerusalem Post*

In September, I began to look for an apartment in Jerusalem and heard that Yossi Goell had been looking for me. I had known him from my youth movement days in American and in Israel. Like many young Labor Unity functionaries, he had begun studying at university in 1957. He earned his way as a night editor at the English-language daily, the *Jerusalem Post*. Yossi believed he had the ideal job for me. "We're desperately looking for a diplomatic correspondent at the *Jerusalem Post*." A reader survey had shown that there was a desire for more information about Israeli politics.

Back then, the *Jerusalem Post* was often a day behind the times. People said sarcastically: "How does *Haaretz* (the competition) always know a day beforehand what's going to be in the *Jerusalem Post*?" The paper was first and foremost lacking in reporters who knew the right people and could get important information quickly. Today we would say they didn't have the right connections. I liked the idea, but I also doubted that my knowledge of English was sufficient. Yossi Goell insisted that we speak to the editor-in-chief, Ted Lurie, that very same week.

At the time, the newsroom and printing presses for the *Jerusalem Post* were still in the building where the paper had been founded [as the *Palestine Post*], in the city center. I was in awe stepping foot into the house, which still showed clear traces of a conflict with the British Mandate government. In February 1948, British soldiers and one Palestinian man had exploded a barrel full of dynamite in front of the printers as revenge for an attentat by the Jewish underground. The printing press had been completely destroyed and the newsroom partially so. The burnt tiles on the wall remained as a witness of this event. In 1971, the newsroom moved into a newly-renovated building in Romema; a former chicken slaughterhouse near the central bus station.

Bombing of the Palestine Post, *1948.*

My interview with Lurie went well and he gave me my first assignment on the spot. I was to write a text on "The Young Turks of Mapai." He was referring to the young men in the labor movement—including Moshe Dayan and Shimon Peres—who had recently protested against the old guard, people such as Golda Meir, who were blocking their advancement. In my best English, which was a bit too grandiloquent for the subject matter, I wrote the text and delivered it to the editor-in-chief the day before Sukkot. His well-meaning critique was: "Content's fine, but the style is unacceptable." It was given to Yossi Goell to edit.

My next story was to find out what was going on with the Mediterranean Colloquium, which was to take place in Florence. In 1958, attempts were already underway to mediate the Israeli-Arab conflict. One of these endeavors was undertaken by then mayor of Florence, Giorgo La Pira. He wanted to host a colloquium that would bring all countries and peoples living on the Mediterranean together at one table. The name of the Israeli delegate was being kept a secret and finding out who would be sent was a delicate matter. Lurie wanted to know how I planned to go about it. "I'll ask Ben-Gurion's office manager, Yitzhak Navon. I know him well, let me call him right now." Lurie was delighted that I had such good contacts and Navon was happy to hear that I was now a correspondent for the *Post*. What is more, he also let me know that Reuven Barkat, director of the international division of Histradut, the organization of trade unions, would lead this delegation. La Pira had set the condition that Israel not send a government official to Florence so as not to scare off the Arab delegates before the talks had even started. The next day, my article was on the front page of the *Jerusalem Post*— no other newspaper had that information.

I quickly understood the influence that newspapers can have. Early the next morning, a high-level official in both the Ministry of Foreign Affairs and the Mossad, who was responsible for contact with Muslim countries, called the deputy editor of the *Jerusalem Post*, waking her up. "Which idiot wrote that I'm going to Florence under Barkat as a mere observer?" They were both incensed that Lurie had given the story to an inexperienced kibbutznik. And they were not the only people inside the newsroom shaking their heads over Lurie's decision. But that same morning, the Israeli Ministry of Foreign Affairs confirmed my report. When I arrived at the newsroom around noon, Yossi Goell was already waiting for me on the stairs: "Good that you only came now. The storm is over." Together, we went into the editor-in-chief's office. "Good work, Ari," Lurie said approvingly and glanced at the clock, which also told the date. "Tomorrow is October 1, the first day of your six-month probation as a political reporter."

For 31 years, from October 1, 1958 to November 30, 1989, I worked at the *Jerusalem Post*. In April 1989, the Canadian company Hollinger Inc. bought the paper. The new owners transformed the *Post* from a liberal daily to a right-wing conservative newspaper. Although they only just made up the majority of shareholders, their CEOs acted like the sole owners. Occasionally, I meet colleagues who still work there today and they look back wistfully at the old days. Since 2004, the paper is again owned by Israelis. Conrad Black and David Radler, the owners of Hollinger, were convicted of fraud related to money they had been entrusted with, and were sentenced to prison in Chicago, forcing them to give up ownership of the *Jerusalem Post*. Even if the paper now takes a more moderate position, its liberal leanings in support of peace in the Middle East is completely passé. Today, the target readers of the *Jerusalem Post* are Jewish immigrants from the United States and Europe, who are often very religious.

The *Jerusalem Post* was founded on December 1, 1932 under the name *Palestine Post*. Its first editor-in-chief was Gershon Agronsky (later Agron) who was born in 1894 in Ukraine, fled from the pogroms with his family to Philadelphia when he was five years old and first came to Palestine in the First World War with the volunteer British Army troops, although he only immigrated for good in 1924. From the beginning, Ted Lurie was at his side as deputy editor. Lurie, born in 1910, was from a Zionist American family. After he graduated from Cornell University with a degree in political science, he and his family immigrated to Palestine. To further their son's career in journalism, Lurie's parents helped finance the paper, for which Agronsky had raised money in England and in

In 1950, the Palestine Post *became the* Jerusalem Post.

Palestine. In their editorial for the first edition, Agronsky and Lurie laid out their main aims: The paper should explain Zionism to British Mandate officials and employees as well as to Arab intellectuals and advocate for the British fulfillment of the Balfour Declaration of 1917, which promised the creation of a "Jewish national homeland" in Palestine. Ted Lurie spoke often about the British Mandate era. Back then, all of the main editors were in a joint committee with leading Jewish politicians, and together they set a unified Zionist course mirrored in the paper's reporting and attacks on the British Mandate government. Incidentally, Zionist journalists like Theodor Herzl or Nachum Sokolov did not have much clout in Israeli daily papers, their style was better suited to the feuilletons.

During the British Mandate period, the *Palestine Post* expanded continually until its daily print run grew from fifteen to twenty thousand. After the state of Israel was founded in 1948 and many British soldiers and administrators returned home, the paper lost many readers. When I joined the *Jerusalem Post* in 1958, it was unclear whether the paper would survive this loss of readership. From the beginning, I believed that the *Post* should be an Israeli paper. It might be in English, but it was decidedly not exclusively for foreigners and tourists. There was another large group of target readers in the country, for example the Yekkes. These Jews, born in Germany and Austria, found it easier to read a paper from left to right and not have to struggle to read the difficult Hebrew letters with no diacritics. There were some German newspapers, but they were modest in scope. In the days before computers and the internet, the *Jerusalem Post* was also the only non-Hebrew source of in-depth information about Israel for the international press and for diplomats. Later, when I became editor-in-chief, my understanding of the paper's role brought me my fair share of criticism, especially and repeatedly from Golda Meir. Any critique of her work, no matter how diplomatically it had been framed, sparked an objection, although she was sanguine about was written in the Hebrew papers; after all, that didn't travel abroad nearly as quickly.

The traditional intimacy between the press and politicians had many disadvantages. Under Gershon Agron's leadership, the relationship was so close that former Foreign Minister Moshe Sharett was given all reports on his parliamentary speeches to read before they went to press, with permission to correct the English. My colleague Moshe Brilliant was so incensed by this practice that he left the *Jerusalem Post* and became a correspondent for the *New York Times*. It was also exasperating that editorials were often written by people who were not part of the paper, including ministers and other high-level government officials.

Ted Lurie was an ambitious editor-in-chief and newspaperman, with a killer instinct for a good story, but he himself seldom wrote. The deputy editor, Lea Ben-Dor, was responsible for editorials. So that she would not be chained to her desk six evenings a week and could travel without worry, she hired a series of "editorial writers" whose backgrounds and allegiances remained mysterious. Lea Ben-Dor had good contacts in high places and had no problems with the fact that these "anonymous" editorialists had been or even sometimes still were members of Israel's secret service. These unknown men worked unabashedly in Ben-Dor's large editorial office and so it comes as little surprise that for many years, the *Jerusalem Post* acted as a mouthpiece of the respective government's opinion.

This role as court reporter did not end until Erwin Frenkel and I took over the editing rooms completely in the fall of 1975. We appointed one of our most talented and educated journalists, Yaacov Reuel, as editorial writer. When he was otherwise engaged, Erwin or I wrote the op-eds, without a byline. It was the start of a new era at the *Jerusalem Post*.

◆

In late September 1958, Dorothy returned from London, in her luggage an impressive dowry for our upcoming wedding: a complete set of kitchen utensils, linens, and dozens of pairs of shoes. We rented a small, comfortable apartment; two half-furnished rooms on the fourth floor of a new building overlooking the valley of Golgotha and the Byzantine monastery. Through a personal ad, I was able to obtain a blue Ford for two weeks from a religious tax official who supplemented his income by renting it. Almost no one at the time owned a private car and there were no car rental agencies at all.

The closer our wedding day came, the more nervous and impatient Dorothy became. Every little thing blew up into a fight. One time, at one of Tel Aviv's few traffic lights, she jumped out of the car and disappeared into a side street. My misgivings grew, but I lacked the courage to cancel the wedding, especially since all of her relatives were already on their way to Israel.

Three days before the wedding, Dorothy and I picked up her parents at the airport. The drive to the Sharon Hotel in Herzliya took over one hour. The hotel stood all alone atop a dune on the seashore; the roads leading there were difficult to pass, you had to take an old dusty street full of potholes and sand drifts. Today, the area is one of the most elegant and expensive sites in all of Israel; numerous countries, including Austria and Germany, have their diplomatic residencies there.

My future mother-in-law Fanny, a tall, dyed-blonde, dynamic British Jew, elegant and bejeweled with numerous diamonds, sat next to me in the front; Dorothy and her father sat in the back. Fanny began to interrogate me at once: "Have you found an apartment yet? And how is your work going?"

"I've been working as a political correspondent at the *Jerusalem Post* for a month," I answered, and also told her about the apartment. She gave an audible sigh of relief and Maurice, thrilled, called out from the back seat: "Splendid! Why didn't you let us know much earlier?" Now they would be able to introduce their future son-in-law to their distinguished guests not simply as a kibbutznik, but as an ambitious member of the illustrious *Jerusalem Post*.

It was of course the Gewirzmans' doing that the wedding took place at the luxurious Sharon hotel. As one of the investors, my future father-in-law received very good conditions for such a large event and he took the opportunity to present his generosity to his family, political friends, and business partners. Two worlds collided at the wedding; very few relatives came from my side, in their stead I had invited around sixty *chaverim* from Hamadia. The ceremony itself was attended only by family and took place in the afternoon in the private home of my uncle Meshulam Rath, the rabbi, in Bnei

Brak, already at the time an ultra-Orthodox town north of Tel Aviv. His daughter Surka aided in Dorothy's ritual preparations and went with her to the mikveh before the ceremony. Rabbi Meshulam himself seldom officiated over weddings, but for me, his great-nephew, he made an exception, a gesture that the Gewirzmans also knew to appreciate. Since my father could not travel from the United States, my brother acted as my witness. Four relatives held the four sides of our wedding chuppah. It was a dignified but simple ceremony; my uncle was a deeply religious and modest man.

Newly wed, we returned to the Sharon hotel for an elegant wedding meal with relatives before the celebrations began. In the hotel lobby, a band played international hits and Israeli folk songs. Joyfully we danced the tango, fox trot, and waltz, but our guests did not really mingle, the Brits and the Israelis both kept to themselves. Later, the doors to the terrace opened, where Maurice Gewirzman had without my knowledge ordered a full buffet. The tables were literally heaving with richly decorated bowls full of salads, platters of lox and herring, and innumerable cakes, fruit platters, and ice cream. Many of my friends from the kibbutz had never in their lives seen such a buffet and literally threw themselves on the delicacies. Months later, people in Hamadia were still talking about the luxurious dinner. The party went on until midnight, when my *chaverim* climbed into their trucks and returned to the kibbutz. Dorothy and I, too, said good-bye to the family and spent our wedding night at Ramat Aviv hotel in Tel Aviv.

For our honeymoon, we visited friends across the country in our rented car. Everywhere, my *chaverim* congratulated me for marrying such a charming woman. I look back particularly fondly on the lighthearted days we spent at Hamadia. To my surprise, Dorothy was very interested in kibbutz life, and she got along splendidly with Avri and Yaffa.

As soon as we got home, I wanted Dorothy to look for work, even though we could have both lived well from my salary. I thought it was important that she be busy and independent. Clara Aran, director of the Knesset library and wife of the Minister of Education, was looking for someone to be in charge of English books and soon Dorothy was the jewel of the library, where she seemed to feel at home. Nevertheless, from the beginning our marriage was strained. I was interested in politics above all else, I was ambitious and highly motivated, and spent long hours in the newsroom. Often I sat in my office on Zion Square until late in the night, laboriously typing up my articles with two fingers. Occasionally Dorothy came by in the evening to pick me up. Usually, she ended up waiting for me for a long time. There were ugly scenes when I came home later than planned and she was boiling with rage and jealousy. On the other hand, Dorothy was never really willing to embrace the relative hardship of life in Israel. She always had a ticket back to London and her parents in her pocketbook.

Sometimes I regret that I had doubts about our marriage so early on, and that I never wanted to commit to having a child together. Perhaps my life would have been different had I become a father back then. As much as I value my freedom, I imagine that a child would have enriched my life greatly.

◆

Despite my new life in Jerusalem, my work at the *Jerusalem Post,* and my marriage, I still felt very connected to Kibbutz Hamadia. I was all the more shaken when this relationship was ruptured in

1959. None other than Avri, my best friend, proposed to the weekly plenary as Kibbutz Secretary that I should be expelled because the two years I had been given to study were now over. This was the first and only time that Hamadia ever threw someone out for this reason; later, hundreds of members never returned without the kibbutz taking any measures at all against them. Recently, I came across an edition of the kibbutz newspaper from 1960 in which one of the founding members, Ariel Renen, criticized my behavior. From the sharpness of his approach, it is clear in retrospect that my leaving had also been traumatic for my *chaverim*. Renen wrote:

> That people leave, is nothing new for us ... Sometimes we remain indifferent, sometimes we are more or less sorry. But generally, we go back to our daily routine without any reaction. But in one case, we had to react before returning to our routine, even if in the end it will be no more than a statistical detail ... Ari was one of the most active members of the kibbutz. He was not one of those people who hid himself in some corner. People listened when he spoke.

Renen went on to recapitulate my history and finally became indignant:

> But then there was a particularly dark hour. Ari demanded, with a pride bordering on vanity, that we put him to the test: "I will prove that one can be a member of the kibbutz and study at the same time." In answer to the reluctance of the kibbutz, Ari urged us to give him the chance to act as a role model ... He failed.

Finally, he expressed regret that my behavior would make it more difficult for others who wanted to study to receive permission.

Even if this decision was understandable from the perspective of the kibbutz, I was deeply offended, for Hamadia had been my home for many years. I was neither personally nor ideologically ready to leave the kibbutz, although in retrospect, being expelled gave a huge boost to my career as a journalist. Of the many hundreds of members who have lived in Hamadia over the decades and left again, I am the only one who remains in regular contact to this day.

Avri and I had no contact for months because of his action. He had wanted to prove that he would not make an exception in this important issue just because of our friendship. But he invited me to celebrate Passover with him and his family on the kibbutz in 1960. We hugged as if nothing had happened.

Meanwhile, my work at the *Jerusalem Post* was beginning to bear fruit. I enjoyed the atmosphere; our open discussions and disputes. There were around forty journalists on staff, most of them young Israelis from English-speaking countries: the United States, South Africa, or Great Britain. There were also a few other Yekkes besides myself: Lea Ben-Dor, the deputy editor in the politics department, the military reporter Ze'ev Shul, and Yakov Ardon and Yakov Fiedler, who headed the Haifa correspondents' office. It did not take long before I was able to add my first byline to an article. Looking through old papers, I found a small story for the society pages. I wrote about Ben-Gurion's passion for walking: every day he spent at in his kibbutz, Sde Boker, he marched seven kilometers out and then back again. Two months, later my comprehensive three-column analysis of the varying Workers' Party factions was published. For many years, the often dramatic developments in Israel's political party landscape, which was rife with splits and reunifications, was the main focus of my work.

In early March 1960, an extraordinary event gave a huge boost to my journalistic career. Slowly, I became conscious of something that had already shown itself when I started at the *Post*: I had good journalistic instincts. This mixture of intuition and the ability to put two and two together landed me many a good story over the years.

As a rule, on Sunday afternoons, the Cabinet Secretary would meet with the press to inform us about the government's plans for the upcoming week. At the end of one of these meetings, he mentioned in passing that Prime Minister Ben-Gurion would be traveling to the United States in two weeks to receive an honorary doctorate from Brandeis University. The news was sensational—no Israeli Prime Minister had set foot on American soil for the past nine years. There was an ongoing diplomatic upset stemming from the United States: Secretary of State John Foster Dulles had never forgiven the Israelis for siding with the British and the French in the Sinai-Suez War in 1956—behind the Americans' backs. I hurried to the editorial office to inform Ted Lurie about the trip. I of course assumed that he, like the other editors-in-chief, would want to attend this important event himself. Instead he asked me: "Listen, don't you want to go with Ben-Gurion to Boston in my place?" I was honored, but unsure; after all, I was still a newcomer. But Ted said: "I went through all of that already during Ben-Gurion's last United States trip, I don't feel like traipsing after him again." He very much wanted to send me, which was a huge vote of confidence since his younger brother, Jesse Zel, worked in New York as correspondent for the *Jerusalem Post*.

I was ecstatic about the assignment and also thought that I could take a week's vacation with Dorothy in London on the way home. I had not been back there since we had met. But instead of being happy, Dorothy went into conniptions. "What? You're just going to go and leave me here alone in stinky cold Jerusalem? And your old father is coming too—you know I can't stand him!" The night was terrible. Dorothy, outraged and impulsive as she was, ripped the few elegant shirts I owned, which I had bought back in New York, to shreds. The next day she accompanied me to a store that sold men's shirts to outfit me for the upcoming trip.

On the evening before I left, I went to the newsroom to check the news agency ticker tape for the most recent reports. A short announcement caught my eye: "German Chancellor Konrad Adenauer will be traveling to the United States soon for a visit. His travels will begin with an unofficial visit to New York before he continues on to Washington, D.C." When I compared the dates, I noticed that Adenauer's and Ben-Gurion's New York visits overlapped by one or two days. It was audacious to think that the two might meet, but I promised Ted Lurie to keep an eye on the situation.

For the first time, I saw with my own eyes the elaborate staging of an official government visit. Even leaving the country we were given a military salute at the airport; all members of the government stood at attention. Ben-Gurion was in the best of moods, his white hair blew in the wind as he crossed the tarmac on the red carpet and entered the waiting propeller airplane. Inside, I was shaking with excitement. I was by far the youngest and least experienced of the accompanying journalists. Ben-Gurion sat in the front of the machine, but once in a while he came to the back to chat with us a little. After landing in Ireland to refill the tank, we arrived in Boston early in the evening. On the morning of the next day, Ben-Gurion received an honorary doctorate for his historical achievements in a solemn ceremony in the auditorium of Brandeis University.

The next morning, we flew to Washington, D.C. The city was

blanketed in snow; it hadn't snowed in March for decades. Night and day bulldozers drove through the streets to plow the main arteries, everything was slowed down by the masses of snow. At the Israeli embassy, we were greeted by Ambassador Avraham Harman, whom I had already met in 1946. He briefed us on Ben-Gurion's itinerary; a meeting with President Eisenhower at the White House was scheduled for the next day. There was no mention of any meeting with Adenauer. I snuck into an adjacent room, called the German Embassy, and asked to speak to the press officer. After some polite back and forth, I asked him outright for off-the-record information on the planned meeting between Adenauer and Ben-Gurion. There was a sudden silence on the other end of the line, but he did not deny that the two would be meeting. In that way, I knew I was on the right trail. The news was sensational—a real scoop.

Understandably, the diplomats wanted to keep the first meeting of a German and an Israeli head of state, fifteen years after the collapse of Hitler's Reich, secret for as long as possible. The option of meeting on neutral territory had been discussed in letters. In recognition of Adenauer's efforts to conclude the Reparations Agreement in 1952, and to follow its provisions to the letter, Ben-Gurion had agreed to meet with him in person. Adenauer had paved the way to this agreement with his September 1951 statement of the federal government, in which for the first time he expressed Germany's willingness to take responsibility for the atrocities committed against the Jewish people: "In the name of the German people, unspeakable crimes were committed that oblige us to make moral and material reparations, both for individual damages suffered by the Jews as well as for Jewish property for which individual beneficiaries no longer exist today."

But the primary and original goal of Ben-Gurion's trip was to attempt to normalize relations between Israel and the United States. Since it was not an official visit, there was no official reception at the White House. Ben-Gurion entered through a side door for his meetings with Eisenhower and Secretary of State Christian Herter. A few other Israeli journalists and I were allowed to accompany him and wait in an adjoining room. There I was, only steps away from the most powerful man in the world while my idol, Ben-Gurion, spoke with him in the Oval Office about the future of Israel. Eisenhower's Chief of Protocol let us know that the success of a meeting with the American President could be measured by the length of the talks. Ben-Gurion had been allotted one hour, but the clock continued to tick, and it was almost two hours before the statesmen ended their tête-à-tête, which was interpreted as a good sign.

That same afternoon, Ben-Gurion met with the Senate and House Committees on Foreign Relations; as an unofficial visitor he could not speak in front of the entire Congress. The head of the committee and host of the meeting was the well-known senator Al Gore, father of Bill Clinton's Vice President. Journalists were not able to attend this meeting, but I had met Gore a few months earlier in Jerusalem. At the time, he had given me his card adding a polite and routine: "Give me a call if you're ever in Washington, D.C." I took him at his word, and Al Gore gave me a report of the meeting. Ben-Gurion had used drastic words to paint a picture of the threat to Israel represented by the arms supply deal between Egypt and the Soviet Union, and he made an urgent plea for American support.

Shortly afterwards, Ben-Gurion left for New York. On the way to the train station, our convoy stopped in Georgetown in front of Secretary of State Herter's private residence. Later it turned out that

Ben-Gurion there secured a promise that the United States would, for the first time, supply Israel with strategically important Hawk air defense missiles. Late in the evening, we arrived in New York and found a note from German Foreign Minister Heinrich von Brentano and Israeli Ambassador Harman. Ben-Gurion and Konrad Adenauer would be meeting with one another the next morning at ten at the Waldorf Astoria hotel.

We journalists were invited to come at eight-thirty a.m. to the presidential suite on the hotel's thirty-fifth floor, where Adenauer was staying. I had no intention of waiting with everyone else for ninety minutes, and so I waited to enter the hotel until a quarter to ten, when I took the elevator directly to the thirty-seventh floor, where Ben-Gurion and his entourage were staying. Ben-Gurion's closest colleagues were waiting in front of his suite: his chief of office Yitzhak Navon, later to become President of Israel; the Israeli Ambassador Avraham Harman and his minister at the Washington, D.C. embassy, Yaakov Herzog; as well as the Director General of the Prime Minister's office, Teddy Kollek. Everybody gave a quick hello and Kollek filled me in on the morning's events. There had been a disagreement between Harman and German Foreign Minister Brentano: Harman wanted Adenauer to go to Ben-Gurion and not vice versa. But Ben-Gurion proved to be very unfussy and immediately said: "Of course I will go to Adenauer, he's ten years older than I am."

Navon and Ben-Gurion held a conversation that sounded a lot like an auction. Ben Gurion said: "two-fifty," Navon replied: "five hundred." Ben-Gurion hesitated and said first that the sum was too high, and that two hundred fifty was more suitable. It later turned out that the two had been discussing how many millions of dollars they could demand from Adenauer as supplemental development aid for Israel. Ben-Gurion knew that the final installments of the 3.45-billion-mark payments dictated by the Reparations Agreement would be made in 1964. That made it all the more critical to extend the agreement for ten further years. Naturally the money could not in any way make up for the suffering of the Jews in the Holocaust, for which reason many survivors in Israel were opposed to the payments. On the other hand, Israel desperately needed the support to help with the huge flow of immigrants coming to the country. In 1960, the Israeli government had spent the entire payment for goods from West Germany and afterwards was unable to order the large number of supplies still needed.

Soon American security personnel arrived and asked Ben-Gurion if he could take the stairs down to the thirty-fifth floor, as the elevators were fully blocked by all of the journalists in the hotel. "I'm happy to walk," Ben-Gurion said and his retinue, which I joined, followed. Entry to Adenauer's suite was being controlled by one German and one Israeli security guard. The latter, Yoske, I knew well. "*Mamzer*" he said and, bastard or not, waved me into the room as the last person.

Adenauer came to the vestibule to meet Ben-Gurion. The two men of state, seventy-four and eighty-four years old, one with a mane of wild white hair, the other tall and haggard, formed an unforgettable picture. I was surprised by how heartily the two greeted one another, as if they had known each other for years and as if the painful past played no role between them. They immediately retired with the interpreters to a salon; the rest of the Israeli delegation was invited to a sumptuous buffet. I hung back discreetly in the vestibule and took the opportunity to observe the members of the delegation. There was the German press secretary Felix von Eckardt, whom I knew by name because he had said during his recent trip through the Middle East that reparation payments to Israel would most certainly not be extended after they ran out in 1964. Eckardt was going through a list with a German security guard, then he got up his courage and turned to Ben-Gurion's military attaché, whom I knew well, a former kibbutznik originally from Vienna, Chaim Ben-David. Eckardt was very polite and said he had been unable to find my name on the list. Ben-David didn't hesitate for a second: "That's Ari Rath from the *Jerusalem Post*—he's accompanying us." Eckardt was visibly surprised: "Is it customary for journalists to participate so intimately in political events in Israel?" Ben-David countered cleverly and said that the Israeli delegation had no problem with my attendance: "We are your guests. You will have to decide on the matter." Clearly the German did not want to provoke any headlines by throwing me out and after some back and forth, Eckardt approached me to chat.

After an hour, a hint of crisis arose between the German and the Israeli consultants. Adenauer's personal assistant, Josef Wilhelm Selbach, was going back and forth between the Israeli delegation and German Foreign Minister Brentano. The problem was the wording of the separate closing statements that Adenauer and Ben-Gurion were to make at the end of their talk. One sentence in Adenauer's statement held out the prospects of continued support for Israeli from Bonn after the 1952 reparation agreement ended. Heinrich von Brentano was vehemently opposed. In the end, both sides insisted on asking "the old man"—as both the Germans and the Israelis called their respective heads of government. Selbach and the acting envoy Yaakov Herzog went in to Adenauer and Ben-Gurion, I spontaneously followed a few members of the delegation into the negotiation room. Selbach brought forth his complaint and was immediately interrupted by Adenauer: "Write what the Israelis propose, we've discussed all of this with one another already." The talk between the two heads of state had been friendly. In a memorable moment, Ben-Gurion said to Adenauer:

"In Israel, they say that one day you were walking with your grandson Konrad and asked him what he wanted to be when he grew up. 'Federal Chancellor, of course' he answered. And you replied firmly: 'That's not possible, because two Adenauers cannot be Federal Chancellor simultaneously.'" Adenauer laughed and answered: "You know, Mr. Ben-Gurion, I was told the same story about you and your grandson." In 2001, when Teddy Kollek turned ninety, at the opening of the Konrad Adenauer Conference Center in Jerusalem, I met Adenauer's grandson Konrad in person. I told him the anecdote, which he had heard often, but never from someone who had been there.

It was over one week later—Ben-Gurion was already on his way back to Israel and we were making a stopover in Oxford—before Yitzhak Navon gave me permission to publish the details of the negotiations in the *Jerusalem Post*. No other journalist had such detailed information about the course of the talks. In Germany, the Federal Foreign Office at first even tried to deny that Adenauer had promised Ben-Gurion a loan of five hundred million dollars, at the time the equivalent of roughly two billion German marks.

Today, it is unimaginable how long it used to take before news from the United States found its way into Israeli papers. Anything that happened in the United States after three p.m. you could read about in Tel Aviv or Jerusalem two days later. Often it took one and a half hours just to send a telegraph about sensational news. After

I had supplied the *Jerusalem Post* with information, I gave what I could to my colleague Shalom Rosenfeld, deputy editor-in-chief at *Ma'ariv*. Since 1958, he had been giving me important tips at the weekly government press secretary briefings.

Apart from the many impressions I gained, the trip had been a journalistic milestone for me. I learned how important it is to treat confidential sources confidentially and I learned from personal experience how adversarial journalists could often behave with one another. At the very beginning of the trip, I had met Amos Elon at the hotel bar in Boston. At the time, he was a correspondent for *Haaretz* in Washington D.C, later he became a respected writer. Two days later, I had an important meeting scheduled with the American vice secretary of state for Middle East affairs, Armin Meyer. This meeting had a certain cachet, because back then Israeli journalists almost never had access to high-ranking officials in the Department of State. Elon claimed that he had a similarly important interview and proposed that we trade information afterwards. My talk with Mayer had been off-the-record. When I met Elon again that afternoon, I told him about our confidential conversation and asked him what he had found out. He prevaricated: "It looks like they coordinated their answers, my source told me the exact same thing." The next day, Israeli Ambassador Harman called me up, incensed: "How could you do that? Your conversation was not to be published!" Amos Elon had turned my information into a three-column front-page article and cited Armin Meyer verbatim, as if he had interviewed him himself. I was so ashamed, I wished the ground would open up and swallow me. I had learned an important lesson about the value of loyalty and trust in journalism.

◆

Four weeks later—I had spent the promised vacation with Dorothy at the in-laws in England—I was back in Jerusalem. Back then, parliament still met in an old building on King George Street and most of the information that passed between politicians and journalists was exchanged at the Knesset restaurant. One day, I saw Arie Dissenchik, editor-in-chief of *Ma'ariv*, his deputy editor, Shalom Rosenfeld, and Ted Lurie sitting together at a table. They waved me over and Dissenchik thanked me for the many reports that I had given his paper in New York. Suddenly he turned to Ted and asked: "So Ted, how much do you want for Ari if we took him as our political and diplomatic correspondent" Ted, clearly uncomfortable, answered: "You'll have to ask Ari himself." Dissenchick offered me an astounding sum, especially since *Ma'ariv* was "*the* newspaper of the country," as their somewhat pretentious slogan claimed. With over 100,000 copies, they certainly had the largest circulation of all papers in Israel by far and the paper was read mostly by Israelis. The *Jerusalem Post's* sphere of influence, with a circulation of 18,000 at the time, paled in comparison. But I didn't hesitate for a second. I thanked him for the honor and explained that I would stay with the *Post*. I felt a loyalty to Ted Lurie, whose trust had opened such huge opportunities for me, and I never regretted my decision, although back then I would never have believed that I could become editor-in-chief of the Jerusalem Post, since English was not my mother tongue. But since *Ma'ariv* desperately needed someone, I offered to rewrite my articles for them slightly until they found someone to fill the post. For two or three months, I wrote for both newspapers. Most of my coworkers could not understand why I had turned down such a generous offer.

In the fall of 1960, Ted Lurie promoted me to news editor and one year later to managing editor. I also rose in the estimation of my coworkers, since the *Jerusalem Post* rose in the public's estimation, also due to my numerous exclusive reports. Our colleagues at *Haaretz* were less happy, since they were often rebuked by their editor-in-chief, Gershom Schocken, when important news was in our paper first—making us increasingly more important.

◆

In 1961, my marriage to Dorothy ended for good. All of our attempts had failed to resolve our conflicts. But the rabbinical court that we appeared before to obtain a divorce urged us to reconcile. And so we in fact tried again. We went to eat in a nice restaurant, but the chasm between us could not be bridged. One day, I returned home to a completely empty apartment. Dorothy had packed all her things and all of our furnishings and household goods and had moved to her aunt in Herzliya. A few weeks later she went back to England and filed for divorce. In 1962, I was again a free man. I had no more contact with Dorothy after that. She found a job in the tourist industry and was married two more times. As strange as it perhaps sounds, although we were married, no sentimental feelings linger regarding this relationship. Other women were more important in my life. But I did feel like the failure of my marriage was one more of so many dashed hopes—proof that all women to whom I formed an attachment would leave me again. After that, I never again fully committed to a woman. From that point on, I was married to the *Jerusalem Post*, a relationship that lasted 31 years.

That is not to say that I joined a monastery after the divorce. For five years, I was together with Malka Rabinowitz, a reporter from the news desk. Malka was from New York and had come to

Jerusalem after university. She was already working at the *Post* when I started. Since we were both journalists, we had none of the conflicts I had had with my ex-wife. We both sat in the newsroom until late at night, afterwards spending hours with friends and colleagues at the famous Fink's Bar, which sadly closed in December 2006. Both of us loved the legendary locale and its one-of-a-kind owner, Dave Rothschild. Dave had been born in Bavaria and was a spirited and very temperamental barkeeper. He would let regulars keep a tab for weeks on end, but if he didn't like someone, he threw them out of his bar without a second thought. Photos of his guests, some of whom had paid their bill with their picture, decorated the walls of the tiny space, which was always packed. Every evening, artists, journalists, and politicians from Israel and abroad gathered there. It was a whiff of the big wide world in a Jerusalem that was still very provincial.

Malka and I got along well but I did not want to make a commitment, which taxed our relationship so much that we began seeing less and less of each other. One evening, Malka told me that a religious Italian man had proposed to her. I begged her not to marry and to stay with me until I could make up my mind. In April 1967, I even agreed to go see a couples therapist with her. But the Six-Day War began before our therapy did. For four months, I was in the army and when I returned to my desk in September 1967, Malka had made the decision on her own and had left me. We remained friends, but I realized how deeply wounded she had been after Ted Lurie died. When his successor was to be chosen, Malka mobilized colleagues to vote against me.

Managing Editor in Turbulent Times

Being the news editor of an Israeli paper was an interesting job at all times, but perhaps never more so than in the early 1960s. After the 1956 Suez Crisis, the country entered a relatively long, relatively peaceful period. The storms that blew in were from the political front. By the second decade of Israel's independence, large segments of society had achieved a standard of living comparable with that of Central Europe. In the suburbs of Tel Aviv and other cities, attractive residential areas sprung up, with elegant one-family homes. Traffic became more and more difficult to navigate on the narrow main roads, as the number of vehicles grew each year. There were always many buses on the road, and traveling between Jerusalem and other cities in the ever-growing Tel Aviv metropolitan area became an onerous task. Between Hadera and Gedera, two cities fifty kilometers north and south of Tel Aviv respectively, grew a bloated, densely populated, and highly industrialized zone. Today, over two thirds of the country's population lives in this area. Agricultural land, in particular the country's characteristic orange groves, fell victim to the building mania of Israeli and international companies. The kibbutzim in the region profited enormously from this economic development and began to erect gigantic shopping malls and high-tech industrial areas on their precious arable land.

With growing prosperity, from the early 1960s the large class of construction and industrial workers built a petit bourgeois social stratum. Our ideal of a socialist Israel was increasingly divorced from reality. And new waves of immigrants began to exert more influence. Alongside Holocaust survivors, hundreds of thousands of Sephardic Jews entered the country, driven out as new governments were founded in Morocco, Yemen, Iraq, Egypt, and Tunisia. Meanwhile, Ben Gurion's vision of Israel as a giant melting pot was only partially realized. All immigrants did learn Hebrew, give their physical labor to the country, and serve in the military, but they gave up neither their very different way of life nor their religious orthodoxy.

◆

On May 23, 1960, together with representatives from all of Israel's newspapers as well as foreign correspondents, I was unexpectedly called to an urgent meeting of parliament in the provisional Knesset building in Jerusalem. David Ben-Gurion had important news for us. He went up to the lectern and declared: "I must inform the Knesset that not long ago the security services found one of the great Nazi war criminals." After a dramatic pause, which brought the suspense in the room to a pitch, he gave us a name: "Adolf Eichmann, who was responsible along with other Nazi leaders for what they called the final solution to the Jewish problem, that is, the extermination of the six million Jews of Europe. Adolf Eichmann is already under arrest in Israel and will soon face trial in Israel, in keeping with the laws governing justice for the Nazis and their helpers." The news was like a bolt of lightning. Everyone in the audience stood up spontaneously and broke into applause, breaking completely with parliamentary protocol.

For eleven months, Adolf Eichmann was held in a police fort near Haifa, where he was interrogated daily by Avner Liss, a Berlin-born Israeli police officer. The light in Eichmann's cell burned twenty-four hours a day. On Sunday, April 11, 1961, the time came: exactly eleven months after his arrest on Garibaldi Street in Buenos Aires, the trial against the mastermind of the "final solution" began in Jerusalem. He was to stand for his actions in front of three Jewish judges. The judges had completed their study of law in Germany and therefore sometimes corrected the official interpreter.

I had a seat not far from the bulletproof glass booth in which Eichmann sat. A gaunt man with a balding head, he was of middling height and wore a dark suit, white shirt and tie, and black horn-rimmed glasses. Eichmann seemed like any government official, nothing remained to remind me of the severe and powerful SS officer in front of whom I trembled when, in September 1938, he stamped my German passport at the Office for Jewish Emigration at the Rothschild Palace in Vienna.

There is no dearth of in-depth reports on both the trial itself and its impact on Israeli society. For the first time, the entirety of Israel's population was forced to face the Shoah head on. Until then, many of the immigrants from the Maghreb and Iraq had been somewhat stand-offish with Jews from Europe. Many of the reports of the suffering in the camps and the persecution of European Jewry were so horrific that they sometimes seemed implausible. Since Israel did not have a public broadcasting station until 1968 and the courtroom was much too small for the throngs of visitors, the daily trial testimony was also broadcast on a screen in a large room in the Ratisbonne Monastery next door. Among the hundreds of people who lined up every morning to get a seat in the room were many

Sephardic Jews, including workers from the *Jerusalem Post* print shop. I was good friends with some of them and was very interested in their observations of the trial. I saw for myself how their attitude towards victims of the Shoah changed from week to week. Some of them even apologized to their colleagues for having had so little empathy with them beforehand.

The trial also had an impact on our work in the newsroom. To prepare for our reports, we put up a long table in the editorial offices for editors who were appointed to work mainly on this story and dubbed it the "Eichmann desk." Instead, that reporting took up so much space for months, in the end almost every desk was an Eichmann desk. Gabriel Bach, the deputy prosecutor, whom I knew well, often met with our reporters in the breaks to explain the finer legal points of Eichmann's hearing. He knew that the foreign press was following our commentary closely and that our reports were often cited.

The fact that Eichmann had been abducted and taken to stand trial in Israel was controversial abroad, but the German government and the German press recognized the legality of this action. It was also the first time that the German government sent an official delegation of observers to Israel. Simultaneously, the German Federal Press Office opened a branch office in immediate proximity to the Gerard Bechar Theater, where the trial took place. The international interest in the trial was staggering. Reporters came from across the globe, whereby German journalists were in the majority. Daily, we met in the courtroom and in the bar which had been set up extra at the behest of our thirsty English colleagues. In the evenings, we all went together to Fink's Bar. Observers were learning details about the camps not only from the trial; the past was omnipresent.

One episode in particular I remember as if it were yesterday. On the first day of the trial, Chief Prosecutor Gideon Hausner quoted a song in his indictment, "Shtiler, Shtiler," whose moving text references the mass murder in the Ponary forest, near the Lithuanian city of Vilnius:

> Quiet, quiet, let's be silent / Dead are growing here / They were planted by the tyrant / See their bloom appear / All the roads lead to Ponar now / There are no roads back / And our father too has vanished / And with him our luck.

I had learned the song from friends who had survived the Shoah and come to Palestine after the war, and had taught it to many of my mentees in the youth movement. And so I sang it for my German and British colleagues that evening in Fink's Bar. I had barely finished when a young man waved at me from the end of the bar: Alexander Tamir (Wolkowsky). I knew that he was a musician; to this day he is a well-known pianist and musicologist. He told us that in 1942, one of the few survivors of the Vilnius Ghetto at the age of eleven, he had composed the music for that song. For all of us who were there, meeting Tamir was incredible; many of the journalists wrote about it for their papers.

Paradoxically, the Eichmann trial provided me with the opportunity to get to know and also become friends with many Germans. For example Hans Stercken, the German Federal Press Office aide for Western and Southern Europe, and head of the official delegation of observers. Stercken and I held many intense conversations about the complex relations between Germany and Israel. I liked Stercken, who was only two years older than I and who had served in the Wehrmacht after graduating from Gymnasium, but we often fought bitterly because he, like so many of his generation, claimed never to have known anything about the mass murders during his stint as a soldier. In contrast, his assistant Luise Bauch was ashamed of her own and her country's Nazi past. I was impressed that she had had the courage to leave her family behind so that she could follow the Eichmann trial up close. Occasionally we went on day trips together—trips on which we had long conversations and I for the first time began to have an inkling of how torturous it could be for the children of Nazi persecutors to face their family's guilt.

One of the social highlights of that period were the regular meetings of German and Israeli reporters at the house of the inimitable *Dawar* reporter, Vera Elyashiv. She came from a Polish-Russian family and had survived multiple concentration camps. Nevertheless, she believed that the trauma of the Shoah could only be overcome through personal meetings between Germans and Jews, a conviction that I shared completely. Her circle of close friends included the TV reporters Peter Schier-Gribowsky and Joachim Besser, with whom we spent many nights discussing the question of why German society had repressed its Nazi past for so long. Vera Elyashiv's openness did not make her only friends; many of her Israeli colleagues accused her of being in cahoots with the Germans. But in fact, the Eichmann trial was a turning point in terms of Germans facing their history—and regarding relations between Germans and Israelis.

◆

It was also an era of great turbulence in Israeli domestic affairs. A new generation of politicians was rebelling against Ben-Gurion's authoritarian leadership style and vying for power. From fall 1960, public debate was again dominated by what was known as the Lavon

Affair. The conflict had been sparked by the failure of a covert Israeli-backed operation in 1954. British and American targets in Cairo and Alexandria were to be bombed in an attempt to prevent negotiations between Egypt and Great Britain on British withdrawal from the Suez Canal. Eleven Egyptian Jews were brought to trial in Egypt, two of whom were executed and two of whom committed suicide in prison. In Israel, a debate arose on who had given the command for the failed operation: Minister of Defense Pinchas Lavon or Binyamin Gibli, chief of the military secret service.

Until 1954, Ben-Gurion had lived a reclusive life in Sde Boker, while still taking an active part in politics. Then he was reelected as Prime Minister in the 1955 parliamentary elections. He rejected the ministerial committee's conclusion, which had absolved Lavon of responsibility for the failed covert operation, so that the affair festered for years. Ben-Gurion was strongly criticized for his implacable position on Lavon. On January 31, 1961, he handed in his resignation, but continued his campaign against Lavon. In the parliamentary elections of November 1961, Ben-Gurion once again won the majority, but the conflict had considerably weakened the Workers' Party and their allies. The press, especially *Ma'ariv*, also mobilized against Ben-Gurion. He finally resigned once and for all in June 1963, leaving government and passing on his official duties to then Minister of Finance Levi Eshkol.

The *Jerusalem Post* was one of very few newspapers that took Ben-Gurion's side. To this day I believe he was justified in insisting that the affair be reexamined by a legal commission. Later, even the legal counsel of the Mapai Party, Yaakov Shimshon Shapira—who at the time demanded that Ben-Gurion and his supporters be suspended from government as "neo-fascists"—pushed through a law in his role as Minister of Justice that made it possible for the Supreme Court to set up an investigative commission in particularly important cases.

The conflict reached its apex at the Spring 1965 Workers' Party Convention in the Mann Auditorium, Tel Aviv's concert hall. Because of the importance of this date, the *Jerusalem Post* sent four editors to cover it, and all the other papers also sent their best people. Prime Minister Levi Eshkol, who for decades had been a close associate of Ben-Gurion, who in fact had named Eshkol as his successor, turned to Ben-Gurion and said: "Give me some credit. Our party must agree on a compromise in order to avoid a schism." Moshe Sharett, suffering visibly from cancer, was pushed onto the stage in a wheelchair and began to mercilessly settle the score with his party comrade. You could see in his countenance the effort it cost him as he accused Ben-Gurion of suppressing opposing opinions with his authoritarian leadership style. After his speech, sixty percent of the delegates voted against the appointment of a new investigative committee—a huge defeat for Ben-Gurion. Afterwards, I spoke with Teddy Kollek and Yitzhak Navon, both of whom had tried to no avail to stop Ben-Gurion from splitting the party. Once he had made up his mind, he did not change it. A few days later Ben-Gurion and seven of his followers, including Moshe Dayan and Shimon Peres, left the Mapai Party and founded their own party, Reshimat Poalei Israel, the Israeli Workers' List. The *Jerusalem Post* dubbed the new party "Rafi," by which name it is known to this day.

These details remain etched into my memory because they dominated the political landscape for months in the early 1960s. People were demonstrating in the streets for and against Ben-Gurion. The founder of the nation, who until then had been an unconditional idol, was suddenly cursed and criticized. I still remember one striking cartoon from those days: it portrayed a larger than life statue of Ben-Gurion and under it, Ben-Gurion as a small man with a hatchet, hacking away at his own effigy. This schism in the Workers' Party marked the beginning of the end of the years-long hegemony of the labor movement and of Israel's founding generation.

I was very shaken personally by these conflicts, but I always tried to keep my feelings out of my reporting. Shortly before he was named Prime Minister in June 1963, Eshkol gave a long interview in which he revealed many details about his life. He spoke about growing up in Kyiv under the influence of two radically different families: one Hasidic and one made up of wealthy businesspeople. He recalled coming into contact with Zionism at the age of fifteen in Vilnius and deciding for himself that he would migrate to Palestine. In 1914, at the age of eighteen, young Levi Shkolnik arrived without a penny at Petah Tikva, the Gate of Hope. I published some of this conversation in the *Jerusalem Post* under the title "Man of Work and Vision." When I now read the emotion-laden words that Eshkol used to describe his arrival, the half a century that has passed since then makes itself clearly felt:

> The border of the village [Petah Tikva] was marked by an acacia tree fence. Beyond it, there was a knee-deep sea of sand. This green fence is the beginning of the Jewish State, I felt. Towards evening I returned to the main square … The sound of a *shofar* announced the beginning of the Sabbath. To me, it sounded as though the days of the Messiah had come.

Right after his election to the post of Prime Minister, one of Eshkol's aides contacted me and asked me to help him write an English profile of the Prime Minister for the Federal Press Office. Not long after, Eshkol asked me to become his government spokesperson. I might even have agreed had not Golda Meir, who was by no means willing to tolerate a follower of Ben-Gurion in such an important position, intervened.

◆

As political correspondent of the *Jerusalem Post*, I of course delved deeply into domestic politics, but my remit also included representing the paper at important events abroad. In May 1963, when I had not yet been at the *Jerusalem Post* for five years, Ted Lurie allowed me to travel to Addis Ababa to report on the founding conference of the Organization of African Unity (OAU). For the chronically underfunded *Jerusalem Post* it would of course have been much too expensive to send a correspondent themselves, and so I found an elegant solution. Officially, I traveled as representative of the Israeli news agency ITIM, and reported not only for our paper, but also for five other small Israeli newspapers. *Haaretz* sent Seev Schiff, and *Ma'ariv* and *Jehidot* also each sent their own correspondents.

That trip opened a previously unknown world to me. Flying from Tel Aviv to Addis Ababa was complicated. Since the Israeli airline was not allowed to cross over Arab airspace, El Al flew via Istanbul and Tehran. I spent a first stopover of several days in Nairobi. In the spring of 1963, Kenya was celebrating "Uhuru," which means "freedom" in Swahili. As the last East African colony, the British had granted Kenya internal self-government, an important step on the road to independence, which the country attained on December 12 of that same year. Shortly before leaving, I had interviewed Thomas Mboya, a key leader in the Kenyan trade union movement, at the Afro-Asian Institute of the trade union organization Histadrut in Tel Aviv. As so often, a friendship grew out of our meeting, and Mboya invited me to accompany him to the official celebrations. Jomo Kenyatta, Ugandan President Milton Obote Apollo, and Julius Nyerere, President of Tanzania, all gathered together on the large balcony of the stately building belonging to the British general-governor. After a short speech by the general-governor, the African heads of states shook hands and then shouted out to the cheering crowd in the square below them: "Uhuru! Uhuru! Uhuru!" I was incredibly moved by this moment; my memories of the founding of the State of Israel and our liberation from the British Mandate fifteen years earlier came clearly to my mind's eye. After the official government ceremony, I was one of the few white people to celebrate with Mboya's comrades and friends, who went from place to place in their colorful traditional garb, drinking local schnapps and dancing joyously.

Still giddy from the day before, at dawn I boarded a bus to Arusha at the foot of Kilimanjaro in Tanganyika. The trip went through the territory of the Luo, the group of which Mboya was a tribal leader. Every two hours the bus stopped at another beautiful inn, where the atmosphere of colonial days was very present. After a drive of ten hours, I spent the night at the famous Hotel Livingstone in Arusha, even then the starting point for those who wanted to climb Mount Kilimanjaro.

After returning to Nairobi, I continued my flight to Addis Ababa and the founding summit of the OAU. There, too, I had good connections to the conference organizers. I had the luck of an old friendship with Ifrach Dimitros, an Eritrean bon vivant who had spent some of his university days in Jerusalem and later returned to his homeland. He was director of the Middle East Office at the Ethiopian Ministry of Foreign Affairs and had been tasked with management of the conference because of his international connections. We met every evening around six-thirty outside of the newly-constructed congress hall and went for a walk, on which he would inform me about the day's discussions in the varying committees. This was incredibly valuable information, since as Israeli observers of the conference we were not exactly in the good graces of our Arab colleagues. The Egyptians even demanded that Israeli correspondents leave the room when President Nassar was in the auditorium. Emperor Haile Selassie denied this request because the Israelis were accredited for the conference just like everybody else. Finally, a compromise was reached: copies of the press passes of the Israeli participants were made and handed over to the Egyptians. An Egyptian security guard was assigned to each one of us, and they never left our sides.

Unlike today, where every journalist is a miniature telecommunication headquarters unto him- or herself, back then all correspondents fought to be the first person to get their story out into the world. There were only two telex machines at the press center in Addis Ababa. I had an advantage because I was higher up in the hierarchy of waiting journalists, since I was accredited as an agency journalist, who had priority access to the telex. However, our Soviet colleagues monopolized the telex apparatus, causing difficulties for everyone else, and we were soon behind schedule. One day, the conflict escalated. The Ethiopians who acted as liaisons for the international press intervened and said to our Russian colleagues: "You have occupied the telex apparatus for two hours now. Please interrupt your work for twenty minutes so that your Israeli colleague can send in his report." A Russian journalist replied: "You're not telling us what to do, you just climbed down from your tree yesterday." This open racism not only incensed the Ethiopians, it also showed me how little the Soviets' attitude concurred with their ideal of socialist equality. Nevertheless, after a few attempts at moderation, I managed to get the two parties to make peace.

As Israelis, we had been excluded from Emperor Haile Selassie's ceremonial reception under pressure from the Arab countries. However the Emperor invited the Israeli members of the press to a separate champagne reception, so that I too had the opportunity of getting a closer look at the luxurious palace, which had recently been revamped by Israeli architects. I remember in particular the prominent Stars of David on the palace's outer walls: Haile Selassie believed himself to be the successor of King Solomon. The incredible wealth of the Ethiopian dynasty was embodied by the opulent flower gardens and water fountains, and by the emperor's two tamed lions, who strolled free at the entrance to the palace. In his speech, Haile Selassie stressed how much he valued Ethiopia's close cooperation with Israel in the fields of technology, agriculture, and security. At the time, Israel trained the Ethiopian police; their uniforms were similar to Israeli police uniforms and they were armed with Israeli Uzi submachine guns.

The trip to Ethiopia was significant because it was the first time Israeli journalists had been invited to participate in an African conference. This was one of the fruits of the foreign policy begun by Golda Meir. From the late 1950s, she had prioritized close relations with the young independent states of Africa; to this day there is a division of the Ministry of Foreign Affairs for international technological development. Israel's first bilateral relations were established with Ghana, followed by agreements with Ethiopia, Kenya, Liberia, Uganda, and the Ivory Coast. For this reason, our Ethiopian hosts were eager to treat us well.

For the Israeli press, it was exciting to observe the first steps toward independence in these countries. We were all young states, and we hoped to learn from one another. Even then, I was convinced that Israel would only ever be able to approach the Arab countries via its relations with African and Asian countries. In April 1959 I wrote: "The road from Israel to Damascus and Cairo does indeed lead through Burma and Ghana." These alliances with the slowly awakening countries in Africa, and to some extent also in Asia, helped Israel to gain global recognition and respect. I further believe that this policy also played a role in making possible Israel's peace treaty with Egypt's president Anwar Sadat in 1977. Egypt was aware of our links to Africa and also saw itself as an African country. Sadly, today, relations with Africa play almost no role in Israel's political identity.

◆

In the fall of 1964, I went on another key trip to a foreign country, this time to India. The head of the South Asia division at the Israeli Ministry for Foreign Affairs, Michael Elitzur, a former *chaver* from Hamadia, called me up one day and said: "UNESCO is holding a four-week seminar in Nagpur for Asian journalists. We want you to attend as delegate for Israel." Geographically, Israel belongs to Asia; in India, it is considered a West Asian country. The seminar dealt with the question of journalism in developing countries, where democracy and freedom of the press were still in their infancy. It was an honor to be invited to participate. Travel costs were covered by the Israeli Ministry of Foreign Affairs, in Nagpur we would be guests of UNESCO. I looked forward to visiting India and decided to travel the country after the seminar. For an extra one hundred and forty dollars, I was able to extend my ticket. After Nagpur, I visited Calcutta, Kathmandu in Nepal, Benares (Varanasi in the Indian state of Uttar Pradesh), Agra, and New Delhi, where I spent two weeks.

In November 1964, I traveled to Nagpur via Bombay and was one of thirty international journalists to arrive in the city in the heart of India, in the federal state of Maharashtra. Michael Elitzur had given me the telephone number of the commander of Nagpur's military post, whom Elitzur had met when he was in the diplomatic service as military attaché for India in Rangun. At the time, Maharashtra was a dry state, and Elitzur gave me a practical tip: "A bottle of whiskey is sure to open many doors." I had stocked up accordingly in the duty free shop. My spirits were somewhat dampened upon arrival. Our living quarters in a boarding house, which belonged to the Anglican Church, were spartan. In place of doors, the rooms had only heavy curtains, and the showers and toilets were in the hallway. Thanks to having lived on a kibbutz, this bothered me less than it did other seminar participants. Nagpur, despite a population of one million inhabitants, proved to be more like a sleepy village. On Sunday afternoon after my arrival, I asked the receptionist to open a local phone line for me and called Colonel Gupta, who was happy to receive greetings from his old friend Elitzur and promptly invited me to tea. Shortly afterwards, he pulled up in his yellow-brown jeep and brought me to his comfortable house next to the garrison. My acquaintance with the Colonel and his wife, a well-known poet with many contacts in India's literary and journalistic worlds, opened many doors for me.

The seminar itself was led by Jacques Léauté, a professor of journalism from Strasbourg to whom I owe my knowledge of bringing journalistic transparency and integrity to societies with deep social rifts. Later, this knowledge helped me to remain unprejudiced when reporting on the large waves of immigrants from the Soviet Union, and on the second generation of Moroccan and Iraqi immigrants. Alongside the practical exercises and lectures, I also profited greatly from meeting colleagues from all parts of India as well as from Burma, Japan, and the Philippines. When I look back at this seminar and the contacts I made there with diverse colleagues, it occurs to me that compared to journalists today, our horizon was very broad. Naturally, news moved infinitely more slowly than it does now, but the insights that we gained from our experiences in foreign countries and societies gave us an irreplaceable fundament that I believe stands up well to today's journalistic practice. Of course, then and now there were and are brave correspondents who report from danger zones without hesitation and risk their lives in the process, but these days it is unusual for young journalists to expand their horizons through extended travel. It is the kind of investment that does not bring quick results on the cutthroat media market. And how little journalistic quality is treasured today can be seen in the many free tabloids that may someday become a serious threat not only to journalism, but also to democracy.

My travels through India left me with mixed feelings. The country had four hundred and fifty million inhabitants at the time and the synchronicity of wealth and bitter poverty, and the unbridgeable gap between social classes were hard for me to accept as a former kibbutznik. Scores of children in rags begged on the streets of Bombay, Calcutta, and Old Delhi, while the families of more well-to-do castes and government officials lived in the lap of luxury, waited on by dozens of underpaid servants. Since India and Israel had both gained independence from the British Empire in 1948, Jerusalem was hoping to establish good relations with the largest democracy in the world. Although Indian Prime Minister Nehru had recognized Israel de jure, he refused to enter into diplomatic relations with our country. The official justification was the conflict regarding Kashmir in the north of India, which both Muslim Pakistan and majority-Hindu India claimed for themselves. Nehru contended that full diplomatic recognition of Israel would cause all of the Arab countries to turn against India. As a compromise, Israel had been allowed to set up a consulate in the 1950s. The Israeli Ministry of Foreign Affairs decided to open this consulate in Bombay, assuming that we would soon be able to establish an embassy in Delhi, which however did not happen for many years.

Often on my journey I was welcomed because many Indians were curious to meet an Israeli journalist. My first important contact in New Delhi was a close friend of the wife of Colonel Gupta from Nagpur, Preminda Premchand. She worked as a correspondent for the Voice of America radio broadcast and was married to General Premchand, Commander of the UN Mission to the Congo from 1960 to 1964. After our first meeting, she invited me to a reception for officers of the Indian UN troops, where she introduced me to the General Secretary of the Indian officers' academy. We had a long conversation, after which he invited me to brief his officers on the situation in the Middle East, at the time an almost unheard-of step for such a high-ranking institution. Preminda Premchand also introduced me to the personal assistant of Indira Gandhi—in 1964

Gandhi was Minister for Information and Broadcasting in Prime Minister Bahadur Shastri's government. She promised to organize a meeting with Ms. Gandhi for me. The editor-in-chief of the *Indian Express*, a paper that was friendly to Israel, advised me to get her permission for Israel to instate an accredited foreign correspondent in Delhi. Such a position would be more helpful than an ambassador in terms of making contacts in Delhi.

One day later I was invited to Indira Gandhi's residence on Safdarjung Road at eight a.m. to observe her half-hour audience. This was a tradition of her father Nehru, which Gandhi had continued: receiving citizens from across the country so that they could bring forward their concerns. It was one of the most imposing displays I have ever seen. Over fifty women and men stood in a large circle in the garden. In her elegant sari, the minister went from one to the other and listened attentively to their problem, while her two secretaries took notes. After half an hour, the group audience was concluded and I was asked into the salon. Sighing, Gandhi sunk into an armchair. I asked: "Ms. Gandhi, how can you begin your day with such an exhausting act?" She laughed and answered: "Very true..." She was a woman of uncommon charm and had already been alerted to my request. "We will be happy to provide an Israeli correspondent with accreditation," she said. However it should be a news agency journalist who covered all of Southwest Asia, and not just India. Indira Gandhi then inquired after the political situation in Israel; she wanted to know what people thought about the new government under Prime Minister Eshkol. When I left, she asked me to keep her in the loop on the question of an Israeli correspondent.

More than once I was invited to be the guest of the Jhirad family, one of Delhi's few Jewish families. Ellis Jhirad was Advocate

General of the Indian navy and had close contact to Shastri's office manager. The two agreed to provide me with the opportunity to accompany the prime minister on the long walk from his office in parliament to the assembly hall. The office manager introduced me to Shastri and I spoke a sentence I had carefully composed: "I have been in India for some weeks now, and I very much hope that we will one day have the opportunity to recreate on the political, diplomatic level such warm and intimate relationships as I have enjoyed privately during my stay." Shastri answered: "I share your hopes, for we value Israel's achievements in the areas of agriculture and technology." When we parted, he shook my hand and looked me directly in the eyes. He allowed me to report that he sent warm greetings to Israel and hoped for the development of fruitful and peaceful relations between the two countries. Then Shastri disappeared into the assembly hall. His secretary, who had remained behind, immediately warned me: "That was all off the record," and threatened, "If you cite his sentences, I will deny that you ever met the Prime Minister." Not until after Shastri's death was I able to write about this episode in an obituary.

On December 24, 1964, I celebrated Christmas for the first time in my life. Preminda Premchand had invited Hindus, Christians, Muslims, and me, the only Jew, into her home. There was a Christmas tree decorated with golden ornaments and candles, and presents for all the guests. Together we sang in English: "Silent night, holy night." On January 10, I returned to Israel. I had extended my stay in India so that I would not have to be in Jerusalem on my fortieth birthday. I did not see why getting older was any reason to celebrate. However our night editor, Charley Weiss, one of my best friends, thought differently and had organized a surprise party after the fact.

I wrote a long report on my journey for the Ministry of Foreign Affairs in which I proposed sending an accredited journalist to New Delhi. The report was—as I heard from those close to her—carefully studied by Golda Meir and next to my suggestion she noted: "Implement!" The Israeli secret service Mossad was also interested in such a connection, but it was very clear to me that only a journalist of integrity should be considered for the position. In the end, the project fell flat for financial reasons. Nobody was willing to invest the thirty or forty thousand dollars that it would have cost to support such a position.

Today, Israel and India have good relations. But it took a long time to establish them, and most of that time the countries were in a love-hate relationship. I traveled three other times to India, on my way to Japan and Manila, rekindling my contacts from that first journey. For many years, Indian friends visited me in Israel, and I helped them by providing contacts in Israel and Europe.

The Grand Old Man's Personal Aide

Elections had been set for November 1965, and David Ben-Gurion had entered the race as frontrunner for the newly-founded Rafi Party. In July, Shimon Peres called me up and said: "Ben-Gurion gave his OK." At first, I had no idea what he was talking about, then it became clear that they wanted me to support Ben-Gurion's campaign as his personal aide. Yitzhak Navon, who had managed his office for many years, was himself running as a candidate on the Rafi list. Peres had already spoken to Ted Lurie and made a deal with him that I be granted a four-month leave from the *Post*. A few days later, I ran into David Landor, also formerly from Vienna, who was director of the Federal Press Office. Landor had helped Teddy Kollek achieve his position. He was horrified to hear about my new job: "Ari, how could you do that, ruining a promising career in journalism by becoming campaign manager for Ben-Gurion? That's a huge mistake!" I answered: "Don't worry, I'll return to the paper and continue to be a trustworthy, objective journalist." And that is what happened.

For me, working together with people whose life work I admired deeply, and still admire to this day, was an unforgettable experience. Already as a teenager, I had been inspired by Ben-Gurion's fiery speeches at party conventions and public rallies. Later, as a member of the press corps, I had accompanied him

Ben-Gurion and Ari at Kibbutz Sde Boker, 1970.

on official visits: 1960 to the United States and Great Britain, and 1962 to Scandinavia. In those days, I also lived on Ben Maimon Street 18 in Rehavia, only a few houses from the Prime Minister's residence, and so often met Ben-Gurion's wife, Paula, who also accompanied him on official visits. Life was slower then than it is today and there was plenty of time for conversation. In June 1963, one day before the transfer of power to the new Prime Minister Levi Eshkol, Paula invited me into the house for a "kutch-mutch," her word for a chat. She hadn't told Ben-Gurion, and so I had to hide in her bedroom until her strictly proper husband—on his last day in his official capacity—had left the house. Paula was already packing and preparing their move to Tel Aviv. She was known as a capable housewife and was the enfant terrible of public life in Israel, since she never minced words, even when she knew, like this time, that I would be publishing our conversation in the *Jerusalem Post*. Paula complained that Ben-Gurion's followers and aides had not taken her warnings seriously enough and had not prevented his resignation.

Then she told me how she had met Ben-Gurion as a young nurse in New York in 1915, marrying him two years later. Paula was completely open with me and gave me a tour of the house. She proudly showed me the kitchen furniture, which she had painted herself, and the table on which she served Ben-Gurion his breakfast every morning. It is an odd feeling to be made privy to a statesman's private life. Unlike his wife, Ben-Gurion never bothered with the banalities of everyday life; he used every free moment to read or to develop his political visions. He left the day-to-day business of politics to his aides, Teddy Kollek or Yitzhak Navon. To the end of his days, Ben-Gurion kept two private apartments, a large but simply furnished wooden house in Kibbutz Sde Boker, and his two-story one-family home in one of Tel Aviv's workers' settlements that had been built in the 1930s. He commuted back and forth between these two places.

During my assignment, I had free access to Ben-Gurion, more so even than Paula. While I organized his appointments, she took care of all meals. She was convinced that the health of her husband, who had been a weakly child, was largely dependent on his eating a large portion of ham every day. I still remember the surprise of the Norwegian Chief of Protocol in 1962 in Oslo, when she instructed him to by no means forget to serve Ben-Gurion a large plate of ham at breakfast. "If we had known that," he said to me, "we wouldn't have flown in kosher meat from Copenhagen extra for him." In Tel Aviv, Paula even kept a whole ham hock in a separate refrigerator.

As Ben-Gurion's aide, I had two main duties: I helped him with his daily correspondence and, with him, managed his electoral campaign. Ben-Gurion insisted on answering every letter and every last message personally and by hand. He wrote his answers on a carbon copy notepad and carefully archived the copies. We also had two or three large rallies every week at which he presented his political visions. His speeches were always unscripted. Usually, they ended in him badmouthing the "immoral" Eshkol government—as he repeatedly called it—for their stance in the Lavon Affair. Even his closest supporters were extremely critical of his campaign. More than once, Shimon Peres asked me to try to get Ben-Gurion to be more moderate; he was certain that this rhetoric would scare voters away. And so, before every appearance, I tried to find quotes from other candidates on which Ben-Gurion could focus his ire. My efforts were in vain, he did not end his tirades. Moshe Dayan even threatened not to stand for nomination to the Rafi list if Ben-Gurion did not start conducting a more positive campaign. Ben-Gurion always agreed to change his ways, but he never kept his promises.

During the hours that we spent traveling from Tel Aviv to his kibbutz, Sde Boker, or to one electoral rally or another, he often surprised me by recounting nostalgic memories of his early years in Palestine. Whenever we drove to the South, he insisted on making a detour from Tel Aviv to Jaffa Port, where in 1905, at the age of nineteen, he had arrived in the country from Płońsk, his birthplace on the Polish-Russian border. Repeatedly, he told how he had marched all alone for hours through the sand dunes, longing for his father. Ben-Gurion had lost his mother at the age of ten. His father, Avigdor Grün, was a lawyer and the head of an early Zionist movement. He had prepared his son for a life in Palestine, but himself remained behind for a time when his son immigrated to Eretz Israel. Ben-Gurion had had a difficult time when he first arrived in Palestine. He did farmwork for Jewish settlers in Central Palestine and became ill with malaria. He ignored the doctor's advice to return to Europe, regaining his strength on his own and then joining a pioneer group in Galilee, working for Jewish farmers in an agricultural settlement west of Tiberias. They drained swampland and freed the barren land from stones to create arable land.

I could easily imagine how life had been for Ben-Gurion. Although I had come to the country thirty-three years later, there were many similarities in our stories: the early loss of our mothers, the longing for our families, the hard labor of the early years. On our long car trips, I also learned many details of his vision for Israel's future. For example, he criticized what he saw as the "illogical" structure of Tel Aviv and its six satellite cities. It made more sense in his opinion to incorporate them into larger administrative units, so that not every small town had to finance its own municipal administration and its own fire station. Nothing has changed in this respect to this day because local political functionaries are unwilling to reign in their power. Ben-Gurion also often got upset about the confusion that resulted from the streets in every town being named after the same great Zionists. This led to Arlosoroff, Jabotinsky, or Weizmann Streets in close proximity. That, too, has not changed, just now they have been joined by Ben-Gurion Streets.

He had an obsession about securing Israel's future by developing the Negev, the at that time almost completely unpopulated south of the country. On the way to Sde Boker, he told me proudly about his early days as a member of the kibbutz in the 1950s. Convinced that he should set a personal example, the founder of the country and Prime Minister took a leave of office for two years in 1953 to raise sheep in the desert. Ten years on, Ben-Gurion still got enjoyment out of the astonishment that this act had met with among his colleagues in the cabinet as well as the general public. But his decision did in fact give an enormous boost to the development of the Negev and many new immigrants settled in the south. The desert city of Dimona later became the center of Israeli nuclear research and technology. In the twenty-first century, over half a million people live in the region and many planners believe that it is the area of Israel with the greatest potential for development. However the question of how to deal with the Bedouin tribes that traditionally live in the Negev has not been conclusively settled. Many of them refuse to give up their nomadic lifestyle and move into villages with houses and modern infrastructure.

Ben-Gurion was also able to implement an idea that many had dismissed as insane: the founding of a university in Beer Sheva. I remember the moment when his opponent Pinchas Sapir from the Mapai Party arrived at Ben-Gurion's home one afternoon despite the acrimonious election campaign. While he did not speak with Ben-Gurion, he asked Paula to give him the news that enough money had been raised in the United States to build the university. Today, Ben-Gurion University is one of the most prestigious in the country.

I also sometimes accompanied Moshe Dayan to rallies and so got to know him better as well. Unlike Ben-Gurion, who never traveled without a driver and a security guard, Dayan drove his green Saab himself; only after a particularly exhausting appearance would he let me take over the wheel. We had many intense discussions about politics but also about our personal lives. He had recently left Eshkol's government in solidarity with Ben-Gurion and had since then been heading a large fishing business belonging to the Histadrut, the federation of trade unions. After his many years as Chief of Staff of the Israeli Defense Force and subsequently Minister of Agriculture, he was now living a civilian life and loved talking about women and archaeology. Dayan told me about his numerous affairs and about his great love for the wife of a well-known lawyer, whom he married after divorcing his first wife, Ruth. His archeological exploits made equally good stories as he had had more than one adventure on his forays into the coastal region or sneaking onto construction sites in his illegal search for valuable antiquities. The garden of his home in the Tel Aviv suburb of Tzahala resembles a museum with its priceless sarcophagi and Roman statues.

◆

During the electoral campaign of 1965, Germany and Israel established diplomatic relations. There was a backstory to this historical moment, which I had followed closely as *Jerusalem Post* correspondent. When Adenauer met Ben-Gurion in March 1960, they had signed a top-secret agreement promising the delivery of used American NATO tanks from Germany to Israel. These deliveries were discovered by Egypt in early 1965, leading to a diplomatic scandal. Cairo threatened to retaliate by recognizing East Germany. To Israel's indignation, the German government immediately stopped the deliveries. To appease Israel, West German Chancellor Ludwig Erhard sent Kurt Birrenbach, a Member of Parliament, to Jerusalem to negotiate fair compensation. The mission was highly classified and Birrenbach's presence in Israel was refuted, but I knew from the manager of the King David Hotel that there was going to be a midday meeting with him there.

I waited in front of the small dining hall. Shimon Peres, then Vice Minister of Defense, emerged first, followed by Kurt Birrenbach and Felix Shinnar, director of the reparations mission in Cologne. Peres prevented me from speaking to Birrenbach. That evening in the paper's offices, just as I about to write up the meeting, an item came in on the agency news ticker: the official East German newspaper, *Neues Deutschland*, had reported that Birrenbach had been a member of the NSDAP, the Nazi party, from 1933. Birrenbach would have to make a statement on this accusation immediately if he wanted to continue his mission. I contacted his Israeli liaison at the Ministry of Defense and insisted on speaking to him on the phone that very evening. Birrenbach's justification could be read in the *Jerusalem Post* the next morning: As a student, he had had to join the party. However he emigrated to South America in 1939 so that he could marry his fiancé, Ida, a "half-Jew" under the Nazi's classification. Until 1954, he had worked as a Thyssen representative in Argentina. Birrenbach was able to continue his negotiations.

On August 19, 1965, Rolf Friedemann Pauls began his tenure as Germany's first ambassador to Israel despite substantial protest. Pauls had been an officer in the Wehrmacht, where he had earned the Knight's Cross of the Iron Cross, and his first diplomatic post had been during the war, as military attaché to Turkey. Even Prime Minister Eshkol and Foreign Minister Golda Meir had reservations about him, but acquiesced when German Federal Chancellor Ludwig Erhard made it clear that should Pauls be rejected, he would refuse to accept Israel's first ambassador to Germany, Asher Ben-Natan. Ben-Natan had been a Nazi hunter after the war as a Mossad agent in Austria.

Soon after his arrival in Israel, Pauls asked for an audience with Ben-Gurion; he had a letter to give him from Konrad Adenauer. Ben-Gurion invited him to come on Saturday afternoon. When Paula told me this, she was quite dismissive. Ben-Gurion should meet Pauls in a hotel, she said, she didn't want any German diplomats in her apartment—and a war veteran at that. In the end she relented, but she greeted the ambassador in a shabby housecoat. And naturally the first question she asked him was where he had lost his arm. The conversation was awkward and remained tense until we retired to Ben-Gurion's study. Paula called after me to tell the photographer to wait until she returned. After a short interlude, she entered the room carrying a tray with coffee and pastries. She was wearing an elegant suit and was hospitality personified.

Pauls handed over Adenauer's letter, in which he announced his intentions to visit Ben-Gurion in Israel in 1966. Then the two spoke about the state of German-Israeli relations, but that was not the only subject touched upon. Ben-Gurion was worried about the military situation in Europe. He wanted to know how the German government and NATO planned to respond to the threat posed by the Soviet troops stationed in East Germany. Pauls answered calmly: "The presence of heavily-armed American troops in West Germany is the best guarantee for our security. The Soviet government would never dare attack."

It was easy to like Pauls, and I was confident that he would form good personal contacts. For many years, we met each other on his frequent visits to Israel, which he continued even as ambassador to Prague and Washington, D.C. I was all the more shocked when I read the book by former Israeli Ambassadors Asher Ben-Natan and Niels Hansen, *Deutschland und Israel. Dorniger Weg zur Freundschaft* [Germany and Israel: The Thorny Path to Friendship] which contained excerpts from Pauls' classified reports to the German Federal Foreign Office. Pauls wrote: "We need to make it clear to the Israelis that we see through their constant appeals to our moral responsibility. That they say 'moral,' but mean 'fiscal.'"

◆

New President of Israel, Yitzhak Navon (left), speaking with Ari at a press conference upon entering the presidential residence, 1978. Photo: Dan Hadani.

The November 1965 election ended, as expected, with a resounding defeat for the Rafi Party. Weeks prior to election day, ill humor had begun to spread among both candidates and supporters. Despite prominent personalities among its members—alongside Ben-Gurion and Moshe Dayan, Shimon Peres and two of Israel's future prime ministers, Yitzhak Navon and Chaim Herzog, were also on the list—the party won only ten of the Knesset's one hundred and twenty seats. Forty representatives from the Mapai Party and its allies were elected and so formed the governing coalition. We were of course disappointed, but consoled ourselves with the fact that Teddy Kollek and his "List for Jerusalem" had won the municipal elections. It was the beginning of what would become a twenty-eight-year term as mayor of Jerusalem.

For Ben-Gurion, the Knesset elections signaled the end of his political career. The left parties did however end up merging—after a marathon of negotiations—in January 1968, when Mapai, Achdut Avoda, and Rafi united to form HaAvoda, the Labor Party. The party leadership met with Ben-Gurion to attempt a reconciliation, but Ben-Gurion remained adamant: "I will not join your new party." Stubborn as he was, he founded his own party and his National Party gained three seats in the 1969 election. By that time, Ben-Gurion was already very weak. Paula had died in January 1968 and he himself had chosen her burial site—at the lip of the Zin River Canyon near Sde Boker.

I visited Ben-Gurion regularly until the end. In September 1970, Ted Lurie and I drove to Sde Boker to interview him for our Rosh Hashanah special edition entitled "Peace and the New Year." At a reception on the previous evening, the director of the American Cultural Center in Jerusalem, Joan Dickie, had asked whether she could accompany us on this trip. Joan waited in the shadow of some young trees in front of Ben-Gurion's house while Ted and I spoke with him about the future of the territories administered by Israel. His opinion was crystal clear: "Except for Jerusalem and the Golan Heights we should return all the territories if there will be peace. I am still for this ... If there is peace, we will return most of the territories. Without peace we shall keep them." But he also spoke about personal things, including Paula's death. When we left, he showed us her room and said: "I still haven't gotten used to the fact that she's no longer here." Ben-Gurion gave me permission to take his photograph. He pulled a comb out of his pocket and tried to get his mane under control. Afterwards, I introduced him to Joan Dickie. Despite his grief, he immediately took an interest in her and asked where she was from. "From the Bronx," she answered, a borough of New York with many Jewish neighborhoods. This roused his curiosity even more: "Are you treated well here as a new immigrant?" I whispered to him: "She's from the embassy." Back then, the Americans never sent Jewish diplomats to Israel, and so Ben-Gurion blurted: "Oh, then you're a shiksa," immediately apologizing for using the disparaging term for a non-Jewish woman. Then he told her about his daughter-in-law Mary, a nurse whom his son Amos had met in an English military hospital and later married: "I tell you, she's a better Israeli patriot than some Jewish women."

In 1971, the year of the "great reconciliation," I met Ben-Gurion again. On the occasion of his eighty-fifth birthday, around Sukkot, the entire cabinet, headed by Prime Minister Golda Meir, traveled by helicopter through the fall heat to Sde Boker and held a special session in Ben-Gurion's honor in the kibbutz library. I was one of very few participants who was neither a member of the government nor a high-level official. Ben-Gurion, marked by his age, greeted his former associates and also his harshest critics warmly, even letting some of them hug him. The fierce political conflicts of the previous years seem to have been forgotten; Israel's first prime minister was no longer a controversial figure. It was the final highlight of a political career that had lasted almost seven decades.

Golda Meir and Ben-Gurion shared the chair of this unique meeting of the cabinet. Meir loudly sung Ben-Gurion's praises for his role in the founding and building of the State of Israel. Perhaps it was her way of showing regret for how she had once attacked him when the party split. Her words sounded empty to me, since only five years earlier she had refused to chair the honorary committee to prepare the celebrations for Ben-Gurion's eightieth birthday. What is more, as General Secretary of Mapai, she had forbidden the leading party members from taking part in the celebrations in Sde Boker.

In May 1973, I visited Ben-Gurion in his house in Tel Aviv. His caretaker no longer allowed any journalists to see him, but he recognized me and bade me to come in. Then he asked: "You weren't born here. When did you come to the country?"

"Before I had even turned fourteen."

"Then you came with your parents?"

"No, I came alone with a Youth Aliya group."

"That must have been very difficult. I came to the country when I was nineteen and I pined horribly for my father." I was touched by how clear his memories of his youth in Palestine had remained.

I had come to talk with him about the twenty-fifth anniversary of the founding of Israel. He did not want to make any predictions about Israel's future or how the country would or should look in twenty-five years hence. But he answered without hesitating my question about the main tasks ahead for the coming years. After the Six-Day War, he had pushed for the return of all Israeli-administered territories with the exception of Jerusalem and the Golan Heights. Now he had changed his mind: "That was then, right after the war, on condition that peace, true peace, would come right away. But peace did not come, to this day they don't want to make peace with us, *halas*—finished. So there is no peace and we must do certain things." Then he added: "We should seriously set about establishing as many settlements as possible in the West Bank, but not by displacing Arabs."

I also asked him about Israel's social and religious problems. I was curious whether he had changed his opinion about civil marriages. Ben-Gurion himself had only had a civil marriage in the United States, but as prime minister, he had given the rabbis a monopoly over marriages. "It is better to maintain the unity of the nation in every respect. Many Jews who come here from other countries would not be able to accept marriage without a rabbi. Most marriages in Israel are consecrated according to Jewish law and in cases where this is impossible, people can go to Cyprus and get married there in a civil ceremony."This decision has had dire consequences that reach into the present.

When I took my leave of Ben-Gurion after two hours and descended the steps from his study, I knew that I would not see him again. It was the last interview that Ben-Gurion ever gave a reporter. It was printed on May 6, 1973; on December 1, 1973, the grand old man died.

Following the Yom Kippur War, the whole country had fallen into a depressive state. Like many other people, I had been called into active duty with my reserve unit. We were stationed on a hill near Jericho. One day, I was listening to Kol Israel (the voice of Israel) on the radio when suddenly the program was interrupted for a death announcement. That never happened; usually deaths, even those of famous people, were announced on Saturday evening after Shabbat. The voice of Ben-Gurion giving one of his rousing speeches came over the radio. The twenty or so members of my reserve unit all stood around my car, the doors opened wide, listening one last time to his words. Strange, I thought, here we've won the war, but our mood is so downbeat. And it's the voice of a dead man who for the first time after so many weeks is raising our spirits and imparting a modicum of hope.

Ben-Gurion's closed coffin was laid out in front of the Knesset, draped in the national flag. From the large somewhat elevated site there's a view of Jerusalem up to the Old City. Thousands of people from all walks of society waited patiently for their turn to pay their last respects to the former Prime Minister. I, too, said my goodbyes. As a soldier, I was able to accompany the transfer of the coffin to Sde Boker, where Ben-Gurion was buried alongside his wife. Today his grave is a national site of mourning, and every year on his yahrzeit there is an official memorial attended by high government officials and key members of Israeli society. This tradition has also been kept by his opponents, including right-wing politicians like Ariel Sharon and Menachem Begin who fought bitterly with him when he was alive.

The grave of Ben-Gurion and Paula is also the final site of the documentary about my life, made in October 2004 by Helga Embacher from the University of Salzburg and film director Hannes Klein. The memory of this man and his historical achievements made a deep impression on my life. Without his decisiveness, the State of Israel would never have been founded. Even if the state of Israeli society today has strayed very far from Ben-Gurion's vision for the country, causing me no amount of worry, I still hold his oft-cited words close to my heart: "In the land of Israel, anyone who does not believe in miracles is not a realist."

Between the Front and My Desk

In November 1965, I returned to the *Jerusalem Post*. Ben-Gurion's electoral defeat had also left its traces in our editorial offices. Mapai Party functionaries had for many years been complaining about our support for Ben-Gurion. A special session of the party leadership, including Prime Minister Eshkol, the General Secretary of Histadrut, Aron Becker, the head of the Jewish Agency, Louis Pinkus, and party secretary Golda Meir, agreed that Ted Lurie should be dismissed and the functions of both Lea Ben-Dior and myself should be limited. There was also criticism from the newspaper's supervisory board, which included representatives from the Workers' Bank and from a group of American Jews, the Israel Investors Cooperation. In the end, the demands for dismissals were rescinded, but an additional second editor was assigned to the paper in 1966 to ensure oversight of the paper, Francis Ofner. Ofner came from a city on the border of Hungary, had studied law, and had worked in journalism since his immigration to Palestine. Later, he was a correspondent for the Springer publishing house for many years. I was surprised that Ofner agreed to take this post as Mapai's "commissioner," since he had always been a vocal supporter of Ben-Gurion. He continually assured us how much he valued our work, which in our day-to-day work in the newsroom revealed itself to be nothing but lip service. He was in a permanent conflict with Lea

Ben-Dor, and we all hoped to soon get rid of Ofner again. In fact, he stayed only until May 15, 1967, when Egyptian troops marched into the Sinai Peninsula, escalating the crisis that would soon after become the Six-Day War. The front page of the weekend magazine in which we discussed this event was illustrated by a close-up of the Knesset. In the front you could see a section of the government table, behind it in the representatives' seats sat the giants of the Rafi Party including Ben-Gurion and Moshe Dayan. The photo was an expression of our hopes for reconciliation between the divided parties. Ofner took one glance at the magazine and stormed into my office, railing at me for using that cover photo. Shortly afterwards, he went to Tel Aviv to get a feel for the current political situation. As fate would have it, a few days later exactly the event that we had foreshadowed with the image took place: the political pressure led to a grand coalition government of all political parties. Menachim Begin, the right-wing national politician, became Prime Minister for the first time and Dayan was named Minister of Defense. And Ofner never stepped foot in our newsroom again.

◆

The year 1966 was remarkable for a number of meetings with key German figures. The first was Konrad Adenauer, who came to Israel on the occasion of David Ben-Gurion's upcoming eightieth birthday. Adenauer himself was already ninety years old and had given up his office as Federal Chancellor of West Germany three years previously. However he remained a member of parliament until his death in April 1967 and was still active in the national and international political arena.

The visit, twenty-one years after the end of the war, was a

delicate matter, as illustrated by an episode on the first day of his trip. Immediately after his arrival, a dinner was planned for Adenauer in Prime Minister Levi Eshkol's house. Eshkol's secretary of state, Yaakov Herzog, had prepared a speech in which the Germans were taken severely to task for their past. Adenauer, who was given the text to read beforehand, was indignant: "It is completely inappropriate to speak to me in this way." He threatened to leave if the speech was read as is. Eshkol's advisor rewrote the speech completely, putting Adenauer's service to Israel at its center. The former Chancellor said in his reply: "We have done everything in our power and have delivered every proof that we are making an effort to overcome that period of atrocities, which no one can undo. But we should now leave those times in the past. I know how hard it is for the Jewish people to accept this. But if good will goes unrecognized, no good can come of it."

I immediately got in touch with Josef-Wilhelm Selbach, Adenauer's aide, to schedule an interview with the former chancellor. Selbach suggested meeting at the Galei Kinneret Hotel on the Sea of Galilee, also one of Ben-Gurion's favorite places. I followed Adenauer's convoy in my own car from Tel Aviv to Nazareth and further to Tiberias. At sundown, Selbach met me in the hotel lobby and brought me to Adenauer on the terrace. The former chancellor greeted me warmly: "I know I promised you an appointment and I'd like to keep my promise, but I implore you: allow me to enjoy the peace and beauty of the Sea of Galilee with my daughter. You know for yourself how turbulent the past few days have been." He promised me an in-depth interview at a later time. I was touched by Adenauer's humanity, besides, I could well understand his exhaustion.

Two days later, I accompanied Adenauer to Sde Boker, where he met David Ben-Gurion for the first time since their meeting at the Waldorf Astoria Hotel in New York six years earlier. Although both men were now retired, the conversation in Ben-Gurion's modest wooden house revolved at first only around developments in Israel and in Germany. In contrast to Adenauer, Ben-Gurion had fallen in esteem, even among his former followers; his upcoming eightieth birthday was in fact being boycotted by the governing Workers' Party. In his eyes, this visit was therefore a particular honor. The meeting was extremely friendly, which should in part be attributed to the presence of the Israeli interpreter Mike Shinnar, whose father Felix knew Adenauer well, since he was director of the Israeli shopping mission in Cologne. Adenauer seemed particularly interested in understanding how a kibbutz worked. And so Ben-Gurion gave him a tour, including the sheep barn and the children's houses, where children grew up separately from their parents.

As always, Adenauer wore a suit, a vest, and a tie—a strange sight in the laid-back atmosphere of a kibbutz. The two men had their lunch together with Paula in the dining hall, where Adenauer sat comfortably among the *chaverim* who had just returned from working in the fields. In the afternoon, he returned to Tel Aviv by helicopter while I tried to coax my old Vauxhall to drive back quickly enough to attend the reception that Ambassador Pauls was giving at the Sheraton. A wide area in front of the hotel had been closed off and police in riot gear were holding back a crowd of demonstrators, including many members of partisans' associations who were demonstrating in the roads leading to the hotel. A German journalist commented: "I can't stand to watch Jews hitting other Jews in order to protect us Germans." The mood inside the hotel was celebratory but tense and in the moment that Adenauer stepped into the lobby, a former ghetto fighter ran up to him, threw anti-German flyers at his feet, and cursed him and the Israelis who had come to the reception. Nevertheless, hundreds of Israelis had gathered in the hotel, leaders from all areas of public life. Only a few years earlier, just the idea of a reception like this, where, moreover, mostly German was spoken, would have been considered utopian by some and a nightmare by others.

Around ten p.m., Adenauer awaited me in his suite in the adjacent Hilton Hotel. He apologized that I had had to wait so long and gestured for me to take a seat on one of the low sofas. He looked at me sternly through his piercing steel-blue eyes and before I had gathered my thoughts, demanded curtly and somewhat impatiently: "Please ask your questions."

"What did you think of the protests?" I wanted to know. Adenauer reacted self-assuredly: "I would have been very surprised if it had been any different. These protests are not directed at me personally, but at the country that I governed for many years." He seemed certain that these would be the last large-scale anti-German protests in Israel, an assessment that would later prove to have been correct.

"Please lay down your pen," Adenauer soon requested, because he wanted to speak freely. He went on to speak openly about his impressions of the trip: "I have taken a great personal interest in the fate of the Jewish people. That's why I wanted to come here and see for myself what is going on here and whether the population is satisfied." He had clearly been impressed by his visit with Ben-Gurion, and by the construction of the city of Beer Sheva in the middle of the desert. Nevertheless, he had a warning: "I probably do not need to explain to you that you are envied by your neighbors, and envy does not bring friends, but holds many dangers."

Adenauer left a strong impression on me. But I am angry with myself to this day that I allowed myself be so intimidated, that I never asked the truly explosive questions. For example, it was well-known that Adenauer was a patron of the political career of Hans Globke, who was first Undersecretary of State and then Chief of Staff of the Chancellery under his administration. And even at that time it was no secret that Globke's career was a textbook example of continuities in the German post-war government. As a legal scholar and as section head in the Reich Ministry of the Interior, Adenauer's close advisor had been involved in the creation of Nazi legislation, including the Nuremberg Race Laws. During the war, he had drafted the legal foundation for the disenfranchisement of Jews and the expropriation of their property in Czechoslovakia. It is as yet unclear whether and to what extent he may also have been involved in the deportation of Jews from northern Greece. There were also misgivings about the past of Adenauer's spokesman Karl-Günther von Hase, later ambassador to London from 1970 to '77, and from 1982 general director of the German public broadcaster ZDF.

One month later, I met a German politician who was less well-known on the international stage, during his eight-day trip through Israel. Surprisingly, it was the office of Golda Meir, who had reservations about relations with Germany, that called me to propose that I interview a young politician from the Social Democratic Party (SPD), Helmut Schmidt.

Schmidt was chain-smoking in the lobby of the King David Hotel in Jerusalem when I went to meet him. He greeted my warmly and was pleasantly surprised when I told him that we could speak

German, although his English was prefect. He proudly reported on his conversation with Golda Meir, which had lasted for two hours rather than the one that had been scheduled. Later, Golda Meir invited Schmidt, together with his wife and daughter, into her home to give her party comrades the opportunity of hearing his opinions. Two days before leaving for Israel, Schmidt had caused quite a stir at the SPD convention in Dortmund, where he was elected speaker for security and defense issues, a position with far-reaching strategic ramifications. It was presumed that if the Social Democrats won the federal election in 1969, Schmidt would be given the post of defense minister, which is exactly what happened. That was followed by a term as Minister of Finances from 1972, and from 1974 to 1982 Schmidt governed West Germany as Federal Chancellor.

Schmidt was decisive in his opinions: "We [West Germany] do not need and should not ask for nuclear alliance. What we do need is the right of veto on the use of American nuclear weapons stationed on German soil. We should be partners in the preparation of nuclear planning to be coordinated with German interests." Schmidt claimed that some members of the conservative Christian Democratic (CDU) governing party in Bonn shared this opinion.

We then discussed the state elections in Schmidt's home of Hamburg, where in 1964 the newly-founded far-right National Democratic Party (NPD) had won 3.9 percent of the vote. Schmidt believed that the party's success was linked to the fact that the top candidates of both SPD and CDU, Herbert Weichmann and Erich Blumenfeld, were Jews or had Jewish ancestry. I was shocked that Schmidt was not more outraged about this open display of antisemitism. But he believed that the NPD was no more than a passing phenomenon; after all, in 1949 three far-right parties had already imploded. That assessment proved false in the long-term, even if for decades the party was no more than a marginal player on the political landscape. But since reunification they have been very present, especially in the former East German states, and repeatedly they have managed to garner more than five percent of the vote, ensuring them seats in state parliaments. For years, there have been demands that the party be banned, most recently and emphatically after a far-right terror network was uncovered in Thuringia in 2011, but these efforts have not met with results to date. In 2012, the party is represented in the state parliaments of both Mecklenburg-West Pomerania and Saxony.

Finally, I asked Schmidt about his thoughts on his journey through Israel. He was particularly impressed by the pioneer spirit and the dynamism of the military: "Your army gets the most for its money by investing in equipment. It knows to concentrate on the most important expenditures and to disregard less important things like comfortable living quarters and unnecessary drills."

At the time, it was unusual for the Ministry of Foreign Affairs to host an official dinner in honor of a German politician. As chance would have it, it was a survivor of Theresienstadt who hosted such a dinner for Schmidt. Seev Sheck, director of the Israeli ministry's division for Western Europe, in his speech called Schmidt "a courageous fighter for democracy, a friend of Israel, and a paragon example of the new Germany." In answer, Schmidt expressed his hopes that the two social democratic parties—SPD and Mapai—would form close ties in the future. He expressed regret that he had so often encountered a negative image of Germany on his journey. The mood at the dinner was informal and convivial, and Schmidt made a positive, open impression on all who were present. That same year, he joined the German-Israeli Society, which had recently been founded in Germany.

Nevertheless, Helmut Schmidt did not always support Israel's best interests. For example, during the 1973 Yom Kippur War, the Willy Brandt government, to which Schmidt belonged as Minister of Finances, did not give permission for oversize American cargo planes to land at American Air Force bases in Germany. In Israel, this was interpreted as failure to render assistance, since the planes, which carried weapons and ammunition, needed to replenish stocks and were instead forced to land on much smaller and more dangerous bases on the Azores. Although the Israeli Labor Party was in power until 1977, Israel had to face the fact that, paradoxically, it received more support from the Christian Democratic German government than it did from the Social Democrats. One exception was the pro-Israel demonstrations in the spring of 1967 by German Young Socialists in the weeks of the crisis that preceded the Six-Day War. These demonstrations made a positive impression in Israel and were a key factor in the gradual shift of the country's attitude towards West Germany.

Furthermore, when a debate arose on the sale of German Leopard tanks to Saudi Arabia, Helmut Schmidt, Federal Chancellor at the time, was one of the supporters of this transaction. This action led Menachim Begin, on the campaign trail at the time, to attack Schmidt sharply, accusing him of greed and underlining his past as an officer in the Wehrmacht. Begin also criticized the fact that, in the Nazi era, Schmidt had attended trials of the "People's Court" as well as executions. The German Federal Chancellor defended himself vehemently against these charges, and I thought it credible that Schmidt would not have been able to refuse the orders to witness these events. I did not learn until later that Schmidt had had a Jewish grandfather. Later a friend of his told me that Schmidt refused to use this fact as an argument against Begin's accusations. The conflict put a significant strain on German-Israeli relations, especially after Begin became Prime Minister in May 1977. Only when Helmut Kohl became Federal Chancellor 1982, because Schmidt lost his tenure to a vote of no confidence, did Germany definitively refuse to sell Leopard tanks to Saudi Arabia because of the possible threat to Israel.

Nevertheless, Schmidt remained a sought-after discussion partner as a political commentator and consultant even after losing his post at the Chancellery. I was therefore delighted in May 1991 that I was able, in my capacity as advisor to the Jerusalem Foundation, to secure his attendance at an international symposium on "The Middle East after the Gulf War" on the occasion of Teddy Kollek's eightieth birthday. Only a few weeks previously, American President George Bush Sr. had ended the war against Iraqi dictator Saddam Hussein with a precarious ceasefire. Helmut Schmidt and French Member of European Parliament Simone Veil were to speak on the European dimensions of these developments. Twenty-two years had passed since my first meeting with Schmidt. In preparation for the conference we had spoken on the phone and written letters multiple times, so that he almost seemed like an old friend when he arrived at the King David Hotel in Jerusalem. But his visit also gave me insight into why Schmidt had the reputation as an arrogant loner. He refused to take part in preparatory meetings about the symposium agenda. Instead, he retired smoking to the piano in the hotel bar and noted casually: "You'll tell me later what I need to know."

My last personal contact with Helmut Schmidt was after the

assassination of Yitzhak Rabin in November 1995. Schmidt had met Rabin in 1975, when he was the first Israeli Prime Minister to visit West Germany. Both belonged to a younger generation of politicians who tried to approach problems pragmatically and unemotionally, so that their relations were friendly despite their differences of opinions on the Israeli-Palestinian conflict. As editor-in-chief of the weekly newspaper *Die Zeit*, Schmidt asked me to write Rabin's obituary, while he himself wrote an op-ed.

♦

In the Fall of 1966, German publisher and media mogul Axel Springer also visited Israel at the personal invitation of Teddy Kollek. It was his second visit, he had been to Jerusalem the year before to attend the inauguration of the Israel Museum. I got to know him in 1966 because Kollek invited me to accompany him on this trip. Springer's first stop was a visit to the Jerusalem Town Hall, where Kollek brought him to the balcony of the conference room. It had a view over the street to the Old City wall only fifty meters away, which was filled with landmines and guarded by Jordanian soldiers. Israelis were not allowed to pass there. It was a highly symbolic gesture, for Springer had just built his new publishing house on Kochstrasse, directly adjacent to the Berlin Wall. Kollek told Springer that this barrier strengthened his resolve to leave the Jerusalem Town Hall exactly where it was and not to build a new one elsewhere, although plans had been made to do so. The Town Hall of Jerusalem remains at that site to this day. In the early 1990s, Kollek did have a large new building constructed, with an expansive plaza. The historic town hall now houses only a few offices. The formerly mine-strewn street is today the main artery connecting the two parts of the city. Since the fall of 2011, the light rail runs through it.

That same evening, Teddy Kollek invited Springer to dinner in his private home, although he lived in a modest two-bedroom apartment. Tamar, his wife, had prepared a buffet. At this event, I had the opportunity to once again observe Kollek in his element. He was a genius at collecting donations and he asked Springer for his support to build a library and auditorium in the Israel Museum. He promised to do all he could to have the library named after Springer. This promise later caused Kollek no end of difficulties; even among his closest friends there were many who thought it inappropriate to name part of a national institution after a German sponsor.

I was surprised by the humor and openness that Axel Springer displayed in conversation. I could of course have been suspicious of a German whose publishing house was known for sacrificing principles and ideals to cater to the tastes of its millions of readers. But I was mollified by his charm and his loyalty to Israel. His feelings for Jerusalem seemed to me somewhat irrational—perhaps a mixture of religious sentimentality and empathy for the problems of a divided city. Springer insisted on spending most of his time in Israel in its main city, and he visited almost every corner of West Jerusalem. Not until 2012, when I went to an exhibition in the Jewish Museum in Frankfurt, did I learn about a biographical detail in Springer's life that adds a further dimension to his commitment to Israel: His first wife, with whom he had a daughter and whom he divorced in 1938, had been Christian but also the daughter of a Jewish mother, making her a "half-Jew" in the eyes of the Nazis.

Springers commitment to Israel was not only expressed through his financial generosity—his publishing house, too, exhibited an unusual loyalty. To this day, everyone who works there must sign a contract stating that they will contribute to the reconciliation between Germans and Jews and that they support "the existence of the Israeli nation." As far as Israeli public opinion was concerned, Springer's staunch support for Israel especially in times of acute threat took precedence over his wrongdoings, of which there are undoubtedly many, for example in connection with the reporting on the murder of the leftist student Benno Ohnesorg on June 2, 1967. But while outraged students in Germany called for the expropriation of the powerful Springer corporation, in many Israeli circles, on the eve of the Six-Day War, Springer was seen as a friend who could be relied upon.

After Axel Springer's death in 1985, his widow Friede continued the tradition of maintaining close ties to Jerusalem. Among the many initiatives that she supported, the Friends of Youth Aliyah was particularly close to her heart. I met Friede Springer in 1993, when I attended a moving commemoration of the sixtieth anniversary of the Youth Aliyah at the Springer building in Berlin. Ernst Cramer had invited me as a keynote speaker, but he mentioned only my work as former editor-in-chief of the *Jerusalem Post*. I surprised the audience by speaking about my own defining experience with the Youth Aliyah as a child. I ended my speech with the sentence: "To this day we think proudly and with affection of all those people who took care of us when we needed care so urgently."

The event was the beginning of a professional friendship with Ernst Cramer that continued for many years. Cramer had immigrated to America before the war, and he had achieved an impressive career as editor-in-chief of the *Welt* and a key figure in the Springer emporium. We saw each other for the last time in person on January 27,

2008, at a commemoration of Holocaust Remembrance Day in the Bundestag, the German parliament. Cramer was standing near me and called over: "You see Ari? The fact that we're both here is our victory over Hitler." On my eighty-fifth birthday, he wrote me a hand-written letter that I never got a chance to answer; he died soon afterwards, shortly before his ninety-seventh birthday.

These meetings with German politicians and journalists in the 1960s convinced me that David Ben-Gurion's attitude towards the Germans had been right. He was of the opinion that there was not a new Germany, but another Germany. In a 1968 interview on the subject he told me: "The Germans are like everybody else. Not the Nazis, but the Germans. ... Jews too have their failings, and one is that they do not have enough understanding of *mamlakhtiyut*—the essence and needs of a nation-state." Ben-Gurion's vision of coming to an understanding with post-war Germany and building up Israel as a normal nation were his main driving forces.

As someone born in Vienna, from the beginning I compared the Germans to the Austrians. I repeatedly asked myself why it was so difficult for my former compatriots to face their past in a similar manner. From 1952, Germany paid reparations and also individual pensions to victims of Nazi persecution. Austrian Jews in contrast received no restitution at all for many years, since Adenauer rightly believed this should be under the aegis of the Austrian government. Many Nazi leaders, such as Ernst Kaltenbrunner and Arthur Seyss-Inquart, not to mention Adolf Hitler himself, had been Austrian.

Only one year after the Second Republic of Austria was founded in 1955, Israel quasi absolved Austria of all responsibility for Nazi crimes by taking up diplomatic relations with the country without hesitation. For many years, I was incensed by this characteristic of Israeli politics: the readiness to sacrifice morality on the altar of pragmatism. Today, I recognize that these policies made it possible for thousands of Holocaust survivors in displaced persons camps in Germany to immigrate to Israel, and later also 270,000 Soviet Jews. Israel needed good relations with Austria, a transit country, if they were going to smuggle Jewish immigrants into the country. Yet in contrast to Germany, not until 1995 did Austria set up a national foundation that attempted to compensate Nazi victims by giving them a small pension and restitution for a fraction of their wealth. My father, for example, received neither restitution for the business he had lost, nor a pension for the torture he suffered in the concentration camp and the consequences it had for his later health. His only pension was from his American pension plan, which he had paid into from the 1940s. Israel should have demanded concrete restitution when it established diplomatic relations with Austria in 1956. To this day I do not understand why Nahum Goldmann, president of the Jewish World Congress, did not do so.

As part of the reparations agreement made with the German government in 1952, individual reparations were made as well as payments to Israel. But equally important in my mind was the Germans' willingness to face their historical responsibility. For example they founded the Federal Agency for Civic Education in 1952, which in 1963, two years before diplomatic relations were established between the countries, began to fund study trips to Israel. Thousands of people in key positions to disseminate ideas—officers, teachers, professors, artists, journalist, and social workers—have taken part in these programs. To this day, the agency offers six study trips to Israel per year. For many years, I followed the work of this agency closely as an advisor, but often also as a speaker at one of their seminars in Israel or in Germany, and so I have experienced the invaluable work of this institution first hand. Because the Nazi past is dealt with so much more openly and self-critically in Germany, especially in Berlin, for many decades I felt more at home there than in Austria. For me, the turning point did not come until Austrian Chancellor Franz Vranitzky visited Israel in 1993 and spoke unmistakably about Austria's share of responsibility for the crimes of National Socialism.

◆

In the spring of 1967, once again there were political skirmishes on the border between Israel and Syria. Despite the conflict, on Friday April 7, a ceremony took place to inaugurate the memorial forest planted near Nazareth and dedicated to Winston Churchill, attended by two guests of honor: his daughter Mary Soames and his son, *Sunday Times* journalist Randolph Churchill. On that Friday, there had been particularly fierce air battles on the Syrian/Israeli/Jordanian border. At the time, I worked not only for the *Jerusalem Post*, but also occasionally for the American news agency Associated Press (AP). Naturally, the air battles had to be reported to AP immediately. Back then, all correspondents shared two telex machines at the main post office on Jaffa Street. Since I worked regularly with one of the telex operators, despite the high costs I asked him to set up a dedicated line to one of the AP offices in Rome or Frankfurt. I ran back and forth between the post office and the Federal Press Office, where reports from the front came in, and so passed on to the AP almost simultaneous reports of the air battles, in which our air force shot down five Syrian MIGs.

In those hectic hours, I got a call from Ted Lurie's wife, Zilla:

"Ari, it's very important; Randolph Churchill just called me. He's looking for someone who can give him information on the political situation in Israel." Ted Lurie was abroad at the time. "Zilla, I have to keep handing in my reports, I can't get away now," I explained to her, "but I'll try to come a little later." And so that afternoon at four-thirty, I met with Randolph Churchill—the spitting image of his father—in his suite in the King David Hotel. At his arm was a large glass of scotch and a mug of milk. "I understand you know your way around," he said to me, and told me that he was to interview Ben-Gurion at Sde Boker for the *Sunday Times* the next day. His editor wanted him to talk to Ben-Gurion about the Lavon Affair. Since Churchill knew little about Israeli domestic politics, he wanted me to provide him with background information. I advised against bringing up the Lavon Affair, and proposed that he instead ask Ben-Gurion about his strategic vision for the Middle East. He then asked me to find a tape recorder for him. The next afternoon, Randolph Churchill returned from Sde Boker, his conversation with Ben-Gurion had gone very well and he invited me for a drink. Two weeks later, I received a telegram at the news office: "My son Winston arriving soon to report on the tensions. Please help him. Randolph Churchill."

But first, there were the celebrations for Independence Day. Every nineteen years, the Hebrew and the Gregorian calendars are aligned. And so in 1967, the dates of Independence Day were again the same as they had been in 1948: both May 14 and 5 Iyar. Like every year, a large military parade was planned, this time in Jerusalem. However, since there were very strict stipulations in place in connection with the ceasefire, there could be no demonstrations of heavy artillery or of the air force. To make up for the smaller parade, there would be a sounding of the Tattoo in the stadium of Hebrew University near the Israel Museum. It was the luck of my reserve unit to have been chosen to participate in that year. In the weeks leading up to the Independence Day celebration, every day we had three or four rehearsals of the choreography for the Great Tattoo, a completely ludicrous event. Each of us, men in the prime of life between the ages of thirty and forty, had to carry colored lanterns on our shoulders to create a light spectacle.

Two days before the performance there was a dress rehearsal. Over the stadium loudspeakers, the radio moderator Asariah Rappoport recited a poem written before 1956 by national poet Nathan Alterman. In one stanza, Alterman warns the Egyptians not to try attacking Israel again if they don't want a repeat of the events of 1948. Right after the dress rehearsal, I called the office of Prime Minister Levi Eshkol, to point out the political explosiveness of the text. The office must have intervened with the organizers, because at the official event, Rappoport refrained from reading that stanza.

On Monday May 15, I went to Jerusalem to see a concert by Arthur Rubinstein in honor of Independence Day. I had difficulty concentrating on the music; I had an uneasy feeling that was exacerbated when I saw General Chief of Staff Rabin leave in the middle of the concert. After the concert I hurried to the newsroom. The news agencies had just reported that two Egyptian tank divisions had left Cairo and were heading towards the Sinai peninsula. Supposedly, President Nasser's marching orders had been founded on false reports from the Soviet Union that claimed Israel had mobilized troops on the border to Syria. This news item also acted like a powder keg in the *Jerusalem Post* offices.

On Friday May 19, I came down with a high fever, which was

unusual for me; nevertheless I went on a bus tour of the Gaza border that had been organized by the Federal Press Agency. On that day, on the orders of UN General Secretary U Thant, the Blue Helmets who had been stationed there on a UNEF mission were withdrawn. Tensions between Egypt and Israel had increased to the point where Thant could no longer guarantee the safety of the peacekeeping troops. The Indian commander of the UNEF troops transferred military control to the commander of the Palestinian Liberation Army (PLA). I watched with great trepidation as the UN flag on the border to Israel was taken down and Palestinian soldiers hoisted their black, white, red, and green flag. Although the Gaza Strip was under Egyptian administration, President Nasser gave the PLA free reign. Now, two armies were directly facing one another; a mere spark could cause the powder keg to explode.

Because of my fever, I decided to stay home on Saturday. Friday evening, the young Winston Churchill called me from Tel Aviv, he was very eager to meet me the following day. He was supposed to write an article about the tensions in the Middle East for the British tabloid *News of the World*, but he knew almost nothing about the history of Israel. And so I invited him to come by my house on Saturday afternoon. I made chicken soup and not only explained the history of Israel to him, but also told him that his grandfather had called for the first partition between Palestine and Transjordan in 1922. As a curious person, I was fascinated to speak to the grandson of such a great historical figure. We also discussed the perhaps upcoming war. Churchill asked: "What are you waiting for? Why don't you attack?"

After the end of the Six-Day War, young Winston Churchill was the first person to write a book about the events. His name opened every door for him; generals literally lined up at the Hilton in Tel Aviv to give him their perspective on the war. Later, Churchill invited me to his house near London and pointed to a new, round swimming pool: "That's my book on the Six-Day War," he said proudly. In 2001, I was able to help him secure a long interview with Prime Minister Ehud Barak for the *Welt am Sonntag*.

◆

By the end of May 1967, nobody doubted that there would be war, although the Israeli government tried to keep the public calm. When the Egyptians closed the Straits of Tiran in the Red Sea to Israeli ships on May 22, Israel Galili, a minister with no department, called upon the editorial offices of all Israeli newspapers to play down their reports on the incident. The government was still hoping to resolve the conflict through diplomatic channels with the help of the Americans. In my commentaries, I expressed hope that the upcoming journey of Foreign Minister Abba Eban to Paris, London, and Washington, D.C. would bring us the support we needed. But Eban's trip was at best a partial success; only American President Lyndon B. Johnson made some vague concessions. The greatest betrayal in my eyes was the total rejection by de Gaulle, who for years had been one of Israel's staunchest allies, along with his warning that Israel should not under any circumstances be the first to open fire if we did not want to jeopardize our arms deliveries from France. I was less surprised by the disinterest of British Prime Minister Harold Wilson.

After Eban reported that the American government still hoped to form an international armada to break through the sea blockade, Eshkol's government decided to cancel the attacks on the Gaza Strip and the northern Sinai that had been planned for May 27. Thousands of reservists had already been sitting in their tanks with the motors running, expecting marching orders, and both the troops and high-level officers were disappointed. Friends who had already been called to the front told me on the phone that the general staff had threatened with collective resignation. Shortly afterwards, Nassar declared that his basic objective was the "destruction of Israel." To calm the population, on May 29, Prime Minister Eshkol held a speech on the radio, but it ended up sounding anything but confident. When he stumbled over a word with a double meaning and had to repeat himself, it sounded like stuttering—a fatal mistake that increased the pressure on him even more. From the inception of the crisis, we at the *Jerusalem Post* and also the editors of other papers had been demanding that Eshkol step down from his role as Minister of Defense and pass the office on to former chief of staff Moshe Dayan, who had experience in military matters. On May 30, Egypt and Jordan signed a mutual defense pact. King Hussein put his military under Egyptian command and invited Iraq to station troops in Jordan.

In light of these developments, two days later Eshkol agreed to form a grand coalition government and Dayan took over the Ministry of Defense. As a result, for the first time, the nationalist right-wing politician Menachem Begin, whom the Workers' Party had ostracized for years, received a governmental office. As chair of the national-liberal Gahal block, he became a minister without a department. That decision to declare former underground terrorists fit to govern after nineteen years would prove to be a decisive mistake that severely weakened the Workers' Party. Ten years later, in May 1977, Begin's party, Likud, would win the elections and he would become Prime Minister.

On Saturday evening, June 3, 1967, Dayan held his first press conference as Minister of Defense, which was broadcast live on radio. Asked how long he would tolerate Egypt's blockade of the Straits of Tiran he answered: "I'm not standing here with a stopwatch." Many foreign journalists, including my new friend Winston Churchill, who had been reporting on the tensions for days, decided to fly home for a few days. Dayan's diversionary tactics panned out: On June 5, Israeli bombers flew in from the west over the Egyptian air bases in the early hours of the morning and demolished ninety percent of Egypt's air force before it ever left the ground. The war against Egypt was in this way de facto decided in its very first hours.

I myself was a technical sergeant in the Six-Day War, in an infantry regiment that had been assigned to the Jerusalem Brigade. Although my job as editor-in-chief of the *Jerusalem Post* was classified as essential, I insisted on enlisting. As I explained to Ted Lurie: "Nobody is indispensable. I have to do my duty." I still felt terrible that I had not been on the battlefield in 1948, and I did not want to fail to fight this time. Many people who know me as hard-headed and opinionated can I'm sure hardly believe that I have no trouble submitting to military discipline. The moment that I trade my civilian clothes for a military uniform and move into a barrack or a military tent with fifteen soldiers, my attitude towards life and my values change completely. Suddenly, oily pasta and inferior tea with its aftertaste of metal dishes and detergent are delicacies. I am repeatedly fascinated by the way in which social hierarchies are turned topsy turvy in the blink of an eye: the general director's chauffeur is suddenly an officer and the general director himself a low-ranking private. In a country such as Israel, where the military plays such a key role, this helps keeps social hierarchies fairly flat.

We were armed with three or four heavy 81-mm mortar cannons, weapons that were relatively easy to transport and had a range of five to six kilometers. That meant that in battle, they had to be very close to the front. Ten days before the fighting started, we were stationed near Abu Gosh in the abandoned Neve Ilan kibbutz, where we had drills every day and trained to improve our fitness. Neve Ilan was ten kilometers to the east of Latrun Fort, which had been in Jordanian hands since 1948. On the morning of June 5, our mobilization orders stated, the battle for Latrun was to begin. The evening beforehand, we brought our four mortar cannons into position. We had back-up from *chaverim* from Kibbutz Zor'a, who had pulled their field cannons to our position with one of their tractors. There were also three busloads of infantry soldiers. When we attacked early in the morning, we found that the Jordanian troops had retreated in the night, so that we took the fort without a battle. I was given the order to fire mortar grenades in the direction of the Jordanian soldiers' rearguard, who were retreating through the olive groves to the mountains. Later we learned that none of those shells had hit their target. I was very relieved to hear that; for me, every person is an entire world, independent of their nationality, background, or religion. The next mobilization order had us move close to Kibbutz Ma'ale HaHamisha, thirteen kilometers outside of Jerusalem. A Jordanian unit was positioned on Radar Hill to the north of the kibbutz and Ma'ale HaHamisha had been under heavy fire. We fired back until the arrival of a tank brigade that was on its way to the West Bank. With that, my unit's active fighting was over.

On June 5, the radio remained quiet. The Israeli general staff had made a strategic decision not to inform the public about the course of the war, which fostered feelings of insecurity in the general population. We only knew that the Jordanians had attacked us; we had no idea that the Egyptian air force had been destroyed on the ground and that the war was as good as won. My greatest worry was for Jerusalem. There was only one reserve brigade available to defend the city, because to the end, hopes had been high that King Hussein of Jordan could be convinced not to enter the war. Now we could see from afar that smoke was rising over the west of the city, because Jordanian units were firing on Jerusalem from the Mount of Olives. In the afternoon, I managed to get the editorial office on the line. Ahuvah, the receptionist, had good news for me: "Everything's alright, don't worry." A missile had hit the *Jerusalem Post* building, but the damages were slight. Besides, the newspaper had apparently already received reports about the destruction of the Egyptian air force. In the evening, around six p.m., the large parachute division under the commando of General Motta Gur passed our outpost at a gas station on the main road to Jerusalem. We cheered the elite unit with the red berets as the passed and threw cold bottles of beer to our comrades on the troop transporters. Their unit had been called back from Gaza to defend Jerusalem. Among the fighters were *chaverim* from Hamadia, two of whom did not survive the battle for Jerusalem.

On June 6, Israeli troops marched into the east of the city. Losses were relatively high; to protect civilians and also the holy sites of Muslims and Christians, the army refrained from using heavy artillery. Almost one quarter of the eight hundred Israeli soldiers who lost their lives in the war died in Jerusalem.

On Thursday, June 8, Israeli troops had taken Jerusalem, the West Bank, and the Sinai Peninsula. A delegation of kibbutzniks from northern Galilee hurried to Jerusalem and demanded that

Prime Minister Eshkol also secure the northern border before ending the fighting. Syrians had been firing at Israeli settlements from the Golan Heights. The kibbutzniks were able to convince Eshkol that the Syrians too should be attacked. Before informing his Minister of Defense, Moshe Dayan, Eshkol personally gave orders to General Chief of Staff Rabin and to the general responsible for the north, Dado Elazar. Very early on Friday morning, the Israeli army attacked the well-defended Syrian strongholds in the Golan Heights.

When the fighting ended on the evening of June 10, 1967, I was in Nabi Samuel, an Arab village at the grave of the Prophet Samuel on a hill north of Jerusalem. From there, we could see as far as the large concert hall in Jerusalem where on that evening, somewhat prematurely, the Israeli Philharmonic and Zubin Mehta performed a concert in celebration of the ceasefire. We listened to the music on our small transistor radio. During the intermission, the commentator announced that the last shots had just been fired on the Golan Heights and that the ceasefire was in place.

Two days later, we received permission to return to Jerusalem for a short visit. There were strict searches at Mandelbaum Gate, the former checkpoint between Jordan and Israel, because it had become common for Israeli soldiers—also reservists it should be said—to plunder Palestinian homes and take their valuables home. Televisions, porcelain, and rugs were particularly coveted. From the very first day, many Israeli soldiers acted like occupying forces and humiliated the defeated Palestinians. When their houses were searched, the inhabitants were often made to stand for long periods with their face to the wall. The soldiers simply took possession of houses whose Palestinian inhabitants had recently fled, acting like the new owners. The commander of my division, a friend of mine, had quartered himself in an elegant villa in Shu'afat, owned by the owner of the Jordanian airline Alia—King Hussein had resided there whenever he visited East Jerusalem. The villa was overrun with soldiers who belonged to the division commander's cadre. After we had lived for days on nothing but soldiers' rations, I was delighted to be able to make myself a huge omelet in a fully equipped kitchen. I repressed the fact that I, too, was acting like an occupying soldier in that moment.

◆

On June 27, the Knesset passed an amendment to the Law and Administration Ordinance of the constitution, seemingly only a formal change, that allowed the Minister of the Interior to redraw municipal borders. In this way, East and West Jerusalem were united and the borders of the city were expanded considerably. The mayor of East Jerusalem was discharged.

In the last week of June, I was given a twenty-four-hour leave. Late in the afternoon, still wearing my uniform, I went into the newsroom. There was a lot of excitement about the upcoming answer to the question of the day: When would the border between West and East Jerusalem be opened? Not even fifteen minutes later, a call came from the Federal Press Agency announcing that three border crossings would be opened the next morning at eight. One of them was the Jaffa Gate, which had been walled up since 1948.

So many Palestinians wanted to cross the border that the opening hour was pushed forward to seven a.m. The bloodbath that those in charge had been fearing never materialized; in its place were many moving encounters. For the first time since 1948, thousands of Palestinians now had the opportunity to visit the neighborhoods from which they had been expelled. Fathers went with their children to Baka, Katamon, or the German Colony, rang the bells of the new occupants of their former homes and asked permission to show their children where they had grown up. The Palestinians were particularly amazed by the traffic lights on Jaffa Street—there was not yet anything of the kind in East Jerusalem. Officially, they were only allowed to visit Jerusalem, but younger Palestinians jumped into a bus at the first opportunity and went to Tel Aviv to enjoy the beach.

A few days later, the landmines were removed from the entrance to the Wailing Wall. On Shavuot, thousands of Israelis flocked to this holiest of Jewish sites. Shortly afterwards, in a cloak-and-dagger operation, the Mughrabi Quarter was bulldozed to create a large plaza in front of the Wailing Wall. This action was condemned not only by Palestinians, but also by many liberal Israelis. The inhabitants were barely given time to pack their few possessions before being loaded onto trucks in the middle of the night and brought to alternative housing. In the newsroom, too, we had bitter fights about this action. Because most of the *Jerusalem Post* team supported this step in principal, my friend the night editor Charley Weiss left the paper after more than fifteen years as editor. He became a correspondent for Voice of America.

Most of my contact to and friendships with Palestinians developed after 1967. Some encounters were intimate—I was invited into private homes in East Jerusalem, Bethlehem, Nablus, and Jericho—for example with Anwar Nusseibeh, whom Ted Lurie knew from *Palestine Post* days. Nusseibeh had studied law in Cambridge and came from one of the oldest Palestinian families in Jerusalem. Traditionally, his family keeps the key to the Church of the Holy Sepulcher. Nusseibeh had lost his left foot in the battles of 1948. He was Jordan's Ambassador to the United Nations and has held many important posts in the Jordanian government over the course of his life, including Minister of Defense during the Six-Day War.

In August 1967, Ted Lurie wanted to rekindle their Mandate-era friendship and brought me with him to their meeting. Nusseibeh's home, an Arab nobleman's house from the nineteenth century, is cattycorner to the American Colony Hotel. His wife, who organized demonstrations in front of the Damascus Gate every Friday in protest of the Israeli occupation of Jerusalem, gave us a reserved greeting and led us to her husband in their elegant living room, appointed with Levantine and Western furniture. Lurie and Nusseibeh exchanged memories and soon we were talking about the current situation. Nusseibeh complained that the Israeli administration had immediately ousted the mayor of East Jerusalem. To secure a good foundation for relations with the Palestinians, he should have been permitted to retain his office, perhaps as vice-mayor for East Jerusalem. One thing that Nusseibeh said remains ingrained in my memory: "We learned our lesson from 1948. This time we will stay and we will not leave. Because whoever leaves their home, never gets it back again." We sat together until midnight and drank more than one glass of scotch. To this day I have fond memories of the honest and open conversations that I have had with this highly-educated gentleman.

In 1981, we were both participants of the first Israeli-Arab conference, which was organized at the initiative of George Assousa, a Jerusalem-born, Greek Orthodox Palestinian astrophysicist. As one of the two chairs of the conference, Nusseibeh moderated the first meeting, in which the participants introduced themselves. When my colleague Shalom Rosenfeld spoke and said that the Israeli State had grown out of the ashes of the Holocaust, a British journalist interrupted loudly: "Do we really have to hear a lecture about the Holocaust again?" Anwar Nusseibeh immediately jumped in and reprimanded him: "I will not allow you to trample on the feelings of our Israeli participants!" He threw the journalist out of the room.

Anwar Nusseibeh died in 1984; for his great services to the Palestinian people he was buried in a grave of honor on the Temple Mount. I was one of the very few Israelis among many hundreds of Palestinian mourners at his funeral. For me, too, his death was a day of mourning. If many more people were as willing to build bridges as he was, we would be much closer to peace today.

Another dear Palestinian friend from this era was Mahmoud Abu Salef, editor-in-chief of the newspaper *Al-Quds*. Abu Salef was an imposing, tall, well-groomed man. His education, his impeccable manners, and his influential position in East Jerusalem combined to make his elegant house in Shuafat, a suburb of Jerusalem, a popular meeting place of the Palestinian political and intellectual elite. His blonde wife, whom he had met while at university in Germany, was the perfect hostess. Every few months he invited me to meet with influential Palestinians, either in his home in Shuafat or at his house in Jericho, which was surrounded by a magnificent garden planted with orange and lemon trees. Like many wealthy Palestinians from East Jerusalem, he spent much of his winter and spring there, because the climate is friendlier than in Jerusalem. We hoped back then that our personal connection would lead to mutual understanding and in the end contribute to peace. Because *Al-Quds* was politically moderate, the paper was looked down upon by Yasser Arafat and the PLO.

Occasionally, we were also able to offer Abu Salef practical help. One day he called me up with a problem: "Ari, can you please do me a favor? We ordered printing paper on time, but it wasn't delivered." I didn't hesitate for a moment. I spoke with Ted Lurie and quickly answered: "Your people can come now and pick up six rolls from our printer." Abu Salef thanked us effusively; without paper he would not have had a newspaper the next day. Another time he had a confidential favor to ask during the local elections in Jerusalem in the fall of 1969. Teddy Kollek was running for mayor with his list "One Jerusalem." As residents of East Jerusalem, Palestinians were able to vote in local elections even though they were Jordanian citizens; Abu Salef was therefore eligible to vote in the election. One hour before the polling stations closed at nine p.m., he called me up and asked whether I could pick him up from his newsroom and drive him to the polling station. He had been wrestling with himself all day about whether or not he should support an Israeli candidate. Finally, he had decided to vote for Teddy Kollek, but he did not want to be recognized and so could not drive with his conspicuous white Mercedes. The polling station was in a school in Sanhedria, an ultra-Orthodox Jewish neighborhood on the former border to East Jerusalem. We arrived at the very last minute. Since the religious poll workers knew that every vote by a Palestinian would be for Teddy Kollek, they tried to prevent us from going in. I insisted on our right to entry. The police on the scene reacted with disinterest to our scuffle with the officials, in which we in the end prevailed, finally managing to enter the polling station with Abu Salef.

In the days after the 1967 ceasefire, I also met Anan Safadi, who freelanced for the *Jerusalem Post,* for the first time. He was from Bet Shean, from where he had flown with his family to Nazareth as a ten-year-old. Safadi earned his living selling cars, but he dreamed of a career as a journalist. From the early 1960s, he regularly supplied us with news and reports from Nazareth and Galilee. Shortly after the end of the Six-Day War, Safadi appeared in the newsroom in person and introduced himself. He had decided to relocate with his family to Jerusalem, because he presumed that it would be the center of all important decisions. I was impressed by his resolve and I wanted to give the bright young man a chance. It was easy to convince Ted Lurie to hire him, because we desperately needed an Arab-speaking journalist to make contacts in the new territories. Very soon, he was indispensable to all the editors. His articles and his contacts with Palestinian journalists and politicians were a great boost for the prestige of the *Post*. More than ever, we were cited by foreign newspapers. Safadi proposed that he regularly listen to Jordanian, Syrian, and Egyptian radio broadcasts so that we could include Arab sources in our reporting. In this way, he repeatedly managed to get news even before the agencies had hold of it. Over the years, we developed a close friendship.

In September 1967, I also met Elias Freij, a Greek Orthodox councilman from Bethlehem. Teddy Kollek had invited him to his office in Jerusalem, and asked me to join them later in order to create a direct contact between Freij and the *Jerusalem Post*. The topic of their talk was the first Christmas in Bethlehem under Israeli occupation. For the first time in nineteen years, it was possible to access the Church of the Nativity via the main street, which meant the procession of Roman Catholic bishops from Jerusalem to Bethlehem could also take place. Kollek and Freij calculated that there would be thousands of Christian pilgrims coming, and Freij was hoping that in the lead-up to this event we would write positive articles about the peaceful atmosphere in Bethlehem.

From the very first moment I met him I was taken with the

charisma and power of this small round man, who put all his energy into improving the quality of life for the population of Bethlehem. Like Teddy Kollek, he too set up a foundation that sought international donations for the upkeep of holy sites in his city. The foundation was supported in the main by wealthy Palestinians from Bethlehem who lived in exile. In 1972, Freij was elected mayor. My connection to him remained unbroken even in difficult political times. I visited him many times in the Bethlehem Town Hall and in his private home on the road to Hebron. Freij also came to our newsroom, where he discussed with our staff possibilities for the peaceful coexistence of Israelis and Palestinians.

Every year, Freij hosted a huge Christmas reception at the Holy Land Hotel in Bethlehem. A highpoint of his efforts towards understanding was the attendance at this event of Prime Minister Yitzhak Rabin and Minister of Defense Shimon Peres in 1975. In 1976, Freij ran into our newsroom clearly upset and asked me to contact Peres's office for him immediately. He wanted to prevent the upcoming mayoral elections in the West Bank, because he expected only PLO candidates would win—a potentially fatal development for the peace process. However the elections took place and Freij was reelected—the only candidate who was not a PLO member. In 1995, Arafat even named him Minister of Tourism for the Palestinian government. Freij is a well-known name in Bethlehem to this day—one of the large souvenir shops next to the Town Hall, which sells typical olive wood carvings with abalone inserts, is run by his sons.

Back then, I shared Moshe Dayan's pragmatic political conviction that the territory we had captured should not be permanently occupied, and I supported his "open bridges" policy. Palestinians should not be cut off from their neighbors in Jordan, which would exacerbate their already difficult situation by obstructing their export markets. Mid-July was the beginning of the watermelon harvest, one of the top export crops for Palestinian farmers in the West Bank. Since both the Allenby bridge near Jericho and the Damia bridge north of Nablus had been blown up in the war, a delegation of Palestinian melon growers went to Dayan to explain that there were only two narrow passages where the large trucks full of melons could cross the river. Dayan recognized the problem and ordered the repair of the bridges over the Jordan, which quickly resulted in a large jump in the exchange of goods and tourists. Former inhabitants of the West Bank who had in the meantime moved to other Arab countries were given permission to visit during the holidays and inhabitants of the West Bank were allowed to work in Israel. In this way, relations with the people in the Israeli-administered territories were normalized relatively quickly.

Jerusalem's mayor, Teddy Kollek, also tried to make concessions without undermining fundamental Israeli interests. Although schools in East Jerusalem were under the jurisdiction of the Israeli Ministry of Education, he stood up to fierce resistance from Golda Meir to ensure that Palestinian students could follow the Jordanian curriculum. Only with a leaving certificate recognized by the Arab world would they later be able to study in Cairo, Amman, or Beirut. Kollek also approved of allowing Palestinians to put up their own war memorials. As he once explained to me, he believed that they would never respect the monuments for our soldiers if they were not allowed to mourn their own fallen soldiers. To this day there is a memorial for fallen Jordanian soldiers, unnoticed by most of the population, on the road to Jericho not far from Damascus Gate.

The results of the mayoral elections of 1969 clearly showed that Kollek's policies were supported by a key segment of the Palestinian population. Kollek received eight thousand Palestinian votes when he ran for reelection, a notable percentage of the seventy thousand Palestinians living in East Jerusalem.

In 1966, Kollek set up the Jerusalem Foundation to further the collection of international donations. He realized that Jerusalem's population did not have anywhere near the means for the upkeep and development of its many important sites. Over the years, the Jerusalem Foundation has supported numerous educational, cultural, and municipal projects that support the peaceful coexistence of Jews, Muslims, and Christians. During the twenty-eight years of his tenure—only in 1993, at the age of 82, was he succeeded by Likud politician Ehud Olmert—he was able to modernize the city considerably, and every year Jerusalem hosts hundreds of thousands of visitors from across the globe. Kollek is rightly popularly known as "the greatest builder of Jerusalem since King Herod."

◆

In the new political situation after 1967, we needed to rethink the aims of the *Jerusalem Post*. I thought back to Gershon Agron and Ted Lurie's op-ed from 1932, in which they expressed their hopes that the paper would further understanding between Jews and Palestinians. Now I wanted our newspaper to act as a bridge between Israelis and Palestinians. I believed this should be reflected in, for example, our choice of wording—a decision that was in part rejected by some editors. I for example refused—and refuse to this day—to refer to the conquered territories as "Judea and Samaria." And in order to avoid the problematic term "occupied territories,"

I invented more neutral wording: "administered territories." I remember many loud exchanges with a religious night editor who absolutely refused to use this phrase. Repeatedly he tried to refer to Palestinians as "inhabitants of Judea and Samaria."

We created a new post for news from these "Israeli-administered territories"—the "West Bank reporter," whose job it was to report on the increasing problems that the Israeli conquest had caused for over three million Palestinians. In this context I would like to mention our "Lost and Found" column, where we tried to help Palestinians whose cars had been expropriated by Israeli soldiers.

Writing about the year 1967 today, I have been thinking deeply about why my empathy for the Palestinians and my hopes for a just peace are founded in this era of all times. Why didn't my sense of injustice regarding the way so many Israelis treated the Palestinians awaken much earlier? I did have a dormant feeling that something was wrong in the country, but it did not truly come to the fore until 1967. The mood in Israel was almost euphoric at that time. The fact that our military had been victorious over three enemy armies in only six days led many Israelis to entertain fantasies of becoming a great power. They saw themselves then, and see themselves to this day, as the "Lords of the Land," as Akiva Eldar and Idith Zertal so aptly named their analysis of the Israeli settler movement since 1967. To this day, I am devastated by and ashamed of how many of my fellow citizens, often the descendants of victims of pogroms and persecution, have themselves become persecutors without a second thought. Being driven out of my homeland as a child is something I will never forget, and I have no trouble imagining how it feels to be forced to capitulate to those who are more powerful.

The year 1967 also marks the beginning of Israel's calamitous settlement policy. On conquered Palestinian territory, with the tacit permission of every Israeli government to this day, an enormous network of Jewish settlements was established on the West Bank. Fanatic settlers destroyed olive groves that were decades old and provided Palestinian farmers with their main source of livelihood. Despite the "Three Nos" agreed upon at the Arab League summit in Khartoum in September 1967—no recognition of Israel, no negotiation with Israel, and no peace with Israel—which destroyed the possibility of any compromise, nevertheless very many Palestinians back then, in both the West Bank and Gaza, were still willing to act pragmatically. For example, one Palestinian initiative to set up a parliamentary representation of Palestinians in the West Bank agreed to cooperate with the Israeli military administration. But the early death of Prime Minister Levi Eshkol in February 1969, and the fact that he was succeeded by Golda Meir, nipped these attempts at reconciliation in the bud. Eshkol had been ready to give the Palestinians autonomous self-government as a step towards peace. In his last interview with *Newsweek* magazine in February of 1969, Eshkol said on the future of the West Bank that a few stones would not create obstacles on the way to peace. But before the end of this conversation, he collapsed from a heart attack.

I last saw the Prime Minister in January 1969. His aides had convinced him to show himself in public again despite his illness and he went out to greet a delegation of British Zionists at the King David Hotel. His health was clearly very bad; his cheeks were sunken and his face was a shade of pale gray. He spoke with effort and left the group very soon after giving a short welcome in English. Afterwards, we spoke a few words. I wished him a speedy recovery and encouraged him to rest. Eshkol thanked me for breaking the

Sabbath on that cold Saturday so that a report of his appearance could be printed the next day. One month later, he had died.

His successor, Golda Meir, did not even believe that there was such a thing as the Palestinian people. Repeatedly she stated: "They are Arabs like all other Arabs."

It was the first time that the sudden death of a moderate Israeli politician halted progression on the path to peace. But it was not to be the last time. In November 1995, the Oslo peace process failed after Yitzhak Rabin was assassinated by a fanatical religious law student. And, finally, in January 2006, the clinical death of Ariel Sharon, who at the end of his political career sought a peaceful compromise with the Palestinians, paved the way for the nationalist right-wing government that rules over Israel today and blocks any hopes of peace.

In the summer of 1968, while the euphoria following the Six-Day War was still strong, Israel was badly shaken by the Soviet invasion of Prague on August 21, 1968, which quelled the Prague Spring. We had sympathized greatly with the attempts of the Communist Party of Czechoslovakia under Alexander Dubček to instate "socialism with a human face." Across Israel there were demonstrations against Soviet despotism and the invasion of the Red Army. You could hear Arik Einstein's song, "Shir shechalamti al Prag" (A song I've dreamt of Prague), on every corner. The lyrics dramatically describe Soviet soldiers trampling over Prague and express hope that a new spring would soon come to the city.

My sympathies for the Czech people went back three decades to the time when, in March 1939, Hitler occupied the remaining Czech Republic in defiance of the September 1938 Munich Agreement. Only nine years later, the Czech government, at the behest of the Soviet Union, supplied the young Israeli state with desperately needed weapons and combat aircraft. For that reason, I was eager to visit Prague for a few days as soon as possible to see for myself what was going on. I faced great difficulties, since the Soviet Union had broken off diplomatic relations with Israel as a result of the Six-Day War. However, in July 1969 a convenient opportunity arose. The Austrian embassy invited me to visit Vienna—an invitation that I had refused multiple times in the past and was tempted to refuse again this time since I did not want to go to Vienna as a guest of the Austrian government. And so it was with ambivalent feelings that I accepted the invitation, although the conservative Austrian People's Party (ÖVP) was the sole governing party. As I had hoped, with the help of Leon Zeon from the Vienna Verkehrsbüro, a tourism organization, I was able to obtain a three-day tourist visa to Prague. A press visa would have needed the approval of the Czech Ministry of Foreign Affairs—which I would certainly not have obtained as an Israeli journalist.

To get a better feel for the mood in the country, I traveled by train from the Franz Josef Station to Prague Central Station. It was a trip full of memories and conflicting feelings; in December 1937 I had taken the same route on my way to Berlin after my bar mitzvah. As chance would have it, I shared a compartment with a Czech journalist and his family. They had flown to Vienna after the Russian invasion and were now returning. I told him about how much sympathy there was in Israel for the Czech people and about Arik Einstein's songs, of which I carried six singles in my luggage, which I happily gave him so that he could distribute them among his friends.

My first stop in Prague was the Czech journalist's association, where my colleague had told me I should be sure to register my arrival. Their general secretary issued a warning: "You're not permitted to work as a journalist with a tourist visa."

"What does that mean?" I asked.

"You are not allowed to conduct interviews, most certainly not with the students on Wenceslas Square."

This ban of course made me all the more curious and naturally I went straight there. Every night, hundreds of regime opponents gathered at Wenceslas Square and laid flowers in memory of Jan Palach, who in January 1969 had self-immolated in protest of the invasion. I felt a kinship with these brave young people who, disregarding both the invader's tanks and a ban on meetings, came together in small bars to protest the new authorities. "We're preparing for a long struggle. Even if it takes years—we have the time and the patience," said one Prague journalist who had impressed me greatly by his calm and fearlessness. "Czechoslovakia will never again be the same country … We have not betrayed the communist ideal … But we demand the right to live our own brand of communism. One that is liberal and democratic." He continued: "One of the very few weapons we have left in our fight against the Soviet rulers is to openly speak our minds to foreigners." I was all the more pleased that I could support the struggle of these brave Czechs by writing two in-depth articles; one political analysis and one report on Jewish Prague.

The German-Jewish culture, which had blossomed in Prague before World War II as it had almost nowhere else, had been almost completely destroyed by the Nazis. Very few Jewish communities survived. To this day, it is they who care for the historical buildings such as the thirteenth-century Old-New Synagogue and the old Jewish cemetery where the tombstone of the famous Rabbi Loew stands. Many memories from my youth returned to me, for although

I had never visited the city, I had been greatly influenced by the stories of the golem and the books by Franz Kafka and Max Brod. I walked alone for many hours through the narrow streets of the extinct Jewish Quarter. I felt like I was on the set of an extinguished world.

◆

For me, one of the most fascinating aspects of my job was that there is no routine in the classic sense. People, issues, and places are always changing; and always, I wanted to report from wherever events were unfolding. Inevitably, working that way comes with a certain disjointedness.

In April 1970, there was a new issue on the agenda. Through the International Press Institute (IPI), of which I had been a member since 1970, I traveled to Manila, the capitol of the Philippines, as an Israeli observer to the founding of the Asian Press Foundation. For many years, Israel had worked towards establishing good relations with Indonesia, since it is one of the largest Islamic countries. But because of Israel's tense relations to its Arab neighbors, Indonesia had remained distanced. Rapprochement appeared to be possible only informally. To prepare for my journey, I spoke with experts on the region, including the Israeli ambassador to Manila and the head of the Asia division of the Ministry of Foreign Affairs. It was known that Indonesia's foreign minister, Adam Malik, had been chosen to give the keynote and I was asked to make informal contact with the Indonesian delegation. That would make it easier for Abba Eban, Israeli Minister of Foreign Affairs, to approach the delegation at the United Nations. Missions such as that, which demanded no little chutzpah, awakened my good-natured ambition.

On the way to Manila, I had to change flights in Bangkok, including checking in again. By chance, three official-looking Indonesians, wearing rounded felt hats (*songkoks*), were in front of me in line; they clearly belonged to Adam Malik's delegation. I had no trouble engaging them in a friendly conversation. Later, I sat next to one of them on the plane, and our conversation became so personal that I told him about my mission. In answer, while we were still on the plane, he introduced me to Malik's personal assistant. On the evening of the first day of the conference, my friendly airplane neighbor came up to me and said: "There is a small room in the corner. Please be there in ten minutes; Adam Malik is willing to meet you for a short talk." I was surprised by the humility with which Malik greeted me; after all, he was a well-known man of state. I passed on our minister's request and Malik answered that he would be delighted to talk with Abba Eban. He then invited me to visit Indonesia. Malik knew that such a visit was almost impossible for an Israeli journalist at the time, and so he added with a wink: "Ask your man in Singapore"—in reference to the Mossad agent responsible for contact to Indonesia—"he'll know what you have to do." Of course I attempted to accept Malik's invitation before returning home, but the formalities proved much too complicated.

There is another reason why my trip to the Philippines has remained so clear in my memory—it was there that I experienced the longest thirty seconds of my life. On April 12, I was in my hotel room on the eleventh floor when suddenly, the building began to sway like a pendulum. An earthquake! From my window I could see hundreds of people fleeing into the street in panic. It would have been completely pointless to attempt to leave the swaying building by the stairs. Instinctively, I decided to stay at the window. If the building collapsed, I reasoned to myself, I would jump out. I was relieved when a young Philippine hotel page entered my room, trembling with fear, and informed me that we were the only two people on the floor. Both wretched, we clung to each other until the horrifying event was over.

◆

The years between 1967 and 1973 were marked by my experiences as a journalist and as a soldier, two roles that I never really felt were in conflict. Soldiers too, when they are alone at their posts, have time to reflect.

The military situation remained tense after the Six-Day War. Until August 1970, there was a real war of attrition at the Suez Canal. Afterwards, although a ceasefire was in place, Egypt and Syria were still secretly preparing for the next war, with the help of the Soviet Union. In September 1970, Egyptian president Gamal Abdel Nasser died during an Arab reconciliation summit. His successor, Anwar Sadat, hoped to recapture Egypt's lost territory through military force, and Syrian President Hafez al-Assad wanted to recover the Golan Heights. Together, the two believed they were strong enough to beat Israel.

In January 1971, although I was already forty-six years old, I was again called to serve in my reserve unit for six weeks. We were to meet at Mount Herzl in Jerusalem, because it could easily be reached by the trucks that were to take us to the harbor of Eilat on the Red Sea. From there, we continued in a large landing craft to the small harbor of Sharm el-Sheikh on the southern tip of the Sinai Peninsula, one of the main Israeli bases in Sinai. The commander of my unit knew that I always drove to my deployments myself in my *Jerusalem Post* staff car, a beige Peugeot station wagon. This time, too, he allowed me to drive alone to Sharm el-Sheikh. That was in fact irresponsible; it meant driving more than five hundred kilometers through the Sinai Peninsula, past the city of Suez and the Gulf of Suez on sand-strewn roads that went almost exclusively through the desert. On the road leading out of Jerusalem stood crowds of young soldiers who were hitchhiking back to their units after the weekend, a phenomenon that repeated itself every Sunday morning. I took two of them to the Mitla Pass sixteen kilometers east of the Suez Canal. The military situation was incredibly tense, no one knew whether President Sadat would renew the ceasefire, which was always limited to three months. All along the canal and south of Suez as well, I saw many tank units and hundreds of troops building military fortifications. If the region had been as fortified in 1973, most likely the Egyptians would never have dared to attack.

After a risky nighttime drive, I arrived at Sharm el-Sheikh at five a.m., shortly before my comrades. Our mission was to guard a new mobile radar anti-aircraft battery on a flat hill that the Americans had recently set up for Israel. My comrades were glad that I had brought a car; it enabled us to take part in the night life of Sharm el-Sheikh. There were already a few small hotels, restaurants, and bars, and even a disco. Israel was turning the city into a tourist destination.

One day, Minister of Defense Moshe Dayan himself came by to inspect the new radar unit. Soon after his arrival, my officer called me into the kitchen tent. "Rath, Moshe Dayan would like to invite you to coffee." Everyone was surprised and I was honored to be given the chance to discuss his strategy going forward with the General Chief of Staff.

In 1973, the radar station that we were guarding was captured by an Egyptian commando in the first days of the Six-Day War. Some of our soldiers died defending it, and many were captured and imprisoned.

In March 1972, I again was called to serve six weeks with my reserve unit in Sharm el-Sheikh. My mortar shell unit was assigned to an infantry company that was completing a landing maneuver on the island of Tiran. The challenge was to transport weapons and ammunition safely in a rubber dinghy and be ready to fire immediately after landing. On the second-to-last day of the drill, our officers made us run through the hills for hours. That evening, Minister of Police Shlomo Hillel was giving a speech. I had studied with Hillel at the University of Jerusalem and had shared an apartment with him for a time in 1957. We did not want to miss his lecture and so we hurried to the lecture hall after the drill. The door was already closed and the Colonel at the door, aptly named Buchhalter—bookkeeper—did not want to let us in. "If you don't obey, I'll have you arrested," he threatened our group of 47-year-old soldiers. My comrades left, but I stayed, and so was arrested and shut into a military police tent for insubordination. The entire action was absurd. After a short while, Shlomo Hillel's assistant came and apologized. But the ordeal was not over yet. On the next day, there was to be a hearing on my case. Two military policemen picked me up and led me to Colonel Buchhalter. Unexpectedly, the Colonel came around immediately; we apologized to one another and I was released.

◆

My private life was reduced to a minimum in those years. I worked every day until late in the night; my friends were in the main my colleagues at the *Jerusalem Post* and my girlfriends too I met at work. Until the paper went to print shortly after midnight, the newsroom was always in a fever pitch, and all that pressure needed to be relieved. Often we played bridge until three a.m., or we went to Fink's Bar for a nightcap. On the weekends, I sometimes drove to Hamadia to visit Avri and other old friends from the kibbutz. Occasionally, I spend Friday evenings at my brother's house in Tel Aviv, where my sister-in-law prepared a feast for Erev Shabbat.

One Saturday in early May 1972, I got a call from the American consul general. I knew him and was happy to hear from him, but he quickly said: "I'm afraid I don't have good news for you." What could it be?

"Is your father's name Josef Rath?"

"Yes."

"And he lives in Zurich?"

I answered in the affirmative again. He had heard from the American consulate in Zurich that Josef Rath had to leave Switzerland immediately. The hotel where my father had been staying for weeks, if not months, had pressed charges with the police because he had stopped paying his bills. He had lost all his money on the stock market and had been arrested the day before. My father had told the police that he had two sons in Israel, at which news the Swiss police expelled him from the country. I immediately bought him a one-way ticket to Tel Aviv. He arrived late in the evening, in his wheelchair as always. The personnel from the Swiss hotel had made no effort to pack his things neatly but had simply thrown everything in large boxes. Despite the unpleasant circumstances, my father was in a very good mood. With his usual dry humor, he told my brother and I that he'd even had a warm shower in the police jail.

He had visited us before in 1949 and 1955, back then with Rita and our sister. To this day I remember our shock when he arrived in a wheelchair in 1955—he had not told us that he could no longer walk—and had to be unloaded from the plane with a crane. His marriage had already broken down to the point that Rita ended her visit prematurely and flew back to Vienna. Most likely she couldn't stomach the idea of having to push him around in a wheelchair for years while putting up with his difficult character. My father returned to the United States alone. When his business with Cuba dried up after the revolution, he closed his paper warehouse in New York and moved to Europe. At first he lived in noble hotels, such as the Savoy on Zurich's Bahnhofstrasse, and then in increasingly smaller hotels until he slowly lost his entire fortune playing the market. Despite his back problems, women continued to flock around him; they pushed his wheelchair and took him on daytrips. My father was not an intellectual, but he read the newspaper every day and was up-to-date on international and Israeli politics. That gave us plenty to talk about, but we never had a conversation about feelings or my difficult childhood. I cared for him, but I can't honestly say that I loved him. His strictness and his silence surrounding my mother's death had simply left too many scars. My friends however appreciated him as an exceptional conversation partner and to his very last days he captivated everyone around him with his charm and his wisdom about life.

From the start, I knew that I would bring my father into my apartment. That changed my life completely, since he needed care around the clock. Furthermore, I lived on the third floor, with no elevator. A caretaker came during the day, and in the last months of his life, the manager of the *Jerusalem Post* cafeteria took him into her home, where she and her husband cared for him. I visited him almost daily until his death on the night after Yom Kippur in September 1977.

Near the end, he complained one day of feeling unwell. The doctor thought he had an ulcer. I carried him down the stairs in my arms and drove him to the hospital. He wailed in Yiddish: "I want to die at home." I hoped he would recover in the hospital, and I consoled him, said goodbye, and reminded him to drink enough. When I returned to the hospital after breaking my fast, his room was empty. They had diagnosed a problem with his heart and moved him to the intensive care unit. I hurried over and found my father in one of the six beds. He woke occasionally, but drifted off again. I stayed near him and sat with the nurses who watched the monitors. At around three a.m. there was an alarm. Doctors arrived with respirators and sent me away. They needed to care for a patient. When I returned to the ICU after around an hour, a doctor was waiting for me. The alarm had been for my father; he had had another heart attack. They had not been able to save his life.

The news shook me to the core. I stood for a long time alone in the morgue in front of the small package of white shrouds that was my father. Because he had died on a Friday, I had only a couple of hours to take care of all the formalities for the funeral, which was to take place on Sunday. My brother flew in from Bonn that day. Almost the entire staff of the *Jerusalem Post* went to the funeral. The director of the *chevra kadisha*, the Jewish burial society, comforted me. "It is a great honor when God calls someone to him in the night of Yom Kippur." He helped me to secure a burial site for my father on the Mount of Olives, from where he can look over the Temple Mount. Although I am not religious, it means a lot to me that his final place of rest is in the most holy of Jewish cemeteries.

After we had covered father's grave with light brown earth and stones, my brother and I said Kaddish. Meshulam knows this prayer of mourning by heart; as an eight-year-old, after our mother's death, he said it daily for six months. With tears running down our cheeks we stuck a small white sign with our father's name in Hebrew and the date of his death into the freshly-dug-up earth. Josef Rath died at the age of eighty-four and four-and-a-half months, I am already older than he was when he died. For a long time, my brother and I stood at the fresh grave looking out from the centuries-old Jewish cemetery to the two mosques on the Temple Mount. My friends and colleagues from the *Post* stayed with us until we had said our final good-byes to our father.

Since then, Abed, the Palestinian caretaker of the cemetery, watches over him. Abed is almost eighty years old, a small, powerful man missing almost all of his teeth who speaks Hebrew well and also some German. He knows that we come to our father's grave every year at his yahrzeit and awaits us at the entrance to receive his remuneration. When my brother appeared alone in October 2011, Abed asked worriedly why I had not come. It is good to know that Abed takes care of our father's grave. I have always been moved by the beauty and the silence of the place. The only bush around throws a shadow on the flat gravestone made of yellow-white Jerusalem limestone. The Hebrew words engraved on the stone say only his name: Josef Rath—loving and beloved father and grandfather.

◆

In June 1973, under extremely dramatic conditions, I met the great man of German social democracy. Willy Brandt came to Israel in

June 1973 at the invitation of Prime Minister Golda Meir; he was the first Federal Chancellor of Germany to come on an official state visit. A highlight of his visit was a tour of the fortress of Masada, the symbol of Jewish resistance and bravery from Roman times. With a group of journalists, I waited early in the morning on the plateau of Masada near the Dead Sea at the spot where military helicopters were supposed to land with Brandt and Yigael Yadin, a well-known Masada researcher, and their entourage.

With much noise and dust the helicopter was about to land—the rotors had already stopped turning—when the enormous aircraft, to the horror of everyone present, slowly rose again. We threw ourselves at the helicopter and hung on to the skids hoping that our weight would keep it on the ground. In the end, its passengers were saved by a one-meter high Byzantine protective wall, which the helicopter crashed into. The crew opened the doors. White with shock, Willy Brandt, Yigael Yadin, and the others disembarked as quickly as possible. Yadin worriedly made sure that Brandt was unharmed. Both men tried not to let anyone see how shaken up they were, and immediately began their tour of the monument, which had for many years been a symbol of Israeli heroism: over nine hundred Jewish soldiers, women, and children had resisted the Roman Empire here while under siege by the Legionnaires. Brandt seemed particularly moved by Yadin's story of Flavius Josephus's historical report: At the orders of the commander of the first Jewish uprising, Elazar Ben-Jair, the heads of all families killed their wives and children and then themselves rather than fall into the hands of the Romans.

Willy Brandt's visit was under an unlucky star. Ever since his *Kniefall* in Warsaw in 1970, a gesture of humility in the face of the Jewish and Polish victims of the Nazi dictatorship, he became the German politician who most enjoyed the favor of the Israeli public. But immediately upon arriving at the airport, Brandt held a speech underlining the importance of a "normal relationship" between Germany and Israel. In Israel, the term "normalization" when applied to German-Israeli relations was interpreted as Germany's attempt to draw a line under the Nazi crimes of the past. The fact that a German Chancellor used these words at his first visit to Israel sparked widespread indignation—also in me. Despite my fundamental liking for Brandt, I wrote a critical op-ed. Israel, I said, expected the first social democratic Federal Chancellor to show more understanding for the suffering that the Nazis had inflicted upon the Jewish people.

Before Brandt's visit was over, both sides had worked successfully to bridge this gap. In his thank you telegram to Golda Meir, Brandt spoke of establishing, "mindful of the burden of the past, ... a new chapter in the relations between our two peoples." He also thanked her for a memorable visit and for the hospitality of the Israeli government, and assured her that the first visit of an incumbent German Chancellor would have great impact on future German-Israeli relations.

I had great respect Willy Brandt, whom I saw as the epitome of a social democratic man of state and fighter for peace. I had hopes that he would make an important contribution to peace in the Middle East, and so was disappointed when he stepped down in May 1974 as a result of the Guillaume Affair. And in fact, as president of the Socialist International, a role Brandt held for well over a decade, he did attempt to promote a peaceful settlement between Israel and the Palestinians.

In 1984, when I accompanied Shimon Peres on a short visit to Bonn, I was able to attend a meeting of the SPD leaders in the "barracks," the SPD headquarters. Willy Brandt greeted the Israeli guests. When we spoke he remembered those dramatic minutes at Masada and also praised the *Post*'s critical reporting on the 1982 war in Lebanon.

Through my contact to Egon Bahr, who played a key role in shaping Brandt's Ostpolitik or Eastern policy, I was able to gain insight into the former chancellor's thoughts on the normalization of relations with East Germany. I was happy that he lived to see the fall of the Berlin Wall in November 1989, especially as he had once been Governing Mayor of Berlin, and I was saddened by his death in October 1992. I had been visiting friends in Munich at the time, and went to Berlin to pay my last respects at Schöneberg Town Hall, where his stately coffin was laid out in the entry in a sea of red carnations and wreaths of red roses. On the day of the state funeral, late in the evening I went to the Waldfriedhof cemetery in Zehlendorf and took my leave by pouring a handful of soil into the open grave.

◆

In late August 1973, once again I took off on a long journey abroad. Back then, when new flight routes were opened, for one year journalists were given the opportunity to try them out on an "introductory flight." Air France had just opened a route from Tahiti to Lima—making it possible to take their airline around the world. To garner publicity for this new opportunity, Air France invited two editors on a test flight: Tommy Lapid, who would later become Minister of Justice and at the time worked for *Ma'ariv*, and me. Normally I always refused such offers, to avoid any possible conflict of interest down the road, but in this case I made an exception, since the trip would also allow me to see my beloved Uncle Jakob again, my father's ten-years-older brother, in Chile.

Jakob and his wife Bassia had also left for New York in the fall of 1940 after their stay in Cuba but, unlike my father, Jakob had never managed to gain a foothold in the city. They had a small grocery in Brooklyn, but although they both worked more than twelve hours a day, they still barely managed to make a living. What is more, my father had fallen out with Jakob completely, so that Meshulam and I could only visit him secretly once a month. Our cousin Dolly moved from Cuba to Santiago de Chile, because there was a small community of German Jews there, and soon after met and married the widowed owner of a lamp store, after which Uncle Jakob's fate took a turn for the better. Dolly brought her parents to Santiago, where Jakob became his son-in-law's business partner and in the end made a modest fortune.

The first stop on my journey was New Delhi, where I renewed my Indian contacts. From there I went to Tokyo, where I met my tour companions and guides: Micky Federmann, Air France's head of PR, and Tommy Lapid, director of the Dan Hotel. Together we flew to Tahiti, with a stopover at Bora Bora Island, whose natural beauty was overwhelming. Then we continued on to Lima. The next day, I traveled alone to Chile to see Uncle Jakob. Aunt Bassia had already died, and Jakob was almost ninety years old. He was confined to his bed and dependent on an oxygen tank, but his mind was as sharp as ever. Every day, he counseled his friends on how to protect their assets in light of the inflation that was raging in Chile at the time.

His step-grandson picked me up at the airport and ardently passed on a warning: "Uncle Jakob said to tell you whatever you do, don't stay at the Carrera Sharon Hotel across from La Moneda, there's been a lot of trouble there." La Moneda, the former mint, was the seat of President Salvador Allende's government. I responded: "My dear boy, I'm a journalist, of course I'll be staying there." On Sunday afternoon, September 2, I checked in. On the Plaza de la Constitución, construction workers were busy putting up a grandstand for the parade on September 4, the third anniversary of the victory of Unidad Popular, the socialist party that put Allende into power. Tractors bedecked in red flags stood at the ready. That first evening, I went to visit Uncle Jakob in his one-family house in an outlying district.

The next day, I had a meeting with the Israeli ambassador, Moshe Tov. There were no taxis because of a strike, so the embassy sent me a limousine and driver, a young Chilean Jew who also spoke Hebrew. The city was covered in slogans, which high school Latin helped me to decipher: "Contra el facismo," "Hurrah for the third anniversary of socialist unity!" Repeatedly, I saw one slogan which I had to get the embassy driver to translate for me: "Contra el golpe"—Against the coup.

I had admired Allende since he had been elected president in 1970. For those of us on the left in Israel, he had put an ideal into practice, instating far-reaching social and economic reforms without introducing a communist regime. He had begun a far-reaching agricultural reform and partially nationalized the banks and industry, in particular the copper mines, which had belonged to U.S. American companies. We also felt a kinship with Chile because it was the only country in Latin America where there had not yet been a military coup.

On September 4, Chile's most prominent socialists gathered for the big parade. My Israeli press pass even won me a spot among the guests on the grandstand. There, I wrangled my way to President

Allende: "I come from Israel and want to congratulate you. We fully support your reform and the socialist front." In no time, I was approached by Allende's media spokeswoman, Frida Modak, who politely but decisively led me away from him. I watched the parade from my new spot and asked Modak whether I could have an interview with Allende. "Call me in the next couple of days," she answered.

My time in Santiago flew by. In the meantime, the hotel had moved me from a small, dark room facing the courtyard to a suite with a view of La Moneda. All of the big papers, as well as the television and radio broadcasters, had sent their correspondents to Argentina to cover the presidential elections, and aside from my colleagues at Reuters, Agence France-Presse, and one correspondent from the Swedish daily *Dagens Nyheter*, there were hardly any other foreign journalists in the city.

My tour guides from Peru had come to Chile for three days, and we went dancing with my family at Santiago's best restaurant and also saw a performance of the Israeli dance company, Batsheva. We enjoyed ourselves immensely, and only those in our group who lived there could tell that the mood in the city was becoming increasingly tense.

Since I had been unable to reach Frida Modak by telephone, two days after the parade, I went to La Moneda in person. The officer at the entrance called her for me. She proved to be extremely uncomplicated and asked me to her office. Unfortunately I would not, she said, be able to speak with Allende, but she could get me an interview with Minister of Defense Orlando Letelier. Dramatically, she declared: "This weekend, the fate of Chile will be decided. Cardinal Raúl Silva Henríquez had organized a meeting between

Allende and the head of the conservative party, Partido Demócrata Cristiano. The outcome of that meeting will decide whether or not a compromise can be reached." The conservatives wanted Allende to promise not to nationalize any more companies. The communists in his coalition were willing to agree, but not the socialist Marxists, further destabilizing the political situation.

The wife of the correspondent from Voice of America invited me to accompany her to a briefing session that the American embassy was holding in a restaurant next to the presidential palace. Our discussion centered around the possible coup. The diplomat, most certainly a CIA agent, said outright: "It is no longer a question of whether there will be a coup; only of when."

Before leaving, I went to say goodbye to Uncle Jakob, but he was no longer in his apartment. His condition had gotten so much worse that he had been admitted to the Santa Maria clinic with a pelvic hematoma. When I entered his room, he opened his eyes and said in Yiddish: "Arile, you have to leave tomorrow." I answered: "Not a chance. I'm not going to leave you here alone. I'll call Lore in Caracas and I'll wait until she gets here." My cousin Lore was fifty-eight years old at the time and somewhat timid. In light of the instable political situation, she did not want to fly to Chile. "Lore, it's your father!" I admonished her, and so she came to Santiago on September 9 to care for him.

On September 11, Lore called me early in the morning; she had just heard the news: "The coup has started. They've already taken the Port of Valparaíso and they're marching towards Santiago. Please be careful." I ran to the window. The Plaza de la Constitución in front of the palace was completely empty. By nine a.m., a small group of around sixty supporters had gathered there, and President

Allende went on the balcony to address them. Then, green buses pulled up and the carabineros drove away; soon after, the presidential guard left the palace. Around ten a.m., a number of American tanks from the Chilean army surrounded the plaza. Not long after, the doors to La Moneda opened. A few women and men waving white flags came out and disappeared behind the tanks. Allende, I learned later, refused to leave of his own free will; a decision by which he signed his own death sentence. But he did not want to leave his country as a political refugee. It did not take long before the military began to fire their cannons and machine guns at La Moneda and other government buildings. There was a great deal of return fire.

In the meantime, the hotel management had ordered all guests to leave our rooms and go to the basement. I stayed at the window observing the scene and taking pictures. Later, I gave the undeveloped film to my colleague Saul Eisendraht from *Time* magazine. Suddenly, machine gun fire hit the building only one meter from where I was standing. Shortly afterwards, one of the hotel pages knocked: "Come down to the basement now." Once there, I felt like I was on a stranded passenger ship. At least three hundred people—hotel guests, service personnel, a group of pilots and flight attendants from SAS, and even a few American businesspeople—sat huddled together in the hotel pantry. The kitchen was also in the basement, and so the hotel was able to provide us with food while we killed time playing bridge.

The battle lasted all day. When things had calmed down, around midnight, the hotel director allowed us to return to our rooms. Because we were not allowed to turn on the lights, they gave us candles. My suite did not look good: a stray bullet had hit the wall and covered one of the beds with plaster and dust. However that made me feel more secure; I thought it unlikely that the same room would be hit twice. Nevertheless, I found it difficult to relax. Repeated volleys of shots outside made it impossible. Around six in the morning, I got up. In that moment, the entire room was enveloped in an enormous cloud of dust and I felt a stabbing pain in my left shoulder; blood was pouring over my clothing and the bed. I had been hit by shrapnel from a heavy machine gun. I was looking for a towel in the bathroom to stop the bleeding when my telephone rang: "Are you OK," Lore asked on the other end. "Yes, yes," I said, and then hurried to the hotel lobby to find the doctor. He spoke some English, looked at the wound, and declared: "You have had incredible luck. The shrapnel only missed your carotid artery by one and a half centimeters ... And because of the fighting we wouldn't have been able to get you to a hospital." Then he cleaned and dressed my wound. With my left arm in a sling, I caused a small sensation at the hotel.

Two days later, the situation became calmer and I used the two-hour suspension of the curfew to visit Uncle Jakob in the hospital. The doctors there looked at my wound and decided not to operate. To this day, I carry a piece of shrapnel in my shoulder as a souvenir of those tumultuous days in Chile.

Uncle Jakob had by then recovered considerably. Lore wanted to return to Caracas, but the airports were closed. As a result, I too was stuck in Santiago, but at least I was able to report back to Israel using Reuter's connection. Very soon, a colonel from the Junta ordered all journalists to present their reports to a censor. Luckily, I was experienced in dealing with such institutions. Until the 1990s, when the internet made censorship obsolete, all news items on military and security issues in Israel, whether by Israelis or by foreign correspondents, had to be approved by a military censor. We always grossly exaggerated a few details so that the censor would have something critical to delete. And so after visiting a huge football stadium where thousands of opponents of the regime were being held, I wrote an article on the conditions under which the prisoners were vegetating and used the phrase "horrifying, inhuman atrocity," which the censor was naturally not happy about. "Señor Rath, do you really need those adjectives?" he asked, and was satisfied when I struck them. In that way my readers were still able to learn how gruesome conditions were for the prisoners.

One week after Allende's death, I went into a small copy shop in Santiago to make copies of some papers. I hadn't yet begun when a young Chilean man ran into the shop eager to use the machine right away. In his hand he was holding a document on the official stationery of the president's office—*Presidencia de la República-Secretaria*—which immediately aroused my curiosity. It seemed to be notes by Allende's secretary, who had taken down the president's last words, and the time they were spoken. "You may use the machine first, but I would like a copy of the document," I said to the young man, and he agreed. At 10 a.m.—while I was watching the army open fire on La Moneda from my hotel room—under the title "Dr. Allende in the Toscea Room," the secretary recorded the following words spoken by Allende to his supporters:

> The women and the men who have no way of defending themselves should leave. I order the compañeros (comrades) to leave the Moneda. ... I will not surrender, but I don't want you to be a sterile sacrifice. ... Revolutions are not made by spiritual cowards; that's why I am staying. Everyone else should leave. I am not going to resign. I thank everyone for their support. The men who want to

help me fight can stay. I have with me here two daughters who have no reason to stay here. They must leave.

On the back of the paper was a second note, written in another hand, headed "Allende in the basement to his daughters" with his words to children Beatriz and Maria Isabel. The time noted was a quarter past eleven, fifteen minutes after the Junta's first ultimatum. While I was observing the women and men leaving La Moneda with white handkerchiefs, Allende had been saying goodbye to his family:

> Leave! You have children to protect, who have a mother. I will resist until the end ... I have the word of a military man that they are sending a jeep for you. Please leave. ... Maria Isabel, René, my son... I love you very much. You were the only real thing to me.

Beatriz, who was six-months pregnant, had left La Moneda a few minutes earlier.

Because of the coup, many Jewish socialist families, who had previously had no contact with the Israeli diplomatic mission, felt threatened and sought protection at the embassy. They spent the daytime in the overcrowded consular rooms and at night were sent elsewhere to sleep. Under the protection of Deputy Ambassador Benni Oron, they were escorted to the embassies of Mexico, France, and Sweden.

A few days after the coup, a plane landed with journalists returning from Buenos Aires. Our previously lean press corps grew to fifty or sixty people. Every morning, a Junta spokesman held a press conference at the hotel. One of those morning, I was called out of the meeting; Meshulam had been able to get through to the Carrera Sheraton. He had read my articles in the *Jerusalem Post* and was worried: "Please, don't write such critical things, wait until you have left the country." I had barely walked back into the room when I was approached by one of the military representatives: "Mr. Rath, please report this afternoon to Colonel Bandoli at the Junta Headquarters." He gave the same order to the correspondent from Reuters, who had been standing next to me. That was an alarming signal. The previous day, members of the Junta had arrested the *Washington Post* correspondent for a few hours. I immediately tried to reach Benni Oron, whom I knew from Jerusalem, to inform him of my summons. At the embassy I was told: "Oron is currently having lunch with the director of the Middle East department of the Chilean Ministry of Foreign Affairs," which had apparently survived the coup intact. I found the two men in the restaurant whose name I had been given, and said to Oron in Hebrew: "I've been summoned to the Junta at 3:00 p.m. If I'm not here by 6:00 p.m., you'll have to look for me." Oron asked me to repeat what I had just said in English for his Chilean colleague. He listened carefully and took down my name.

At the appointed time, I reported to the Junta headquarters, a ten-story government building with an imposing lobby that was heaving with soldiers and officers. Hesitantly, I entered the office of Colonel Bandoli, who immediately screamed at me: "Who do you think you are writing news reports? You're not even an accredited journalist!" I responded: "I was already here on September 2 and I was planning on leaving quite a while ago."

"When do you want to leave?"

"As soon as the first Air France machine takes off."

He jotted down the next departure date. Then he barked at me: "See that you are on this flight no matter what. And if I were you, I wouldn't send off any more articles just now." With that warning, he dismissed me from his office. I am convinced that having met with Benni Oron beforehand spared me a worse fate.

I did in fact stop sending articles, but I continued to attend the press tours conducted to show how many weapons the Allende militia had horded. One day, they took us on a tour of La Moneda to show us the Hall of Independence where President Allende had committed suicide. Shaken to the core, I stood in front of the blood-spattered sofa; all of the hopes that I had linked to Allende had been dashed. I managed to get away from the press group and went to search for Frida Modak's room. Her office had been ransacked, but the propaganda posters that she had decorated it with hung untouched on the walls. I took six or seven of the posters, rolled them up with the white side showing, put them under my arm and returned to the hotel to pack. To this day, a Che Guevara poster from La Moneda is hanging in my Jerusalem apartment.

On September 22, Air France resumed operations in Chile. In the morning, the hotel desk called me two hours before I had planned to leave for the airport. "The car you ordered is at the door." I had not called a car; I had not even finished packing. When I went down to the hotel lobby, a driver was waiting who took me to an out-of-the-ordinary taxi; a van of sorts guarded by eight Carabineros with Uzi submachine guns. Apparently the regime wanted to make sure that I really left. Outwardly cool, but with a fast-beating heart, I returned to my room and finished packing. I lay the posters picture-side down on the bottom of the suitcase. In that way, I smuggled them out of Chile in plain view of Junta soldiers. Two hours before the departure of the Air France machine, we arrived at the airport. At passport control, the officer noticed that I had spent twenty days in the country without having done my forced shopping—every day, visitors were compelled to buy five dollars' worth of local wares. And so I was left holding one thousand escudos with nothing to spend them on at the airport. I bought a few items made of copper and was relieved when I was finally sitting on a plane headed for Buenos Aires.

I landed in Argentina on the evening of the re-election of President Juan Perón, who had returned to the country from exile. In 1955, he had been overthrown from his first term in office in a coup led by the Navy, but the government that followed had been unable to stabilize the country. Now Perón had won sixty percent of the vote in the country's first democratic election. People were celebrating in the streets; everyone hoped for better times. That hope was not to be fulfilled, since Perón died only a few months after his re-election.

I spent a few days with my friend and *chaver* Federico Rottenberg, who had gone to Palestine with me from Vienna and also lived with me in the kibbutz for many years. Over the years, it had become second nature for me to write about anything and everything that I experienced on my many journeys abroad. I therefore sent the paper a few articles on the Argentine election, before continuing on to Brazil, where I recovered from the trials and tribulations of the previous weeks on a visit with Adolpho Bloch, a friend of Ted Lurie.

I had met Bloch, owner of the large publishing house Manchete, a few years earlier. He had been born in 1908 and came from a Jewish Ukrainian family that had immigrated to Brazil in 1922. Bloch had started as a printer with a small hand-operated printing press, had had an impressive career as a publisher, and in the end became one of Latin America's media czars. In 1952, he published the first edition of the popular weekly magazine, *Manchete*. The *Manchete* offices were in a beautiful multi-story building built half into the cliffs of Rio de Janeiro; besides the newspaper, the building housed an art gallery and a large cafeteria. Bloch had booked me a small hotel near Ipanema and was also otherwise incredibly friendly and helpful. His chauffeur showed me the city, driving me through all of Rio. I saw the elegant neighborhoods and also the favelas that spread up into the hills.

One afternoon, Ted Lurie called and proposed that I not return to Tel Aviv from Rio de Janeiro as planned, but make a stopover in Vienna. Golda Meier had been invited for a short visit with Federal Chancellor Bruno Kreisky to negotiate the transit of the Jewish Russian immigrants. To his surprise, for once I declined: "I've been traveling for weeks already, changing my flight route will be expensive and this meeting between Golda and Kreisky isn't worth it. I'm coming directly home after Yom Kippur."

The Yom Kippur War
and Its Aftermath

The Yom Kippur War took me by surprise on October 6, while still in Rio de Janeiro. I am not religious but ever since the age of thirteen I do fast and go to synagogue on Yom Kippur. It is a tradition that I have kept throughout my life in memory of my grandmother, Omama Frimtsche. On Erev Yom Kippur, I went for Kol Nidre to the large Ashkenazi synagogue in Copacabana and spent the following day in my hotel. I slept a little and wrote an article for the paper; breaking with my usual habits, I did not listen to the radio the entire day. In the evening, I went to the large Sephardic synagogue for the final prayers and then planned to go to Adolpho Bloch's break-fast dinner, a tradition held in the newsroom to which he invited all of his workers.

Around five-thirty p.m. I stepped into the synagogue, which meant that it was around eleven-thirty p.m. Israeli time. As soon as I entered, I was approached by someone I knew: "What's new with the war?"

I was irritated and thought he meant the civil war in Chile. "War?"

The man said: "Yes, haven't you heard? Israel was attacked."

I said a quick prayer, ran out of the synagogue, and took a taxi to the *Manchete* newsroom. Everyone was in uproar. Adolpho Bloch and his editor-in-chief had decided on short notice to completely update the coming week's magazine. *La Guerra de Yom Kippur* had to be on the cover. It was already Saturday evening and the magazine was set to appear on Monday. The editorial team gratefully accepted my offer to help. Reuters and AP were delivering a continuous stream of reports in Portuguese, which I was able to decipher using the Latin I'd learned at school. I was particularly troubled by a statement by military spokesman Chaim Herzog. He said: "The situation is more difficult; it won't be like 1967. But we will nevertheless vanquish the enemy." I read this between the lines as meaning that this time, the fighting would be long and heavy. To get a better picture of what was happening in Israel, I tried to call the *Jerusalem Post* newsroom. That proved to be impossible, but I did manage to set up a dedicated telex line. In that way, we managed to have a written long-distance discussion with David Landau and Mary Hadar in Jerusalem—or a "chat," as we would say today. We asked each of them to write a mood piece for *Manchete* on the first day of the war. I was tasked with writing an op-ed. I wrote: "We will hold our ground, but this war will last much longer and claim many victims." When *Manchete* appeared on Monday, it included a two-page spread with reports directly from Israel. It was illustrated with agency photos, but *Manchete* itself had an excellent photographer on staff.

"Ari, do you think it's still worth it for him to fly out there?" the editor-in-chief asked me. "Moshe Dayan is sure to have won the war in three or four days."

"Unfortunately, he'll have plenty of time to take photos of the war," I replied.

Israel had been fairly unprepared for the Yom Kippur War.

After the Six-Day War, we felt almost invincible. Defense Minister Moshe Dayan, the hero of 1967, was not expecting further attacks. Israel's intelligence service had mistakenly interpreted Egypt's landing maneuver on a branch of the Suez Canal as a harmless, routine drill. Dayan and Golda Meir had decided against preventive measures, because they did not want Israel to appear as an aggressor in the eyes of the world. Apparently, Dayan had also thought that Israel could easily defend itself against an Egyptian attack.

Naturally, I wanted to return to Israel immediately, but flight connections back then were nothing like they are today, and it was almost impossible to book a direct flight to Europe. The first flight I found left on October 8; an Air France red eye arriving in France on the afternoon of the ninth. I had no chance of continuing on to Israel that same day. El Al, the Israeli national airline, only allowed young men, active reserve soldiers or doctors on board. I was at least able to secure a promising wait list spot on an Air France machine leaving for Tel Aviv on Wednesday, October 10, around noon.

That left me with a bit more than a day in Paris. The French papers claimed that Israel's fate was in the hands of King Hussein of Jordan. *Le Monde* assumed that a third front would open on the border to Jordan, which would make the situation more difficult for Israel. I did not want to spend the day in Paris alone and depressed, and so I decided to fly to Bonn to see my brother. Meshulam and his wife Hannah had just arrived there three days previously; he was to start his position as embassy counselor in October. They did not yet have their own apartment and were living in a boarding house. We sat up all night talking about the war.

The next morning, I flew back to Paris and checked in for the flight to Tel Aviv. The Air France machine had been ready to fly for over three hours, but there was no co-pilot. The pilots and crew were all on the flight voluntarily, since they would be flying over a war zone, which meant it was potentially dangerous and the hours would be extremely long. No pilot could be found until late that afternoon.

I began a conversation with the young man sitting next to me, who introduced himself as Maurice. "Why are you flying to Israel now?" I asked him, "Do you have relatives there?"

"No," he answered. He was originally from Tunisia, but had been working in Paris for many years as a steel wholesaler. "I have been listening to the news non-stop since the war began. I can't just sit here calmly while you're fighting for your lives. So I'm going over myself to see how I can help." His determination was inspiring.

It was around midnight when we reached our destination. Tel Aviv lay in complete darkness, punctuated only by the pale shine of dimmed searchlights. There wasn't a soul at the airport, except for a few people at a small stand the military had set up in the arrivals hall. All able-bodied Israeli men were registered and told to report immediately to a collection camp, where they would be assigned to a battalion. I went up to the major on duty: "You know what it's like when you go to a new unit. I promise you, I'll drive to Jerusalem and by midday tomorrow I'll be with my unit near Jericho." She agreed, took down my name, and let me go.

Surprisingly, the car rental at the airport was open. Since I had left my car in Jerusalem, I had to rent one. Maurice never left my side. What else should he have done? Since he was not Israeli, he could not volunteer to fight. I agreed to drive him to Jerusalem, and also offered to take a couple who had flown with us, an offer they thankfully accepted. But first I wanted to learn more about the current military situation. We therefore drove first to Tel Aviv, to the press center in Sokulov House. The mood was gloomy. The military spokesman shrugged his shoulders when he saw me and said: "Ari, my lips are sealed, but Micha Shagrir and Yirmiyahu Yovel just got back from the Sinai Peninsula." The two were well-known colleagues; they served in the reserves as military radio reporters and had just visited a key section of the front. They looked exhausted. Dejected, they passed on their impressions: "You can't imagine what it's like. Conditions have flipped. The Egyptians have learned from us how to fight. Things look very bad and everything depends on how fast we get reinforcement." They were particularly upset about the official news reports and the censorship: "You have no idea how much of our reporting was simply blocked because we reported too truthfully." I would have loved to have learned more, but I had to go, since I wanted to make a short stop to see my sister Henny before driving to Jerusalem with my travel companions.

A bunch of people were gathered at Henny's house. My brother-in-law Amitai Neeman had just returned a half hour earlier from his reserve service at the airbase Ramat David near Haifa. As a composer and musician, he entertained the soldiers and pilots with his accordion, encouraging them to sing along. He took me confidentially to the side: "All of a sudden we had to interrupt our singing. The General Chief of Staff and Commander of the Air Force spoke in front of the soldiers: 'Now we can all breathe a sigh of relief. Today, thanks to the concerted attacks by the Israeli Air Force, we have stopped the Syrians advance on the Golan Heights.'" I was reassured by the news, it meant that we had averted the worst danger, namely that the Syrians advance to the Sea of Galilee, in the end perhaps even taking Tiberias. Soon I took my leave from my family and drove with my three companions to Jerusalem.

On the winding road, I suddenly saw in front of me the silhouette of large vehicles against the first light of the dawn. Reinforcement, I thought, and prepared to pass. Then I realized disappointedly that the flatbeds were not transporting tanks, but bulldozers. As would become clear that morning, the military was using them to block the street from Jericho to Jerusalem, in case King Hussein decided to attack Jerusalem with tanks.

Early in the morning, we arrived in Jerusalem. I left the couple at the entrance to the city; I myself however did not drive home, but parked the car outside the Old City. I was instinctively drawn to the Wailing Wall. A few dozen young Orthodox men were saying their prayers. Like many religious people, I wrote my wishes on a small piece of paper and stuck it in a crevice of the age-old wall: *Tikvah le'nizachon ve le'shalom*—Hope for victory and peace. Then I brought Maurice to Moriah Hotel and suggested he take over my car rental contract. In the meantime, I had had an idea about what he could do. "If you want to make yourself useful, you should help the reservists who are now traveling through the country in the thousands—trying to get to their deployment sites or back to their families. Best is, you drive in the direction of Tiberias to the north and offer a shuttle service. That way, every day you can provide many soldiers with a short vacation." Maurice was happy to have something concrete to do. In the end, he spent three weeks driving back and forth from Tiberias to Tel Aviv, the newspapers and radio called him the "Parisian angel."

I picked up my car, went to quickly look in on my father, donned my military uniform and drove towards Jericho to my unit, which was again stationed on the hills outside the city. Our job was to stand watch at the Jordanian border, a somewhat unsettling mission since there were no tanks available for our defense—they were all at the Suez-Sinai front or at the Golan Heights. Our defense consisted of volunteer anti-tank units made up of two to three reserve officers who were not assigned to any particular unit and had been given American anti-tank grenades. If the Jordanian army had in fact invaded, we ourselves would have been the living anti-tank defense.

However, I did not spend long with my reserve unit; the editors of the large daily newspapers were being briefed on the war by Minister of Defense Dayan in Tel Aviv and my commanding officer had given me permission to attend. Two days earlier, he had lamented our losses and warned that Israel was facing the destruction of the third temple. Apparently, he had truly been expecting defeat, but his mood had since greatly improved. He told us that it had been possible to stop the Syrian advance on the Golan Heights, and that our troops had advanced in a counteroffensive and were around forty kilometers outside Damascus. During our meeting, Dayan's adjutant passed him a note. He gave a fleeting, sardonic smile: "You probably want to know what this says. I will tell you: Kissinger has informed me that the American government is finally willing to increase their support." Nathan Peled, Minister of Aliyah and Integration, also had news for us, although it had to be kept secret: The Kremlin was going to grant exit visas to 50,000 Soviet Jews. Incredibly, this sensational news did not leak through to the public; the large American media outlets, too, did not want to endanger the emigration.

For a few days, Israel's fate had lain in the hands of the United States of America. A few days after this briefing, when the fighting was already over, I learned that the support that Kissinger had promised had by no means been a sure thing. That information had been passed on to Dayan by my friend Mordechai Shalev. Shalev had a diplomatic post in Washington, D.C. and had led the initial negotiations with the American Secretary of State (Israel's ambassador, Simcha Dinitz, a close associate of Golda Meir, was at the time in Tel Aviv for his father's funeral). I had gotten to know Shalev, an experienced diplomat, when he was spokesman for the Israeli Ministry of Foreign Affairs and we had become friends before he left for D.C. When he was back in Jerusalem for a short vacation in early November 1973, Shalev gave me a call. I paid him a visit without even changing out of my uniform, and he gave me a detailed account of how Henry Kissinger had hesitated before promising support for Israel. The day the war started, Shalev had asked for an emergency meeting. So as not to desecrate Yom Kippur, he walked the three kilometers to the White House, where the top American political and military figures had been gathered for hours in the so-called situation room, following the fighting in the Middle East. Kissinger let him wait in the outer office, which made Shalev feel so humiliated that he lit a cigarette, although smoking is forbidden on fasting days. Kissinger then agreed to replace anti-tank missiles so that Israel could stop the massive attacks on the Golan Heights and the Sinai Peninsula, but he was not ready to promise speedy delivery of spare parts for damaged tanks, or fighter jets or other strategically important machinery to replace the losses Israel had suffered on the first day of the war. The conversation must have been traumatic for Shalev. Tears of anger sprung to his eyes when he told me how Kissinger had cynically reminded him that Israel after the Six-Day War had assumed that its borders were absolutely safe and that we thought could defend them on their own. "In fact, Kissinger wanted to see us bleed, as punishment for, as he said, Israel's hubris." As a

Jew, Kissinger put pressure on Israel in a way that other politicians would not have dared to emulate.

After the briefing with Dayan, I returned to my hill near Jericho that same evening. Often, we listened to the English Jordanian radio station to find out what the enemy side was planning. On Saturday afternoon, October 13, at around two-thirty p.m., the music program was suddenly interrupted: "Stand by for an important announcement." This message was repeated three, four, or five times. I immediately called over our commanding officer. Shortly before three, the Jordanian radio announcer went on air: "His Majesty King Hussein, ruler of the Hashemite Kingdom, hereby declares that he has resolved to join the holy jihad." Immediately we trained our binoculars on the Jordan border and tried to see whether troops were moving towards us. The announcer continued: "In line with this resolution, King Hussein has decreed that tank regiment number forty will provide reinforcement for our Syrian brothers on the northern Golan Heights." We breathed a sigh of relief. His decision meant that Hussein was refraining from opening a third front.

One of the jokes that went through Israeli ranks at the time was as follows: King Hussein made two capital errors during his reign. The first was entering the Six-Day War in 1967—if he hadn't Israel never would have gone into the West Bank or East Jerusalem. The second was not entering the war in 1973—he would have had no problem bringing his troops and tanks to the gates of Jerusalem.

The ceasefire in Sinai on October 28 ended the Yom Kippur War on the Egyptian front; Israeli troops were 101 kilometers outside of Cairo. Positional battles for the Golan Heights continued until the spring of 1974.

◆

More than one sacred cow was slaughtered in 1973. Traumatic memories of the war still reverberate; every anniversary there are innumerable new articles, films, books, and public discussions. My own view, too, has changed since then. From the founding of the State of Israel, most political correspondents and journalists accepted as true whatever was said by the so-called defense establishment. After the 1973 war, they completely lost their credibility and their reputation of competence. This is seen for example in the resounding popularity of the book *Ha Mechdal* ("the failure," published in English as *Kippur*). The four authors, well-respected journalists and military commentators, revealed that many of the claims about Israel's invulnerability were no more than empty phrases—even if we did in the end win the war,

Like many Israelis, I, too, experienced a certain disenchantment, making me more willing than ever before to compromise and make sacrifices. We saw that the fantasies of Greater Israel, which included Judea and Samaria, could not be become reality. One of the main demands of the Labor Party in the 1969 election had been that Israel must at all cost retain territorial continuity along the shore of the Red Sea. Moshe Dayan expressed this in a memorable phrase: "Better to hold Sharm el Sheikh without peace than to have peace without Sharm el Sheikh." Dayan did not step back from this position until the early 1970s, when he proposed that Israel unilaterally retreat from the eastern bank of the Suez Canal. However Prime Minister Golda Meir and the majority of the cabinet rejected his proposal. I have not changed my mind about Golda Meier's government, which I still believe was a five-year period of unusually short-sighted policies. I hold her responsible for grave damage to our young nation.

On November 18, 1973, a judicial commission chaired by Shimon Agranat, president of the Supreme Court, began an investigation into the military preparation for and the defeats of the Yom Kippur War. The parliamentary elections, which had originally been scheduled for mid-October, were pushed back to December 31, 1973. In light of the vehement public criticism of how the war had been waged, a majority of Labor Party members demanded that the list of candidates be reopened so that new people could run for office. I too joined these demands, as did former party secretary and peace activist Lova Eliav. Fatally for the party, Golda Meir and the leading party cadre were in opposition. As a result, hundreds of reservists who had returned from the war staged the first large-scale protest movement against the Labor Party executive, under the leadership of law professor Amnon Rubinstein. This group formed the nucleus of the new center-left party Shinui (change), which would end up playing a decisive role in the change in administration in May 1977.

With a Machiavellian instinct, Henry Kissinger had recognized on the very first day of the Yom Kippur War that it presented an opportunity for restructuring power relations in the Middle East and forcing through American interests. He also saw an opportunity to bring Egypt out from under the influence of the Soviet Union. During the ceasefire negotiations, he was able to convince President Sadat that he would only be able to regain the territory he had lost to Israel with the help of the Americans, and by no means by further wars. Soon after the end of the fighting, Kissinger proposed to the Soviet government that they call for a peace conference in Geneva at the end of the year. Surprisingly, the USSR agreed to convene an international peace conference under the auspices of the United Nations, headed jointly by the United States and the Soviet Union.

On November 5, 1973, Kissinger initiated his strategy of "shuttle diplomacy" in the Middle East. He traveled from Jerusalem to Cairo, Amman, and Damascus to prepare the text of the invitation and coordinate it with all parties—Egypt, Jordan, Syria, and Israel. When he returned, he met—as per usual at the time—for a briefing session with the Committee of Daily Newspaper Editors, a group of around ten editors. Kissinger was a good storyteller, and I greatly enjoyed his description of his meeting with Hafez al-Assad of Syria, whom he had purposefully met with last, as he was known to be a particularly difficult negotiation partner. Assad had unexpectedly proven to be extremely cooperative and accepted the text of the invitation without any changes. At the end of the meeting, he asked Kissinger whether he hadn't perhaps forgotten one key detail. Kissinger did not understand the question, but Assad clarified: "You forgot to ask whether we will take part in the conference." Kissinger replied: "If you agree with the wording of the invitation, I assume that you will participate." Assad however replied: "But we will not attend the conference."

Ted Lurie decided to send Anan Safadi and me to Geneva. On December 21, in the historical building of the League of Nations, the conference on peace in the Middle East was opened, presided over by UN General Secretary Kurt Waldheim and jointly chaired by Andrei Gromyko and Henry Kissinger. The Syrian delegation's table remained empty. For nine day, delegates negotiated on the disengagement of Egyptian and Israeli forces at the Suez Canal. For the first time since 1967, when all Eastern Bloc countries with the exception of Romania broke off diplomatic relations with Israel, the Israeli Minister of Foreign Affairs, Abba Eban, met with Andrei Gromyko for an in-depth conversation.

One day, the Egyptian government spokesman Takhsin Bachir invited a group of journalists, myself included, to an off-the-record conversation. Colin Legum from the British *Observer* asked: "What will happen with Jerusalem?" Bachir answered: "Let's solve the Gaza and West Bank problem first. You will see—the Jerusalem problem will solve itself." I was impressed that a high-level Egyptian government official gave such a pragmatic answer and took it as a sign that President Sadat was willing to think seriously about securing peace, even so soon after the war.

The Geneva conference was my first opportunity to make contacts with Egyptian and Jordanian journalists. I became close with the Reuters correspondent from Cairo in particular. Day in and day out, we sat side by side in the small news agency office from where I sent my bulletins to Jerusalem. Suddenly he turned to me and blurted out: "These idiots—now they want me to report on things they should be asking you." He had been tasked with writing a report on the strength of Israeli troops in Sinai. Together we attempted to piece together the desired information.

The conference ended on December 30, 1973, and the next day I returned to Israel. By chance, I was on the same plane as Finnish General Ensio Siilasvuo. After sharing more than one glass of vodka at the airport bar, he told me that Israel and Egypt were on the verge of a compromise on the disengagement of their troops. Before even boarding, I called in to the editorial offices; the paper would have to change the headline—"Geneva Peace Talks Fail"—since there was now a chance of results.

◆

The Agranat Commission's interim report on the prelude to the Yom Kippur War caused a political earthquake when it was released on April 1, 1974. It accused the army, in particular General Chief of Staff David Elazar and a few high-ranking generals, of multiple failings. The military had not been prepared for war and had also been late in recognizing plans to attack the country. The report refrained from an opinion on the extent to which Moshe Dayan carried political responsibility for this state of affairs. On that same day, as a member of the Committee of Daily Newspaper Editors, I was slated to visit the Golan Heights, where David Elazar would brief us on the military situation. But instead of accompanying us on the flight as planned, he explained the situation while we were still at the Tel Aviv airport; Golda Meir had issued an urgent call for his return to Jerusalem. On his way to the helicopter he said to me: "I'm sure it's about whether we need to mobilize more reserve units."

Midday, my colleagues and I were sitting in the Nafach military headquarters in the Golan Heights, which had been captured by Syrian troops for a time during the war, when rumors began circulating that the Agranat Commission had recommended Elazar's dismissal. By the time we returned to Jerusalem late that afternoon, Elazar had already been let go. There was an uproar over the fact that Moshe Dayan had been exonerated.

Intense debates were held on this question within the Labor Party. Those in the activist wing of the party, Ahdut HaAvoda, were particularly vehement in demanding Dayan's resignation; he however refused to leave his post as Minister of Defense as long as he continued to enjoy the trust of Golda Meir. There was no support for a proposal that I attempted to put forward making Dayan Minister for Peace Negotiations. Since public pressure on Dayan showed no sign of abating, in late April Golda Meir convened an urgent meeting of the Labor Party fraction in the Knesset, which I was invited to attend. To the surprise of all present, she announced her resignation as Prime Minister. That meant the de facto resignation of the entire cabinet, including Dayan.

On June 3, 1974, after the conclusion of ceasefire negotiations with Syria, former General Chief of Staff and Ambassador to Washington, D.C., Yitzhak Rabin, took over the post of Prime Minister; Shimon Peres became Minister of Defense. Rabin was only 52 years old, and I was pleased that for the first time a politician of my generation held the power; Rabin was a charismatic sabra known for his political integrity. Although I would have preferred Peres, whom I had known since 1945 and with whom I had worked closely since the founding of the Rafi party, I thought Rabin was a good choice and that he symbolized a new era.

As Minister of Defense, Peres helped build up Israel's armed forces in the wake of the Yom Kippur War, but the rivalry between Peres and Rabin overshadowed the three years of their administration. Rabin, because he had been General Chief of Staff, resented the fact that he was not both Prime Minister and Minister of Defense, as had been the custom in Israel for many years, and Peres was disappointed that he had only lost to Rabin by a fraction of the Labor Party Central Committee votes—everyone else had been taken by surprise that he had won so many votes at all. In his autobiography, Rabin famously called Peres a "tireless schemer." Considering all that, it is almost a political miracle that the two worked so well together in the second Rabin government, formed in 1992, with Rabin as prime minister and Peres as foreign minister. In the final analysis, it was their harmonious relationship that made the Oslo Agreement possible. Many Israelis remember Rabin and Peres arm in arm at the end of the large peace rally in Tel Aviv on November 4, 1995, singing the peace song Shir LaShalom: "Don't say the day will come—Bring the day!" A few minutes later, Rabin was assassinated.

◆

Because the Syrians did not take part in the 1973 Geneva conference, Kissinger negotiated with them directly on disengagement in the Golan Heights in May 1974. For four weeks, the King David Hotel was the quasi-headquarters of the U.S. State Department. On their first visit to Syria, the American delegation spent the night in Damascus. Having however returned with upset stomachs, Kissinger decided that in the future they would spend the night at the King David and also eat there no matter the hour. That provided Israeli journalists with a chance of obtaining daily first-hand updates on negotiations with Syria. Many years later, he had since left his office as Secretary of State, Kissinger elucidated his negotiation tactics for me during a private visit, illustrating how well he understood the psychology of his dialogue partners: "You have to know the point beyond which your negotiation partner is by no means willing to go. Then you set your own position at a realistic distance from that point—and within these two points, you'll find a compromise." This strategy once again proved itself in the Israel-Syria conflict: The ceasefire border agreed upon at the time exists to this day. Israel returned the city of Quneitra to the Syrians. While Egypt rebuilt its cities along the Suez Canal, Syria decided to leave Quneitra as a ruin—a constant warning and reminder of the wars and the Israeli enemy.

In early 1975, Israel negotiated with the United States on the next phase of the withdrawal of its troops from the Sinai

Peninsula. Kissinger played the role of Egypt's envoy to accelerate Israel's withdrawal, a behavior which I repeatedly criticized in the *Jerusalem Post*. In early March, the Committee of Daily Newspaper Editors, accompanied by the Israeli military spokesman, visited the Mitla and Gidi passes sixteen kilometers east of the Suez Canal, the sites from which the two main streets to Sinai were controlled. The sun was burning down when we landed after two rather uncomfortable hours in a noisy helicopter. The new General Chief of Staff, Mota Gur, and his generals accompanied us to explain the danger it would pose to Israel were we to give up these strategic passes without a peace treaty with Egypt in place. When Kissinger arrived in Jerusalem shortly after, he was extremely disappointed; from the various negotiations he had had the impression that Israel was ready to compromise on this point. In the lobby of the King David, he told the Israeli journalists gathered there that he would be aborting his visit, but that he did not blame Israel for the failure of the negotiations. At the exact same time, the State Department spokesman one story above us was telling a group of American journalists that the breakdown of negotiations was Israel's fault. A few hours later, when Kissinger and the American journalists accompanying him landed in Rome, they cited a "senior official on Kissinger's plane" (the formula behind which Kissinger himself hid) as having said that the American government would be conducting a reassessment of its relations with Israel. In plain English, this meant that the United States stopped delivery of almost all strategic weapons to Israel. Kissinger was putting on the pressure, which had the desired effect. Six months later, in September 1975, we again flew with the same generals to the Gidi and Mitla passes. With the same conviction as before, they told us that as long as Israel controlled the higher ground, giving back the passes posed no threat at all. Sure of a victory, Kissinger returned to sign a new agreement with Rabin, defining the new disengagement lines. In return, the United States promised not to negotiate with the PLO. Ironically, eighteen years later, it was Rabin who, while working on the Oslo Accords during his second term as Prime Minister, became the first Israeli politician to recognize the PLO as a negotiation partner.

One of the political developments of the era that has burned itself into my memory were the mass protests by the then new Jewish settlers' movement. Hundreds of settlers, some armed with sticks and stones, occupied the hill on which the Knesset stood, demonstrating against the precedence that Israel was setting by returning captured territory. Despite a massive police presence, it did not take the settlers long to encircle the building. They threatened Minister Fuad Ben-Eliezer on his way to a Knesset reception and destroyed his car. Only with great difficulty were the police able to control the crowd. Even at the time, I interpreted these scenes as a bad omen for the future of Israel.

Also during the fall of 1975, the board of directors named a new leadership team for the *Jerusalem Post*. I became managing director and editor, and my colleague of many years, Erwin Frenkel, was also named editor. Ted Lurie had died suddenly from a stroke during a trip to Japan in May 1974. To prevent a new editor-in-chief from coming in from the outside, Erwin Frenkel and I insisted that the board of directors name Lea Ben-Dor, who had been second editor for many years, as Lurie's interim successor. Our loyalty was however put severely to the test, as she soon tried to place the former deputy director of the Mossad, Dave Kimche, as new editor-in-chief. The newsroom was in uproar. In the resulting conflict between the staff and the board, Erwin Frenkel and I attempted to gain the upper hand by putting up a united front—a strategy that panned out in the end. Until the paper was acquired by the Hollinger company in 1989, the two of us made a very good team. Our former colleagues, looking back in April 1991, remarked on how well Frenkel, a Harvard graduate born in Germany, and I, the former kibbutznik from Vienna, collaborated despite our diametrically opposed characters: Frenkel the quiet and pragmatic intellectual and me, the stubborn firebrand with a big heart.

Ari on a tour for senior journalists organized by Keren Kayemet (Jewish National Fund), 1982. Photo: Dan Hadani.

Hopes and Setbacks

After decades in power, in May 1977 the Labor Party lost the election. Menachem Begin, the right-wing nationalist opposition politician who had already made eight unsuccessful bids at Prime Minister, finally won at his ninth try. He was eager to perform an historical act. He could no longer found the State of Israel, David Ben-Gurion had beaten him to it. But he could be the first Prime Minister to make peace with a neighboring Arab country. However, as a former nationalist terrorist, he was lacking the necessary diplomatic connections. And so he asked Moshe Dayan to join his government. Dayan was originally on the Labor Party list, but since the Yom Kippur debacle, he had been a controversial figure in the party.

Dayan saw his chance for political rehabilitation and became foreign minister. Shortly after the government was formed, he met secretly with King Hussein of Jordan at the house of Lord Mishcon in London. When it became clear to Dayan that peace with Jordan would not be possible as long as Israel had not reached an agreement with the Palestinians, he set his sights on Egypt. Disguised by a wig and sunglasses, Dayan flew secretly to Morocco in September 1977 for a meeting with Deputy Prime Minister Hassan Tohamy to discuss the conditions for a peace treaty and also the details of a possible upcoming visit to Israel by President Sadat. In this way, Sadat knew before his official visit that it would be possible to reclaim

With Egyptian President Anwar Sadat in Ismailia, December 1977.
© *Moshe Millner / Government Press Office, Israel.*

large parts, if not all, of Sinai.

The importance of this rapprochement can hardly be overestimated. The president of one of the most powerful Arab countries was willing to go to the Israeli capitol of Jerusalem—which was not recognized as such by the international community—to speak there to the Knesset and to meet with Israeli political leaders. It was truly a sensation. The other Arab countries retaliated immediately at this provocation. Sadat was quasi-excommunicated, and the League of Arab Nations swiftly moved their main seat from Cairo to Tunis. All international Arab committees divorced themselves from Egypt.

Naturally, the *Jerusalem Post* was on site for the historical action. On November 9, 1977, Anan Safadi excitedly waved me over to him while he was listening to the Egyptian news. He had just learned that Sadat was going to give an important speech to the Egyptian People's Assembly. On that day, our troops had bombed

Fatah outposts in southern Lebanon from the air, and we assumed that Sadat was going to condemn the attack. How wrong we were. To our great surprise, he spoke about peace and said: "I would go to the end of the world to spare an injury to one of our men, much more the death of one. Israel may be greatly surprised to hear that ... I am even ready to go to the Knesset and discuss with them."

We immediately called the Prime Minister's Director General, Eliyahu Ben-Elissar, and let him know what Sadat had just told his parliament. He was excited to hear it and reacted with an Arabic greeting: "*Ahlan wa sahlan*"—welcome! We were the only paper to print this sensational news, and so played our part in a course of events that culminated in Sadat's visit. Two days later, Begin made a declaration of peace for the Arab television and radio broadcasters.

Sadat's visit to Jerusalem came more quickly than expected. On the afternoon of Thursday, November 17, I heard on the radio that he would arrive in Israel that Saturday evening—in only forty-eight hours and not in ten days as I had assumed. I knew right away that we would have to prepare a special issue of the paper for this occasion. Otherwise, top-level Egyptian government officials and thousands of journalists from across the globe would come to report from Israel and not find a single Israeli source of information upon arrival. We at the *Jerusalem Post* could fill this gap and so live up to our international reputation. But how could I explain to Chananya Levin, the religious union steward at our printing press, that his workers would have to break the Sabbath again? I called a meeting with him and cited precedents from Jewish tradition. Interpretations of the Torah allow for a multitude of exceptions: saving a life for example takes precedence over keeping the Sabbath. You can drive a sick person to the hospital although driving is otherwise forbidden. I invoked my uncle the rabbi and convinced Levin that Sadat's official visit belonged in the category "saving life," because peace with Egypt would in fact save many lives. We agreed in the end on a compromise: he would print the issue as long as the machines were not turned on before the end of Shabbat. Luckily, in November sundown is relatively early, and so we were able to print the first thousand copies of our special edition before Sadat's arrival. At the top of the front page, handwritten in Arabic with the English translation below, both in large red letters, the headline read, "Welcome To President Sadat."

However, I believe that this instance of breaking the Sabbath was not without its consequences; extremely religious people have long memories. A few years ago, the former deputy mayor of Jerusalem, Judith Hübner—from the National Religious Party—proposed me for the award "Honorary Citizen of Jerusalem." Every year, this distinction is given to twelve Jerusalem residents over the age of eighty. The evaluation process for this honor is strict and overseen by an independent committee. The influence of Orthodox rabbis on said committee is increasing, and I was not found worthy of the honor.

Around noon on November 19, a Saturday, the entire King David Hotel was declared a high-security zone; only people with a pass from the National Ministry of Security were allowed to go in or out. Every newspaper received one pass, we had reserved ours for Anan Safadi. Because I was friendly with the hotel's owner, I managed to secure two extra passes meant for hotel employees. In that way I was able to move about freely and could carry our special issue into the hotel—over two hundred pounds of paper.

The first Egyptian I met in the hotel was Mohammed Gawad,

the editor-in-chief of the Middle East News Agency, whom I had met in June of that year in Oslo at a conference of the International Press Institute. We had spoken in depth about the new Begin/Dayan government. I'd held that an initiative for peace might now be possible, Gawad in contrast had been much more pessimistic. I will never forget how not even six months later we sat together looking out his hotel room window onto the nighttime lights of the Old City of East Jerusalem, enjoying the historic moment. Gawad admitted to me: "I passed your assessment of the new situation on to Sadat, but I never would have thought that peace was so close."

Today, it is hard to imagine the widespread euphoria and our hopes for a new beginning. Sadat stayed for two days and gave an emotional speech in the Knesset, which he began with "*bismillah*," invoking God, and in which he underlined the fact that he was there on a mission for peace. At the same time he warned even then that long-term peace between Israel and Egypt would not be possible without a just solution of the Palestinian question. But, he continued, in the name of a "just and stable peace ... We welcome you among us [the Arab nations—A.R.] with confidence and security." Sadat met with representatives of all the large parties in order to establish contact not only with politicians from the governing coalition, but also from the opposition. Golda Meir gave Sadat a necklace for his newborn grandchild and asked him in an accusatory tone: "Why didn't you come while I was Prime Minister?"

Accompanied by Teddy Kollek, Sadat went to the Temple Mount and prayed in the Al-Aqsa mosque. People were cheering in the streets and waving Egyptian and Israeli flags. Despite the widespread euphoria, the president was clear from the very beginning that the Palestinian question was the crux of the problem and without a solution, true peace would not be possible. Even before his visit to Jerusalem he had pledged to achieve the "right to self-determination" for the Palestinians, a phrase that elicited Begin's rage each time it was spoken. To prevent this from happening, shortly after Sadat's visit, Begin went to Washington, in his luggage a somewhat absurd plan for autonomy for the "Palestinian Arabs in Judea and Samaria," as he called the Palestinians in the West Bank. It should be noted that this autonomy was meant only for the people, not the land, as if the Palestinians floated in the air like figures in a Chagall painting.

Sadat returned to Cairo after spending two days in Jerusalem. We sat together in front of the TV in the editorial conference room, to see how he was greeted at home. There too, people were cheering and so we decided spontaneously to preserve the memory of the historic events of the past days and the photos of cheering crowds in the streets of Jerusalem and Cairo by publishing a souvenir album entitled *Sadat in Jerusalem*. The publication was in high demand. Sadat himself ordered two hundred copies so that he could distribute them to his guests at the negotiations in mid-December.

In December 1977, political preparations for peace accords were already in full gear. Anan Safadi and I were again chosen to send out joint bulletins from Cairo. We brought the souvenir albums that had been ordered with us, declaring them as personal luggage. As soon as we arrived, the excitement in the air was palpable. The road from the airport to the pyramids was full of people cheering the delegates and observers on their way to the conference. A huge banner over the Mena House hotel, where the conference was held, proclaimed "Preliminary Talks on a Continuation of the Geneva Middle East Peace Conference." Anan and I put our things in our shared room and went to meet our colleagues. As a Jewish-Arab team, we were the object of much attention. At the time, it was unusual for journalists with such disparate biographies to work together so closely. Everywhere, Anan underlined the fact that he saw himself as an Arab Israeli—a stance that met with a lack of understanding on the part of his Egyptian colleagues.

Early the next day, the negotiations began. Eliyahu Ben-Elissar, Begin's Director General, who had also coordinated Sadat's visit in Jerusalem, was the Israeli representative. He was assisted by Meir Rosenne, legal advisor of the Ministry of Foreign Affairs and later ambassador to Washington, D.C. Every evening he gave David Landau and me an exclusive report on the conference's progress—in Yiddish, because he was afraid of bugs.

We enjoyed the friendly atmosphere; the Egyptians proved to be the perfect hosts and made it possible for us to celebrate Shabbat, together with all of the Israeli security staff, with a large meal at which we boisterously sang Hebrew songs. For two weeks, I managed the editorial work from Cairo; every afternoon I wrote a list of the articles that should be published the next day, just like I always did every evening in Jerusalem. David Landau, Anan Safadi, and I wrote detailed reports on the conference every day.

But Anan never felt truly accepted by his Arab colleagues, because he wrote for the *Jerusalem Post* and not for an Arab paper. What is more, he couldn't listen to Arab radio in Cairo, so that an important source of his reporting was lacking. His frustration peaked when he was not invited to press conference of Israeli and Arab journalists for an interview with President Sadat. All of my attempts to convince him not to leave Cairo early despite his disappointment were in vain, Safadi returned home.

The negotiations in the Mena House hotel took place under

time pressure, because Prime Minister Begin, Defense Minister Weizman, and Foreign Minister Dayan were arriving in Ismailia. All of us journalists drove there; while we were waiting for the Israeli government plane to land, I began a conversation with the Egyptian Chief of General Staff Mohamed Abdel Ghani el-Gamasy, the true architect of the Yom Kippur War. He was a very well-educated man and his English was impeccable; he confirmed for me that it never would have come to war in 1973 had Golda Meir agreed to Dayan's plans for retreat and brought the Israeli troops sixteen kilometers east of the Suez Canal.

In the weeks leading up to Begin's return visit to Egypt, Sadat had been upset about the Israeli Prime Minister's inadequate autonomy plan, and so when Begin arrived at the military airport in Ismailia on December 25, he received a very frosty welcome. There were no flags, no hymns, and no guard of honor as per usual at such occasions. Sadat sent his vice president, Hosni Mubarak, to greet Begin, and Defense Minister Ezer Weizman was met by General Gamasy. There was no one of an appropriate rank to greet Foreign Minister Moshe Dayan, because the new Egyptian foreign minister, Ibrahim Kamal, had just been appointed by Sadat a few hours earlier and had not yet been sworn in. His predecessor, Ismail Fahmi, had resigned in protest over Sadat's visit to Jerusalem.

Mubarak accompanied Begin to Sadat's villa, where Kamal's swearing-in ceremony was first on the agenda. The two heads of state then talked for half an hour in private. Since I had already been to the house, I found a spot directly at the entrance so I could get a statement. When the two men came out, I asked Begin in English: "Can you tell us what you spoke about?"

Begin said only: "President Sadat would like to make a

statement." Sadat announced that two joint working groups would be set up: one headed by the Egyptian and Israeli defense ministers to discuss military matters, and one headed by their foreign ministers do deal with political issues. "The military group will convene in Cairo, and the political committee in Jerusalem. The chairmanship of each will alternate." That Sadat had agreed to meet in Jerusalem, the unacknowledged capitol of Israel, was a particularly conciliatory gesture towards Begin.

While the assembled journalists were all running to the phones to pass on this sensational news, Sadat, whose fifty-ninth birthday it was on the day, invited Begin for a one-hour pleasure drive à deux in his convertible along the Suez Canal. I had since learned that the Israeli delegation to Ismailia would be staying in the French Colonial style villa of Ferdinand de Lesseps, the developer of the canal. Since there were only a limited number of rooms, all Israeli journalists were supposed to return to Cairo. Instead however, I hid in the garden of the house. Shlomo Kital from Radio Kol Israel had had the same idea and after the other journalists had left, we went to the guesthouse. They invited us to dine with them and the Egyptians eventually found a single room for us to rent in a run-down neighborhood. The delegations negotiated late into the night, but Dayan and Weizman were unable to convince Begin to agree to compromising with Egypt on the status of the Palestinians in the West Bank and Gaza.

The next day, Sadat and Begin appeared before the international press in the tent that had been pitched for the occasion in expectation of massive interest. At this press conference, the Israeli prime minister made a grave mistake: In the discussion of the Palestinian question, he forced Sadat to refer to the West Bank as "Judea and

Samaria." The phrase alone was an affront to the Egyptians. The disappointment of the Egyptian and Palestinian journalists—of the entire press corps in fact—was palpable. And none were more disappointed than Shlomo Kital and I. Menachim Begin for his part attempted to spread optimism, announcing: "I have come here a hopeful prime minister, and I am leaving a happy man."

When I arrived at the Mena House hotel that evening, I ran into Osama El-Baz, Mubarak and Sadat's advisor, who had just returned from the barber. He came up to me and said: "You have no idea how let down the people here feel."

Nevertheless, Sadat was still interested in rapprochement with Israel, as seen by the fact that he promised the *Jerusalem Post* an interview—his first with an Israeli newspaper. For days David Landau and I waited for a convenient moment, but I could not stay in Egypt indefinitely. And so a few days later, Landau visited Sadat alone at his winter residence, a villa in Aswan on the banks of the Nile. Sadat spoke openly about his regret that, despite his attempts to secure peace, Israel's government was unwilling to give up the occupied territories. He also criticized Israel for being unready to give the Palestinians true autonomy.

Early in January of 1978, President Carter resolved to visit Sadat in Aswan in order to move the peace talks forward. He had formulated his own proposal for a solution to the Palestinian problem: Palestinians should have the "right to participate in the determination of their future." In the lead up to this visit, Alfred (Roy) Atherton, the US State Department diplomat responsible for Middle Eastern affairs, traveled to Jerusalem to garner Israeli support for this almost Talmudic wording. I knew Atherton well and we agreed to print this phrasing in the *Post* as stemming from "reliable sources" to test the acceptance of the Israeli public. It went over well and so Sadat and Carter used what became known as the "Aswan formula" in their joint declaration of January 4. However on the same day, Begin announced the construction of four new settlements in Sinai. He personally wanted to be a part of one of these settlement projects—a disastrous signal for the upcoming discussions.

The negotiations announced by Sadat began on January 18, 1978 in Jerusalem. Begin insisted on being present at the opening meeting, a formal dinner, and continued his confrontational stance by giving a contentious speech. Those of us who were in attendance as Israeli observers looked at one another askance—it was an inauspicious launch of the formal negotiations that were to start the next day. And the next afternoon, it was announced that the Egyptian delegation would depart that very evening. The Egyptian foreign minister, Muhammad Ibrahim Kamel, had recommended that Sadat break off negotiations. Egyptian and Israeli participants alike were appalled. The Egyptian diplomat Osama El-Baz, with whom I had scheduled a meeting, broke into tears when he learned from me that he would be packing his bags.

The discussions in the defense committee were more fruitful, in part because the chemistry was better between Sadat and the Israeli Minister of Defense, Ezer Weizman. Both of their families had suffered in the battles for the Suez Canal: Weizman's son had only barely survived a shot in the head, and one of Sadat's brothers had fallen. Although they were initially mistrustful of one another, the two developed a life-long friendship. Weizman the hawk became a dove; it is hard to imagine that the 1978 peace agreement would have been reached were it not for his absolute commitment. However, there were many long months in between; the conference in Leeds in the spring of 1978 also failed to deliver concrete results, although the mood on both sides had improved greatly since January. But the status of the Palestinians in the West Bank, East Jerusalem, and the Gaza Strip remained a point of contention. Moshe Dayan nevertheless returned from England with the words: "We were unable to make a concrete agreement, but I am now convinced that the Egyptians want peace. Only somebody who is serious about negotiations is so meticulous down to the very last detail."

But it was President Carter who managed to finally broker a compromise between Israel and Egypt during the thirteen-day negotiations at Camp David in September 1978, which led to the signing of a peace accord. In December 1978, Begin and Sadat were jointly awarded the Nobel Peace Prize; on March 26, 1979, shortly after Jimmy Carter went again to Cairo and Jerusalem to make final adjustments, the peace treaty between the two countries was signed in Washington. The Israelis agreed to retreat from the Sinai Peninsula and both countries promised to establish diplomatic and trade relations.

In the era before the internet and cell phones, it was a great deal more difficult for journalists to remain informed about events that took place simultaneously in more than one place. Hence the *Post* tried to have reporters on site at all of the most important places. That also helped us to counter various government press secretaries' attempts to manipulate our reporting. One example of just such an attempt occurred when Wolf Blitzer, our American correspondent, came to Jerusalem with Carter's delegation. A press conference was held in the afternoon at the Jerusalem Hilton at which journalists were told that negotiations had failed and the delegation would be leaving that day. I however believed that this announcement was a targeted lie meant to increase pressure on the Israeli delegation. I myself had been at the King David that same afternoon, having been invited for drinks with the Israeli ambassador to D.C., Eppi Evron, and Carter's closest advisor, Hamilton Jordan. We didn't talk about anything of importance, but I did learn at the occasion that Carter was in fact staying over night and had a breakfast meeting scheduled with Begin the next morning. Hence no final decision had in fact been made. It was a classic example of attempted media manipulation. In this case, the *Jerusalem Post* was the only newspaper that published a balanced story. In the end, an agreement was in fact found the next day and the path to peace had been smoothed. On the flight back to D.C, Carter's press secretary had to apologize for the false information and was soon replaced by someone else.

I attended the ceremonial signing of the peace treaty as a member of the Israeli press corps that accompanied Begin to Washington on a government plane. In my luggage, I carried five copies of the souvenir album *Sadat in Jerusalem*. It was wonderful to be among the dozens of Egyptian, Israeli, and American diplomats and guests of honor in the White House Rose Garden, all in the best of moods. Thirty-one years and four costly wars after the founding of the country, Israel had made peace with the most important Arab country. Even the loud cries of protests from Palestinians demonstrating in front of the White House were unable to disturb the atmosphere. I stood with my albums behind the main stage at which the signing ceremony was to take place. After the ceremony, Sadat, Begin, and Carter were standing together on the lawn. Without anyone stopping me despite increased security, I went with my thick envelope towards Sadat, since I wanted signatures from all three protagonists for my albums. But it was only in the evening that I was able to collect the signatures, at the gala dinner for over five hundred guests held in a large tent in the Rose Garden. At every table, three Americans, three Egyptians, and three Israelis had been seated; late into the night the band played Hebrew, American, and Arab music.

In March 1979, Israel returned the strategically important city of El Arish on the Sinai Peninsula to Egypt. In the presence of Sadat, Israeli soldiers took down the blue-and-white flag of Israel and Egyptian soldiers hoisted their flag—a first concrete step to retreating from occupied Arab territory. At the conclusion of the stirring ceremony, Begin and Sadat flew to Beer Sheva to begin negotiations on autonomy. Soon after, despite great resistance from the settlers, ten settlements in the northern Sinai and the desert city of Yamit were evacuated. Back then, it was still possible for a right-wing government to relinquish occupied territory in order to secure peace.

In early July, negotiations continued in Alexandria. The evening before departure, the American ambassador held a Fourth of July reception at his residence in Herzliya. There I witnessed one of Begin's many instances of pettiness that made negotiations with him so difficult for the Egyptians. I was standing in the garden with Begin, Ambassador Sam Lewis, and a few acquaintances. Begin was riled up: the Egyptians wanted to put him up in Alexandria's brand-new and most exclusive hotel, which was called "Falastin"—Palestine. He said disdainfully to me: "You'll have no problem staying at the Falastin Hotel, after all, you're from the *Palestine Post*." He himself insisted on staying at the old Savoy, which was far less comfortable—it didn't even have air conditioning—but carried a less provocative name. The Egyptians for their part had no understanding for Begin's demand. After all, they had participated in the negotiations in Herzliya without complaining that the city is named after the founder of the Zionist movement and author of the book *The Jewish State*.

Although Foreign Minister Moshe Dayan had been one of the architects of the peace treaty, Begin did not appoint him as chief negotiator but instead Joseph Burg, Minister of the Interior and also head of the National Religious Party. Begin saw negotiations on Palestinian autonomy as a domestic policy issue. Dayan was so furious that he resigned. Ezer Weizman retained his position, but six months later, he too stepped down. In a long open letter, he blamed Begin for not fulfilling Israel's obligation to secure peace. From a strategic point of view, Weizman and Dayan should have resigned at the same time; had they done so, it would have brought the government down. Instead, Begin remained in power and little by little all hopes died of making progress in the question of Palestinian autonomy.

Yet while it was clear that grave conflicts were brewing in the political arena, the peace accords with Egypt did make some things easier in our everyday lives. My articles from this period include a long reportage from January 1980 on the opening of the overland route from El-Arish across the Suez Canal to Cairo: "Israel is no longer an isolated territorial island locked in by the land masses of Asia and Africa. For the first time since 1948 it has a main land route open along the Mediterranean coast." At the *Jerusalem Post*, we welcomed this development: "This month the coastal road through northern Sinai will begin to serve the cause of peace, gradually building tourism and trade links between Israel and Egypt and slowly removing the sense of the claustrophobia which was Israel's share until now."

As soon as rapprochement between Israel and Egypt seemed

as if it might be a possibility, I had dreamed that readers would one day be able to buy the *Jerusalem Post* in Cairo. I had already spoken with the large international media sales group Hachette many times, but we could not discuss details until after the peace treaty became official. Soon after its adoption, our distribution manager accompanied me to a meeting with our Egyptian marketers. We crossed the Suez Canal on an improvised ferry constructed from the remains of a floating bridge salvaged after the Yom Kippur War. We and the Egyptian officers and soldiers who managed ferry traffic were all deeply moved by this moment, They waved at us in a heartfelt greeting, crying out *"Salam!"*—Peace! In Cairo, we negotiated an agreement with our Egyptian partners to sell the *Jerusalem Post* at news kiosks in the city center and at the city's large hotels. For a few months—the project never progressed past the trial stage because the effort was not in the end justified by the revenue—Egypt demonstrated in this way that it had in fact opened itself to Israel.

◆

In my private life as well, the late 1970s were a fulfilling time. I remember well the warm spring evening in May 1978 when I attended a reception at the residence of the Swedish ambassador on the occasion of the Swedish king's birthday. I had already said my good-byes when I noticed an extremely beautiful blonde young woman with blue-green eyes near the exit. Assuming that she was one of the Swedish diplomats, I thanked her for the reception. She responded indignantly: "I'm Finnish and I'm a guest here myself. My name is Anneli Halonen, like *chalon katan* (little window) in Hebrew." Her card revealed that she was the vice-consul of the Finnish embassy and director of the Office of Soviet Interests in Israel (after the Six-Day War in 1967, Finland had agreed to represent Soviet interests). Anneli was twenty years younger than I, she had studied political science in Helsinki, and spoke seven languages, including fluent Russian. She went into diplomacy right after completing her studies and had already worked for the Finnish embassy in Moscow and also in the Finnish Ministry for Foreign Affairs. She had been living in Israel since 1976.

Anneli accepted my offer to invite her to dinner sometime in the future, but all of my attempts to reach her by phone were futile. I was told repeatedly by a female voice with a Finnish accent—her mother, it later turned out—"Anneli is in Finland," but further communication proved impossible. I did not see her again until many months later during a farewell reception for the British deputy ambassador, who had extended an invitation for a boat trip along the coast of Tel Aviv. We kissed on the cheek and made plans for me to pick her up for dinner one week later.

At her home in Herzliya I received a rather unusual welcome. Her small dog, Otto, attacked strangers without warning; not even my great love of dogs helped to calm his wild barking. And before Anneli could hold him back, Otto had torn my suit pants.

After this embarrassing welcome, Anneli offered me a drink and then we drove to small restaurant in Jaffa. We had not even turned onto the main street when she said to me in her inimitable direct manner: "If you are taking me out because you think you'll find out something about my work, we can turn back right now. You're wasting your time." In the end, it was a wonderful evening and the beginning of a relationship that, despite many ups and downs, lasted for almost twenty years. Anneli soon became my official plus one and she was a welcome guest at receptions and dinners with Israeli politicians and generals, including Yitzhak Rabin, Abba Eban, Ezer Weizman, and Ehud Barak. She also quickly won a place in the hearts of my family and friends. My brother Meshulam, who in our childhood had protested so vehemently against our father's tie to Maria Hauer—because she was Christian among other reasons—hoped to see us married. He knew that I had never forgotten the drama surrounding Maria. One day, he invited Anneli to talk, and assured her that he would be more than happy to welcome a non-Jew into our family.

Anneli spoke fluent Hebrew and was well-versed in Judaism. We also visited her family in Finland together, with whom I got on well despite our communication difficulties. She is the woman with whom I had by far the longest relationship. When she was recalled from her diplomatic post in 1984 and returned to Helsinki, we even considered marriage. But despite our many shared interests—politics, classical music, traveling through all of Israel, the Sinai, and even Beirut—despite our trips together to Europe, the United States, Mexico, and Venezuela, our temperaments were so different that repeatedly we ended up in huge arguments. In the end, we each lived in our own world and neither of us was willing to reign in our professional ambitions for our relationship. Anneli continued her career as cultural attaché for the embassies in Moscow, Berlin, London, and Washington, D.C. Our last, already somewhat half-hearted attempt to revive our relationship during a trip to Alaska fell flat in the summer of 1995. Since then, we have each gone our own ways, but we remain friends to this day.

The New York psychiatrist I had consulted years previously for other reasons was proven right. Looking at my life story, he noticed that I always tried to have relationships with women where it was clear from the beginning that the relationship did not have much chance of a future. They came from another milieu, were much too young, or were married.

◆

Not long after the peace accords with Egypt were signed, in May 1980, I had an opportunity to become better acquainted with the Austrian chancellor Bruno Kreisky. Kreisky was highly controversial in Israel for two reasons: For one, in September 1973, still affected by the massacre at the 1972 Olympic Games in Munich, he gave into the demands of Palestinian terrorists to close the Schönau transit camp—a key station for Soviet Jews immigrating to Israel. At the same time however, he insisted on Austria's right to allow transit and opened a new camp in Traiskirchen. The second bone of contention was that Austria, under Kreisky's leadership, in 1980 became the first Western nation to recognize the PLO as the legitimate representatives of the Palestinian people.

Kreisky, who had been born into a Jewish family in 1911, first became active in the Social Democratic Party while still at school. He saw himself as an agnostic and in 1931, he left the roster of the Jewish Community. During the era of Austro-fascism he was held for a year in the Wöllersdorf internment camp; he was released in 1936 and was just able to complete his law studies before immigrating to Sweden in 1938. In 1951, he returned to Vienna for good and made a career for himself in the Social Democratic Party of Austria (SPÖ) despite the antisemitic climate in post-war Austria. He played a key role in negotiating with the Soviet Union for the Austrian State Treaty in 1955, and in 1959 became minister of foreign affairs. In 1967, he was named head of the SPÖ, and from 1970 to 1983, Kreisky was chancellor of Austria.

Kreisky traveled to Israel for the first time in 1974, with a fact-finding mission of the Socialist International aimed at informing members about the Middle East conflict in the wake of the Yom Kippur War. It would be the beginning of a long-standing relationship with Yasser Arafat. Before Kreisky arrived, I visited his older brother Paul, who had come to Palestine in 1938. Paul Kreisky had a slight mental disability, lived in Jerusalem with a Bukhari foster family, and sold stationery supplies and other goods door to door. Occasionally he came to the *Jerusalem Post* offices and I bought tea cups from him or other tchotchkes. Contrary to malicious gossip, Kreisky always acknowledged his brother's existence and sent him monthly support via the Austrian embassy. Paul told me: "You know, we were both free thinkers in the '20s, and we both became members of the Socialist Party. But when I saw how many former socialists defected to the Nazis after the civil war of 1934, I decided to go to Palestine." There he became religious and he always wore a kippah.

In 1974, I observed Kreisky only from afar; I first met him at a meeting of the Socialist International in Haifa in 1978. At that conference, there was a half-hearted reconciliation between Kreisky and Golda Meir, who had never forgiven him for closing Schönau. In 1980, Kreisky invited me to Vienna for the official celebration of the twenty-fifth anniversary of the Austrian State Treaty. There were other exiled Austrians in attendance alongside many prominent politicians. It was a very upscale event; all guests were put up in the Bristol Hotel, and I attended with Anneli. The celebrations ended with a large reception in the Belvedere, with free-flowing champagne and an elegant buffet. When Kreisky saw the beautiful woman at my side, he made a beeline for Anneli. "*Küss die Hand*" (kiss your hand) he said with inimical Viennese charm and introduced us to many of his guests.

A few days later, I met the federal chancellor in his office in the palace on Ballhausplatz for a long interview that appeared in the *Jerusalem Post* on May 30 under the title "Understanding 'Kaiser Bruno.'" Kreisky greeted me warmly but immediately warned me that we might be interrupted: "I'm putting the finishing touches on a special Socialist International mission to Tehran, together with Swedish socialist leader Olof Palme and Spanish socialist leader Felipe Gonzalez." During the course of the revolution in Iran, Islamist students had taken 52 American embassy workers hostage in December 1979 and held them for months while international diplomacy strove for a peaceful resolution to the crisis.

Then Kreisky concentrated his attention on me. He was well-versed in Israeli and Middle Eastern politics, which he knew as well as he did events in Austria. I began our talk with the provocative question whether he had more sympathy for the Arabs than for Israelis. He negated this notion decisively, calling it "sheer insanity": "I am not a Socialist to have this kind of attitude. My concern for people and other nations' fates is part of my socialist principles. We have to solve the Palestinian problem because I see no other way for Israel's existence." Kreisky believed it would soon be possible to buy nuclear weapons on the free market; which would threaten the very existence of Israel. "Even today there are radical Arab regimes which would like nothing better than to wage another war against Israel, because that is the only thing that holds them together. One must counter this trend by coming to terms with the Palestinians. This is the only way out," he stressed repeatedly. To my surprise, Kreisky also expressed respect for Begin's stance, while criticizing him roundly for a policy that made all attempts at rapprochement impossible. This was not a popular view in Israel at the time, but it proved to have been accurate, and in fact still is. He then asked me how his brother Paul and his nephew in Israel were doing, before turning again to his initiative to save the hostages in Tehran.

In January 1981, when Kreisky turned seventy, I had an idea: wouldn't it be nice if his brother could pass on his congratulations by telephone. I went to visit him at his foster home and made the suggestion.

"But I already sent him a telegram," Paul Kreisky said.

"But wouldn't you like to talk to him?" I called Kreisky's office and asked: "Is it possible for Kreisky to receive a birthday call from his brother today?"

I could sense the astonishment on the other end of the line, but two minutes later, a friendly voice answered: "Yes, warm greetings from the Chancellor. The best time would be nine p.m. tonight at the Chancellor's home." Paul was thrilled by the response and was so excited that he had already arrived at my office by six p.m. At the arranged time, we both congratulated Bruno Kreisky. Politically curious as always, he used the opportunity to question me closely about the latest developments.

My last meeting with Bruno Kreisky was in 1984, six years before his death, in his apartment in Vienna, where he was recovering from a kidney transplant. Kreisky had suffered from a renal disease for many years and even as chancellor had had to coordinate his travels with his dialysis appointments. He sat in his living room in a blue jogging suit; with his reddish beard and pale skin he reminded me of a pious Jew. And in fact he underlined in that conversation that he had always worried about the future of Israel. Only for that reason had he pushed for recognition of the PLO: "There will be no security for Israel without negotiations with the Palestinians." This opinion put him far ahead of his times.

Today, Kreisky's political achievements are receiving more recognition, and I was glad to see that many events were held in commemoration of his hundredth birthday. My connection to Kreisky's family continued after his death. When his son Peter died in 2010, I said Kaddish at the burial of the urn at the behest of the family.

◆

There are three reasons why the year 1982 stands out for me as editor-in-chief of the *Jerusalem Post*. In spring, we published three open letters that garnered a great deal of attention, written by Palestinian journalist Jamil Hamad. In June, the war in Lebanon began and with it a whole new chapter for our reporting, and in December, the newspaper celebrated its fiftieth anniversary.

Of the many Palestinian journalists I met after the Six-Day War, I was particularly impressed by Jamil Hamad. He was originally from Rafat, south-east of Jerusalem; his family had been forced to leave their native village in the 1948 war and moved to Bethlehem. I got to know Hamad better in 1967 under strange circumstances. The editor-in-chief of the small Palestinian newspaper *Al-Fajar* (the horizon), where Hamad was an editor, disappeared under mysterious circumstances and Hamad was suspected of having had something to do with his disappearance. He asked me to help him prove his innocence, which we were in the end able to do after I arranged a new hearing for him at the relevant Israeli authorities through Teddy Kollek's advisor for Palestinian residents of East Jerusalem. In so doing, I won Hamad's trust and we became friends.

In 1982, Hamad invited me to his home, which lay outside of Bethlehem alone and unprotected, a rather dangerous position for somebody in the opposition. On that evening, we spoke openly about the unbearable situation for Palestinians under Israeli occupation. At the end of the evening we had the idea of formulating Hassad's thoughts in three open letters to King Hussein of Jordan, PLO chief Yasser Arafat, and the head of the civil administration in the West Bank, Menachem Milson. His son translated the letters into English and in May and June we published them, at intervals of a few days, on the op-ed page of the *Jerusalem Post* under the pseudonym Abu Zerr el-Gaffari. Hamad did not mince words. In his letter to Milson he spoke about abuses in the occupied territories; about corruption and injustices suffered by the general Palestinian population. He was extremely critical of the incompetency of the people working in the Israeli civil administration. In his letter to King Hussein on the other hand, he expressed his anger at the corruption in the Jordanian administration. The Palestinians should cease to be the pawns of Jordanian interests in the Middle East: "We are no longer the same people we were in 1967. We think differently than those who live in Amman, Jerash, and Irbid … We have learned what democracy is, and what it is not … The prime minister and members of parliament are not above the law." Finally, Hamad called upon Palestinians to join the negotiations for peace. Hamad's letters found international echo and were reprinted by numerous newspapers including the *Frankfurter Allgemeine Zeitung* and the *New York Times*.

◆

On June 3, 1982, I was enjoying a dinner at the Jerusalem Hilton, a send-off for the German Foreign Minister Hans-Dietrich Genscher, whose visit in Israel had gone very well. I was seated at a table with the Egyptian ambassador, Mohammed Bassiouni, who shared the opinion of high-level Israeli and German government officials that the 1977 peace accords between Egypt and Israel had significantly improved the political climate in the Middle East. We all believed that conditions were relatively stable, despite the civil war that had been raging between Muslim and Christian fractions in Lebanon since 1975. Regularly the Fatah—the fighting wing of the PLO—launched Katyusha rockets from Lebanon, firing at villages and cities in the north of Israel.

On the way home I stopped off at the newsroom to see which items the night editor had chosen for the front page. Automatically, I turned on the radio on my desk, which was just then broadcasting the midnight news. At the very first words, I felt a chill down my spine: The newscaster said that Shlomo Argov, the Israeli ambassador to London, had been shot in the middle of the city by Palestinian terrorists from the radical Abu Nidal group and was in critical condition. I was horrified; the fifty-two-year-old diplomat was a friend of mine—his wife and mother of their three children had traveled with me as a young girl in November 1938 on the *Galilea* from Vienna to Palestine.

I wanted to have the news in the next day's paper at all costs, but the people who operated the Photon machines that we used at the time for typesetting had already gone home. We were the first Israeli newspaper to switch to modern printing methods. Our texts were no longer cast in lead; instead, the graphic designers created a paste-up of the text in columns, which was then photographed and sent to the offset printer. The printers naturally often worked late into the night. I therefore wrote a short report on the assassination attempt on my typewriter. The designers fit the nine-by-four centimeter note onto the front page and the bulletin appeared the next morning exclusively in the *Jerusalem Post*. The June 4, 1982 edition with its hand-typed addition became a collector's item.

I had a foreboding that night that Israel's minister of defense, Ariel Sharon, who was in Romania for a few days' vacation at the time, would use the attack as justification for an invasion by Israel into southern Lebanon. Sharon planned to attack the Fatah units in the Palestinian refugee camps located there.

Only two days later, on June 6, 1982, the Lebanon War began. Three convoys of Israeli tanks and infantry marched into south Lebanon. Journalists were allowed to accompany the rearguard and report directly from the front, as well as from the Lebanese villages that had swiftly been captured. As editor-in-chief, I had to decide quickly which of our journalists would take on this task. They would have only a few hours to prepare and to say goodbye to their families. And they would have to report on topics that were completely new to them: the Palestinian refugee camps, the Shiite Amal militia, which had taken a stance against the PLO, and the representatives of the Christian Phalangists from Beirut, who had become Israel's new allies. Back then, I often cited the saying on the difference between an expert and a journalist: While experts have to know more and more about less and less, for journalists it's the other way around: we know less and less about more and more issues.

Officially, the government declared that the Israeli military would only advance forty kilometers, as far as the Litani River, to prevent the immediate threat to the north of Israel. The intervention was therefore given the harmless-sounding name "Operation Peace for Galilee." Prime Minister Menachem Begin, always somewhat in awe of popular generals, put full trust in the misleading cabinet reports of his defense minister, Ariel Sharon, who tried to mask the true aim of the war: to capture the capitol city, Beirut.

At the time, I was in personal contact with Sharon's deputy, Mordechai Zippori, a reserve brigadier who had been a founding member of the right-wing nationalist Likud-Herut party, but was nonetheless a politician of integrity. Zippori cast doubt on Sharon's reports from the front and also dared to contradict him. In an off-the-record briefing, he speculated that Sharon was planning to advance into Beirut. This information aided our critical reporting on the war, we were able to publish it citing "a high-level government source."

In the last week of June 1982, I went to Lebanon for the first time. To avoid the worst traffic, I left the office on a Saturday at four a.m. with my company car, after writing myself an official letter for the Israeli military authorities on newspaper letterhead. My destination was East Beirut, which was under the control of Israeli troops. After driving north for about three hours, I reached the Gesher Hasiv kibbutz, a few kilometers from the border crossing. All journalists who did not have a permanent entry permit, whether foreign correspondents or Israelis, had to be accompanied from this point by an armed military spokesperson. Luckily, I was assigned my colleague Jakob Friedler, who in civilian life was the director of our Haifa correspondents' office.

After the last border control at the striking white cliffs of Rosh Hanikra, we began a hazardous journey along the coast to Sidon and Damour, and then up the steep roads leading over the Chouf mountains, the heart of Druze country, and finally to Baabda, the high-lying Christian suburbs of East Beirut. We needed two hours for the last eighty kilometers of our journey. Shortly after nine a.m.,

I arrived at the office of Bruce Kashdan, a press attaché of the Israeli Ministry of Foreign Affairs and liaison for the international press corps in West Beirut. On this first trip, I wanted to meet with the representative of the Lebanese Minister of Information, who wanted to connect the *Jerusalem Post* with foreign journalists and Christian intellectuals in Beirut. He hoped that this might lead to a normalization of relations between Christian Lebanon and Israel, before any formal peace treaty.

The drive back led us through numerous Shiite villages in southern Lebanon that were ruled by the Amal militia. During a break for coffee at a village square, I was approached by a tall, handsome fighter who spoke to me in English. He introduced himself as the regional commander of the Amal militia and told me that the Palestinian Fatah fighters did not dare come near the areas they controlled: "The 60,000 Shia in South Lebanon are your true allies. It is in Israel's interest to cooperate with us." We exchanged telephone numbers in order to stay in touch. After returning to Jerusalem, I told Neville Lamdan about this encounter. Shortly before, he had left his post as a British diplomat and had immigrated to Israel, becoming director of the newly-instated Lebanon division of the Israeli Ministry of Foreign Affairs. Upon hearing my story, he invited an Amal militia delegation to Jerusalem in order to build relations with them. However the connection did not last because Bachir Gemayel's Christian Phalangists were strictly against the collaboration.

Begin and Sharon erroneously thought that Israel, after expelling the PLO from Lebanon, would be able in alliance with the country's Christian president, Bachir Gemayel, to establish a new political order in the Middle East. I myself heard Sharon express this hope during the war. On July 23, 1982, Egyptian Ambassador Mohammed Bassiouni held a large reception for Revolution Day in the garden of the Acadia hotel in Herzliya. When Sharon as guest of honor cut the large marzipan torte in the colors of the Egyptian and Israeli flags, he solemnly declared: "Now I know which Arab nation will be the second to make peace with Israel."

Sharon's decision to acquiesce to the Phalangists' demands would prove to have been a grave strategic mistake. It was not long before the Shiite Amal militia, turned down by Israel, gave their support to the radical Shia-Hezbollah instead.

In August, I again went to Beirut, this time with the Committee of Daily Newspaper Editors at the invitation of the military press office. We were led to the roof terrace of the six-story Notre Dame School, where the Israeli Parachute Division was headquartered. General Amos Yaron pointed out the two Palestinian refugee camps in West Beirut, Sabra and Shatila, which you could see easily with the naked eye. "These camps are a thorn in our side," he declared. Clearly, even then the Israeli generals were eager to put down these strongholds of PLO activity and were only waiting for an opportune moment. That came on September 14, 1982, when Bachir Gemayel, leader of the Christian Phalangists, was assassinated in a bombing of Phalangist headquarters during a meeting of his political compatriots. Although the Syrian secret service was suspected of being behind the attack, the Israeli army, supposedly on the sole orders of Sharon, supported by Christian Phalangist units, entered PLO-controlled West Beirut. Two days later, Phalangist soldiers arrived at Sabra and Shatila.

The three days and nights from the sixteenth to the eighteenth of September 1982 mark one of the most shameful episodes in the annals of the Israeli military. Hundreds of Phalangist soldiers under the command of Eli Hobeika carried out a massacre in the camps. They mercilessly murdered Palestinian children, women, and men—sources vary between eight hundred and three thousand victims—while the Israeli army kept the area hermetically sealed and lit up the night as bright as day with rocket flares and spotlights. Later it came out that Prime Minister Begin, at home for Rosh Hashanah, only learned about the attack from the BBC.

The outrage in Israel and throughout the world was boundless. Just a few days after these events I took part in a mass rally that brought three hundred thousand people to the square in front of Tel Aviv's City Hall. Israeli President Yitzhak Navon spoke at this event and—as head of state!—openly criticized the government. Accompanied by thundering applause from the demonstrators, he demanded a legal inquiry into the events. Prime Minister Begin saw no choice but to have the Supreme Court form an investigative commission, which in February 1983 resolved that Sharon should be stripped of his post as Minister of Defense and Brigadier General Yaron should be degraded in rank for three years.

With a heavy heart, a few months later I visited the razed and abandoned camps of Sabra and Shatila while in Lebanon to report on the first peace negotiations between Israel and Lebanon in a small hotel in Halde, south of Beirut. While a preliminary agreement between the two nations was signed, the Lebanese parliament never ratified the peace treaty because the compromise had been negotiated with the Christian party alone. Not until 2000 did Prime Minister Ehud Barak decree that Israeli troops retreat from Lebanon to the international border.

♦

Editor-in-chief of the Jerusalem Post, 1985. (David Ben-Gurion on the large poster in background). Photo: David Brauner.

In December 1982, we celebrated the fiftieth anniversary of the *Jerusalem Post*. In preparation, we formed a committee to organize a variety of events; we wanted to celebrate not only in our editorial offices, but also with the other news outlets and our readers. Our largest event was an international conference on "War and the Media." Its main focus was a comparison of journalistic reporting methods in the Lebanon War and the Falklands War, the latter between Great Britain and Argentina in the southern Atlantic between April and June 1982. While the press had relatively free access to both sides of the front in Lebanon and were able to report almost without restrictions, during the Falklands War journalists were only able to report through the communication network of the British naval fleet. Israel received a good report card in this comparison.

A few of our editors shot a film about the history of the newspaper, which premiered in the presence of President Yitzhak Navon at the Jerusalem Theater. Colleagues from Israeli media outlets and foreign correspondents expressed their admiration of our work. During the fifty years of its existence, the *Jerusalem Post* had created its own niche in the Israeli newspaper landscape and had done much to modernize Israeli media because journalistic language had become so much more objective and precise in English over those years.

One event that meant a lot to me was a gala lunch on a Friday at the King David Hotel for everybody who worked for the paper—editors, journalists, office staff, and printers. As a surprise, I had invited the star comic Tuvia Zafir, who impersonated conservative politicians Menachem Begin and Ariel Sharon in his speech in praise of our paper. Since the two men were nemeses of the *Jerusalem Post*, the performance was a huge hit and the dining hall echoed with laughter.

I had been looking forward to moderating this joyful event, but a personal tragedy made it one of the most difficult tasks of my life. The night before, my nineteen-year-old nephew Adi, the son of my sister Henny, had died of an asthma attack. I had spent the whole night with my family in Tel Aviv and only arrived in Jerusalem shortly before the event, because I knew that my presence was necessary to the celebration. So as not to dampen the mood, I only told my three closest colleagues what had happened, but after it was over I was unable to contain my tears any longer. I quickly said good-bye to my friends and colleagues and hurried back to Tel Aviv. Many people who worked for the paper came to the funeral two days later in support of my family and myself.

Naturally we also brought out a special edition of the paper for the anniversary. I spent two long nights working on a fundamental text that expresses like nothing else I've written the journalistic and political ethos of myself and of the *Jerusalem Post* at the time. To this day, this text, "A Newspaper's Credo," remains particularly important to me:

> Newspapers in modern, free, and truly democratic societies do not merely inform their reading public of newsworthy facts and events. They also try to analyze these events and to comment on them. ... But to be worthy of their office, editors must have the courage to voice their convictions, unpopular though these may be.
> As political parties in modern democracies—both those in power and those in opposition—tend to follow set patterns of establishment syndromes, the press is often called upon to fill the role of an extra-parliamentary opposition. ... [There] are the protagonists of reason and moderation, who believe firmly that Israel must come to terms and seek peace with its Arab neighbors in this part of the world, and specifically with the Palestinians. ... Moreover, fifteen years of Israeli occupation of the West Bank and the Gaza district have already greatly distorted some of Israel's basic social and moral values as it is being turned into a permanent occupying power, exercising control over a population which is growing increasingly hostile. ... This debate far transcends the narrow confines of party politics: it concerns itself with the most fundamental values and principles of social and national revival. As it has been proved so often in the past, Israel owes a great deal of its unrivaled development and political progress to the fact that the voices of reason, moderation, and political realism prevailed at crucial junctures of its recent history. This applies with even greater validity to the major choices facing Israel today.

Together with the overwhelming majority of people in Israel, the *Post* opted for peace five years ago, when Mr. Begin's first government welcomed Egypt's President Sadat in Jerusalem in a rare moment of political wisdom and courage. It was clear then, as it is clear now, that this was to be the first step towards a more comprehensive peace which would usher in a new era in the Middle East.

To achieve peace, Israel must be prepared to give up some of the territories it has held since 1967, not just the Sinai. A nation which has chosen peace is called upon to adopt an overall peace policy, as long as it does not endanger its security. It is therefore incumbent on the government which made the first major step towards peace to be consistent, as it is on the opposition which supported that government. ...

The editors of the *Post* will therefore continue to judge both the government and the opposition on the merits of their policies as they have done for the past seven years, regardless of the personalities who advocate them. In this major national debate, which is uppermost in the mind of every Israeli, the *Jerusalem Post* cannot remain neutral. For keeping silent over the crucial issues which face the nation would mean abdicating its role as a living newspaper.

◆

In the 1930s, the newspaper landscape of Jewish Palestine was vast and varied, building on the tradition of the Middle and Eastern European press. Many Jewish editors had come to Palestine and each political party had their own paper. When a party split into factions, each one immediately founded their own newspaper; without a paper of your own, you could hardly be considered a party. The different party papers had surprisingly high journalistic standards; many even had literary supplements—they were not only political mouthpieces. In the early 1980s, most party papers folded for financial reasons, those of the three religious parties stayed on as the exception.

Two of Israel's major dailies have remained family businesses to this day: *Yedioth Ahronoth* (The Latest News) and *Haaretz* (The Land). *Yedioth Ahronoth*, with a market share of around one-third, was the most-read newspaper in Israel until 2009 and was founded in the late 1930s. It was the first evening paper in the British Mandate and has been in the hands of the Moses family since the 1940s. Despite its popularist style and short news items, *Yedioth Ahronoth* is not a classic tabloid. The paper's op-ed contributors are among Israel's most important leaders of public opinion. In February 1948, the newspaper *Ma'ariv* (The Evening) split from *Yedioth*. After many changes of hand, it is today owned by the Nimrodi family and espouses a moderate conservative course.

In 1939, the small newspaper *Haaretz* was bought by Salman Schocken, a businessman and publisher from Zwickau, Germany. His son Gershom turned it into one of the country's most important newspapers. For over fifty years, until shortly before his death in 1990, Gershom Schocken was the heart of *Haaretz* as its publisher and editor-in-chief; over the years he trained generations of Israel's best journalists. Schocken placed high value on literary sections and supplements in the tradition of the large German dailies, but in the final analysis, no Israeli paper ever achieved the intellectual standard of the *Frankfurter Allgemeine Zeitung*, the *Süddeutsche Zeitung*, or the *Neue Zürcher Zeitung*

Although Schocken had been a political adversary of Ben-Gurion, I respected him for always upholding the freedom of the press, even in times of war. In many important questions, such as the continuous fight against military censorship restrictions, the urgent need for a peaceful compromise with the Palestinians, and censure of the Jewish settlers in the occupied territories, we shared the same opinions. The *Jerusalem Post* was the first paper that Schocken read each morning, having already read the galleys of *Haaretz* in the night. Those who worked for him, many of them friends of mine, told me that that they were taken to task at the daily editorial meetings any time the *Jerusalem Post* had scored a scoop.

We worked hard to have good relations with both evening papers. Although the *Jerusalem Post* was aligned with the Labor Party, I was adamant that our reporting remain independent and critical. That changed drastically in April 1989 when the *Post* was sold and I was let go a few months later. Since then, Israel has lacked a liberal voice for peace in English. I therefore pushed for *Haaretz* to publish an English edition. For almost twenty years now, the English *Haaretz* is published with the international *Herald Tribune*—a huge success and no small competition for the *Jerusalem Post*.

There have been many changes in the Israeli newspaper market over the past five years, ever since the conservative American multi-millionaire Sheldon Adelson began publishing the free daily paper *Israel Hayom (Israel Today)*. The paper reaches almost one-third of Israeli readers and supports the right-wing conservative Prime Minister Benjamin Netanyahu unconditionally—in my eyes posing a huge threat to democracy.

◆

In my personal life, little was more important to me in the 1980s than getting to know Saleh Turujman, who became like a brother to me. Without exaggeration I can say that he is one of the most loyal friends I have ever had. Saleh was born in Jerusalem in 1941 into one of the oldest Palestinian families in the city. His father was a wealthy lawyer with liberal views and a circle of friends in which religion was of no importance. He made some of his money with real estate and also rented to Christians and Jews, for which he was criticized by many members of the Muslim community. He owned numerous plots in the west and the east of the city, the sites of many important buildings erected after 1948. Saleh's father was clearly not expecting the foundation of a Jewish State, because he did not move his money out of the country and even invested in Jerusalem, which would prove to have been a fatal mistake. While in Egyptian exile, for years he was still paying mortgage to the Arab Bank for a house that he had built in 1946 in the Jewish part of the city behind the Mandelbaum Gate, which had fallen into the hands of the Israeli administration for "abandoned enemy property," as did his other plots of land.

In April 1948, Saleh's family left their rented apartment near Mea Shearim in the heart of Jerusalem. They had lived there for many years and had gotten along well with their Christian and Jewish neighbors, but Saleh's parents began receiving threats that the house would be bombed. Frightened, the Turujmans fled to Jordan and later to Alexandria in Egypt, where they lived among many Palestinian refugees. Despite flight and exile, Saleh remembers his childhood as sheltered. He graduated from the renowned Victoria College in Alexandria that had been attended not only by King Hussein, but also by many Jewish students; most of his friends were Egyptian. After school he—and his siblings—went to study in the United States, where he has lived ever since. He has long been an American citizen and for many years has headed an FDA research division for the approval of new medications and food additives. Saleh speaks excellent German; he took courses in Munich and Vienna from 1964 to 1966. His connection to Jerusalem never broke, especially since his parents returned there in the 1980s, to a small apartment in Beit Hanina, a few kilometers north of the city center. I first made Saleh's acquaintance at parties in Jerusalem in the early 1980s; he was extremely social and a welcome guest in our liberal journalist and intellectual milieu. We did not become closer until the mid-1980s, when a mutual friend asked me to help him. Despite his American passport, the Israeli border police had forbid him from entering Israel via the land route from the Sinai. What is worse, they put a stamp in his pass forbidding him to enter at all, whether by land or by air. Saleh was enraged, especially since he had been given no reason for this measure.

I used the opportunity of a conference of the International Press Institute in Cairo in March 1983 to meet with Saleh and think together about what we could do. "This is a case for Ezer Weizman," I thought. As a minister without a resort in the Israeli government, he was responsible for questions regarding Israeli-Palestinian relations. "In Arab countries, there is a tradition of writing letters to the head of the country," Saleh explained to me. He had often had positive responses from such letters. In 1974, for example, he wrote to King Faisal of Saudi Arabia asking for support for his studies and had immediately received one thousand dollars.

We therefore decided to write to Weizman. We worked on the wording of our letter for many hours, anticipating all possible responses, and finally typed the final draft on my portable Hermes typewriter, which I carried with me everywhere. Saleh signed our masterpiece and I brought it personally to Weizman's office when I returned. We did not have to wait long for a response: Weizman was so impressed by our letter that he wanted to meet Saleh Turujman as soon as possible. He also found an individual solution to his problem, together with the Ministry of Interior, which oversees visas. Whenever he wanted to visit Israel, Saleh had his lawyer inform the Ministry of Interior when and where he planned to enter, and he never had any problems crossing the border.

After our meeting in Cairo, Saleh and I became close friends, a friendship that also extended to our families. For years, I regularly visited Saleh's parents in Beit Hanina. Whenever they flew to Washington, D.C. to see their children, I went with them to the airport to make sure they got through security; Palestinian travelers accompanied by Jews are hassled far less than those traveling alone. When Saleh's father died from a stroke in 1995, I looked after his mother. She knew that she could count on me. I was very moved by a conversation overheard at Saleh's wedding in D.C. in August 1997. Friends of his young Polish wife asked his mother why she lived alone in Jerusalem and not with her children in the United States. She answered indignantly: "Whatever for? I am not alone, I have Ari there." Not until she was diagnosed with cancer did she move to her children, where I also visited her before her death in June 2002.

The link between Ezer Weizman and Saleh also remained strong. The two met regularly, even after Weizman became president in 1993. Weizman was forced to resign in the summer of 2000, because he had not declared cash gifts that he had received from a rich friend. Soon after, he was diagnosed with cancer. We visited him before his death at his villa in Caesarea. He came to meet us, walking with the help of Filipino carers. We were both shaken to see this large man, who had always been strong and attractive, in so much pain.

Weizman died on April 24, 2005, a Sunday. Immediately I called Saleh.

"When is the funeral?" he asked.

"In two days."

"I'll be there," Saleh said, without hesitating for a moment. I was slightly worried; Weizman would receive a state funeral and I was afraid that a Palestinian by birth would perhaps not be allowed to attend. But my worries proved unfounded. I called Ruma Weizman, Ezer's widow, to let her know Saleh would be coming. Right away she said: "I'll put your names on the President House list." We were hence able to together take leave of Ezer Weizman, who was buried in a small cemetery in Or Akiva. On the way there, Saleh lost his kippah. Ehud Barak stepped in to help: "I'm wearing a hat, you can have my kippah," he said. After the funeral, we went to the widow's home. Ruma gave Saleh a particularly warm greeting; she was moved that he had come all the way from Washington, D.C. Politics play a subordinate role in our friendship; our views on the situation and the main actors are too similar. We both know that if there were more friendships like ours, peace would have been established in the Middle East a long time ago.

◆

In the early 1980s, a few days before Passover, I received a call from Vicky Meroz, wife of the former Israeli Ambassador to Bonn, Jochanan Meroz: "Ari, would you be willing to one time not celebrate with your family and instead come to our small seder? We're hosting an eminent guest. Richard von Weizsäcker, the Governing Mayor of Berlin, and his wife Marianne will be celebrating the seder with us." I agreed under the condition that I could bring Anneli. It turned out to be one of the most interesting and pleasant seders I have ever attended. Eight of us sat around a round table in the Meroz family's modest Jerusalem apartment; aside from us and the Weizsäckers, the only other guests were the Meroz's son and his girlfriend. We had Haggadahs with both English and German translations. Jochanan, a nephew of the American philosopher and scholar Herbert Marcuse, explained the rituals and the meaning of the stories in the Haggadah, while Weizsäcker listened carefully and asked many questions.

This shared seder in Jerusalem was the beginning of an acquaintance that we kept up also after Weizsäcker was elected the sixth West German President in 1984. His first official trip brought him to Jerusalem for a day. President Chaim Herzog invited me to the reception for his German counterpart and we had an opportunity to exchange reminiscences of that seder.

On May 8, 1985, Weizsäcker held his famous speech in the Bundestag on the fortieth anniversary of the collapse of Hitler's regime:

> The 8th of May was a day of liberation. It liberated all of us from the inhumanity and tyranny of the National-Socialist regime. ... We must not regard the end of the war as the cause of flight, expulsion and deprivation of freedom. The cause goes back to the start of the tyranny that brought about war. We must not separate 8 May 1945 from 30 January 1933. ... There is every reason for us to perceive 8 May 1945 as the end of an aberration in German history, an end bearing seeds of hope for a better future.

I was impressed by the forthright honesty of the speech, which is rightly to this day considered a milestone in the German people's confrontation with their Nazi past. I decided to print the entire speech in English translation in the *Jerusalem Post* on the next day. The press attaché of the German embassy in Tel Aviv thanked me for doing so in the name of the Federal President's Chancellery.

I met Weizsäcker once again in 1992 in Berlin, where he had been invited as a guest speaker by the Zionist charity, Keren Hayesod. Before the event, he had heard from our ambassador Avi Primor that I was also invited, and he asked for a chance to speak with me alone for a few minute before the event. I waited for him at the entrance to the Hotel Kempinski ballroom. Weizsäcker arrived with the ambassador and the host; he greeted me and led me to a quiet corner in the foyer. He wanted to know my assessment of the impact of Yitzhak Rabin's election as Prime Minister for the future of Israel. I explained that chances had improved of reaching a compromise for peace with the Palestinians. Although the people in the conference room were expecting him, he calmly asked for clarification on one detail after the other and remained unaffected by the increasing impatience of his hosts. At that occasion, too, he proved his openness to and interest in Israel.

I thought often of Weizsäcker's integrity in 1986, the year I met the Austrian President, Kurt Waldheim. Everyone was talking about the "Waldheim Affair" at the time, to this day one of Austria's domestic political events that has garnered the most international attention. In the final analysis, it also led to huge changes in the country.

The debate began when Kurt Waldheim, a former Wehrmacht officer and later General Secretary of the UN, decided to campaign for Austrian president. In his biography, the conservative politician made no mention of his time in the Wehrmacht, and so the Austrian news magazine *profil*, the *New York Times,* and the Jewish World Congress did their own research. They uncovered that he had been a member of Wehrmacht units implicated in grave war crimes, including the deportation of Jews. Waldheim denied having known anything about these crimes. As early as May 1986, the Jewish World Congress asked that Waldheim be put on the watch list for suspected war criminals, causing outrage among large segments of the Austrian public. In the months that followed, Waldheim's party, the ÖVP (Austrian People's Party), depicted Waldheim as the victim of a smear campaign. Their strategy was successful, and on June 8, 1986, he was elected President in a run-off. Immediately, the Israeli government recalled Ambassador Michael Elitzur from Vienna; until 1992, the embassy was run only by a chargé d'affaires.

Three months after the controversial election, the city of Vienna invited me for a one-week stay. The invitation was part of PR campaign, "Vienna is different," whose initiators hoped to improve Austria's image abroad. On the first evening, I went to the Akademietheater for the premiere of the revival of "Herr Karl" by Helmut Qualtinger, who had died suddenly only days previously. I accompanied Leon Zelman, with whom I had been friends since the late 1960s. Zelman was born in 1928 in Poland, had survived the Lodz Ghetto and the Auschwitz death camp and was finally liberated, half-starved to death, by American troops in a satellite camp of Mauthausen concentration camp in Austria. In 1946, he went to Vienna, where he was taken in by the Young Socialists. He studied publishing and journalism, founded the annual journal *Jüdisches Echo* (Jewish Echo), and after completing his doctorate, began working at the Verkehrsbüro, Austria's largest travel agency, where he focused on organizing trips to Israel. On these trips, he realized that many former Viennese residents were interested in the city of their birth. Since the journey was too expensive for many of them, Zelman looked for financial support and in 1980 founded the Jewish Welcome Service. He put his stamp on cultural life in Vienna until his death in July 2007 and contributed greatly to creating a climate in the city that today makes it possible for me to live here—at least some of the time.

After the theater, Zelman introduced me to Gerold Christian, Waldheim's press spokesperson. Waldheim's election had led to quite a stir in the Israeli media as well and Christian was eager to make contact with a representative of an Israeli newspaper. He offered to come to my hotel so we could talk, but I was not adverse to meeting him in the Chancellery in the old Hofburg. Our conversation, which lasted an hour, centered around the question of how Waldheim's international isolation could be ended. I used Karl Carstens, a former German President and also President of the Bundestag, as an example. His official biography listed him as a member of the Nazi party from 1934 to 1938, and still he had been officially received with full honors by Menachem Begin and Yitzhak Shamir in Jerusalem in 1978. In contrast to Waldheim, Carstens had not tried to hide his past. Christian agreed that Waldheim would have to respond openly to the charges as soon as possible. At the end of our talk, he assured me once again that "the boss" was not in the house and showed me the State Room of the presidential Chancellery, which had once been Maria Theresia's study.

While I was waiting with Christian in front of the small elevator that would bring me to the exit, the door opened and who stepped out but Waldheim himself. When Christian mentioned my name and the *Jerusalem Post*, Waldheim remembered our meeting in Jerusalem some years previously, where he had been in his capacity as UN General Secretary. "I still have some time before my midday date and would like to chat with you a bit," Waldheim said. I could by no means turn down this proposal and so I followed him back to his study. I asked that Christian also be a part of our conversation, since we had already spoken about Waldheim's isolation. Citing a very recent example, I told the Federal President that Leonard Bernstein, who would be giving a benefit concert the next day at the Vienna Music Society, had publicly threatened to speak his mind should Waldheim appear at the concert. "We have a calendar conflict anyway," Waldheim responded, and proceeded to rage against Edgar Bronfman and the Jewish World Congress. When he stopped for breath I asked him: "But how should this go on, Mr. President?" To my surprise, he changed his tone and became personal: "You have no idea how much this situation torments me." Then he went on to say that he had many Jewish friends in New York. I repeated my advice that he respond to the accusations publicly. "In your speech you will have to acknowledge Austria's partial responsibility for Nazism; with a speech like that you could make history," I said to him. "*Ja*, something like the Weizsäcker speech," he answered. Then he told me that he was planning, as a gesture of reconciliation, to go to the city temple on the Seitenstettengasse on the upcoming Yom Kippur holidays. "Mr. President, I would advise against that," I responded.

I had a strange feeling while we were speaking. Here I was, the Jewish boychick who had been expelled from Vienna forty-eight years earlier, sitting with the President of the Republic of Austria in the Hofburg on Ballhausplatz, taking on the role of critic and advisor. Then I remembered that Waldheim was due to speak on television on October 26, on the occasion of the Austrian national holiday. "That's the perfect opportunity to make an official statement," I proposed. The three of us thought about which points Waldheim should cover in his talk. Christian took notes and both men asked whether they could reach me whenever they needed before the speech. So that the text would reach a broad international audience, it was to be translated into English and French before it was held.

At the end of our talk—it was unclear what had become of Waldheim's midday date—he walked me to the corridor and thanked me. On the way to the elevator, Christian also repeated these thanks and stressed that nobody had spoken so openly with Waldheim about these problems since he had been elected. "You have to understand. Since I work for him I cannot mention these things as plainly," he said.

A few days later I traveled to Budapest and Bonn and returned to Vienna exactly two weeks after our encounter. By chance, I met Christian at the Burgtheater on Friday afternoon. "So, how is the big speech coming along?" I asked him directly, to which he answered sheepishly that they wouldn't be able to make much of an impact; the President had only been given five minutes of airtime. I shook my head incredulously: "It's none of my business, but I assume that the President, as sovereign of the nation, would receive thirty minutes to speak from the public broadcaster ORF if he demanded it." In response Christian said that Waldheim's credibility was also at stake. "Exactly," I answered, the longer he waits to make a statement, the more he forfeits it." Christian insisted on meeting me again the next day, one day before my departure. On that day, October 18, he brought me the President's greetings and renewed thanks. Christian had told him about our meeting. As a result, Waldheim had allegedly changed his plans and now meant to give his speech as agreed upon. His spokesperson and I again went through the diverse points that should be touched upon and then we said our good-byes. On October 26, Waldheim did speak, but only about general issues; calling upon Austria's citizens to do their democratic duty in the upcoming elections. Supposedly, the ÖVP leadership had warned against making any statement about shared culpability so shortly before the elections.

On the international stage, Waldheim became more and more isolated. In April 1987, the United States even banned him from entry as a "suspected war criminal." A few months later, on February 8, 1988, a commission of historians that had been appointed by the Austrian government to investigate Waldheim's past released the results of their research. They had not found evidence of any war crimes committed by Waldheim himself, nevertheless they wrote:

> Even though, as a subordinate in staff positions he had no executive powers, he was excellently informed about the events of the war thanks to his education, his knowledge and as a result of glimpses which he gained as a translator in decisive events of the command, and especially from his activity in the central intelligence service of his army group, and his physical proximity to the events.

The report minced no words, stating clearly: "He repeatedly assisted in connection with unlawful actions and thereby facilitated their execution."

Not until seventeen months after my meeting with Waldheim,

on the fiftieth anniversary of the Anschluss, the Nazi annexation of Austria on March 10, 1988, did he speak on television, on the public broadcaster ORF. The speech contained wording familiar to me from our conversation. Waldheim acknowledged that the Holocaust was one of the greatest tragedies in the history of the world and admonished not to forget that "many of the worst Nazi henchmen were Austrians." He stressed that there was no such thing as collective guilt. "Nevertheless," he stated, "as head of state of the Republic of Austria, I wish to apologize for Nazi crimes committed by Austrians." Because Waldheim had not been allowed to speak at the official state ceremony on March 11, this was the president's only official speech fifty years after the Anschluss. It was not able to salvage his reputation.

As in 1938, the commemoration of the Anschluss also fell on a Friday in 1988. I decided to spend the week in Vienna to see for myself how the Austrians dealt with the anniversary of that fateful day. My memories from my youth were still so present that I wanted to at least confront some former supporters of annexation. Franz Vranitzky, the Social Democrat who had been Federal Chancellor since 1986, also knew that he would have to make a stand on this anniversary. He called an international press conference and declared that the controversy surrounding Waldheim's election had contributed to the large media interest in this anniversary of the Anschluss. And in fact, it was

Franz Vranitzky, 1988.
Photo: Walter Rutishauser.

almost impossible to keep track of the many events, rallies, conferences, and memorials taking place in the city. It seemed as if Austria was making its first earnest efforts, albeit very delayed, to confront its past.

Originally, I had been invited to two lectures in Club Alpha, a forum for discussion headed by Maria Rauch-Kallat, an ÖVP politician who would later become Minister of Health. I had also been asked to give witness testimony by many radio and television broadcasters who wanted to interview me about my memories of Vienna in 1938. After I expressed criticism of a podium discussion after a broadcast by a documentary by Wolfgang Glück on the year 1938, the filmmaker asked me to stay in Vienna one day longer so that I could participate in "Zerreissproben" ["acid tests" literally "rip rehearsals"—trans.] an event at the Theater in der Josefstadt. As in the above mentioned podium discussion about Glück's film, many Austrians who lived through the Anschluss defended the events of the day. Zerreissproben was filmed by ORF and also broadcast in Germany and Switzerland. I am still proud of myself for getting in one important sentence during the event, namely:

> The dramatic collision of German political National Socialism and deep-rooted Austrian antisemitism so accelerated the persecution of the Jews that there was far worse violence in Austria in the first five months after the Anschluss than in the five previous years in the Third Reich.

On the end of the last day of my stay in Vienna, I visited my former sports teacher Franz Stefan from Wasa Gymnasium, whom I remembered as a staunch Nazi. Stefan was born in 1904, but was still in very good health and he greeted me with a firm handshake. I showed him an article from the *Jüdischen Echo* in which I had named him as one of the most active Nazis at Wasa Gymnasium. "Why do you think that?" he asked me, surprised. "Did you ever feel like there was something antisemitic in my teaching?" I reminded him that after the Anschluss he immediately wore the round red Nazi party pin to class, and also that he had openly spoken of his sympathy for the Nazis long before annexation. Stefan became evasive. Asked directly: "Were you a party member, or not?" he prevaricated: "You could perhaps say that I joined verbally. I never signed anything." It was half-lies, fibs, and excuses like these that for decades had made it impossible for me to live in Austria.

It would be another three years until Federal Chancellor Vranitzky would clearly acknowledge Austria's share of responsibility for National Socialism in a memorable speech in front of the National Assembly on July 8, 1991. In this speech, he clearly rejected the thesis that had always been propagated by official representatives of Austria until that day, namely that Austria had been the first victim of Hitler's policy of aggression. Vranitzky declared:

> We have to live with our share of responsibility for the suffering that was inflicted, not by Austria, ... but by some of its citizens on other people and on humanity. ... We acknowledge all the facts of our history and the deeds of all sections of our people, the good as well as the evil. And just as we take credit for the good, we must also apologize for the evil to survivors and relatives of the dead.

In 1992, Kurt Waldheim ended his presidency. He had never been able to free himself from his international isolation and he had had so little domestic success that he abstained from running again. He never changed his views, as was clear from his book *Die Antwort*

(The Answer), in which, in finest antisemitic tradition, he rants against the supposed international power of the Jewish-controlled media.

◆

In the mid-1980s, it became clear that the future of the *Jerusalem Post* as a liberal newspaper was threatened. The group of Jewish-American stakeholders who had invested a quarter of a million dollars for the modernization of the paper in the 1960s, keeping fifty percent of the newspaper's stock in return, was dissolved in the early 1980s. Their shares, worth around four million dollars in the meantime, were held in trust by Koor Industries, a company close to the trade union that promised both to ensure the economic independence of the *Post* and not to sell the shares. When Koor was facing bankruptcy a few years later, the bargaining over the newspaper began—neither the Histadrut trade union center nor the Workers' Bank cared one bit about their pledge. Their behavior not only shattered my belief in the Israeli labor movement that I had grown up in, it also had a huge impact on my working life: I put all my energy and much of my time into an attempt to create a liberal Jewish consortium that would guarantee our editorial freedom. I traveled to Switzerland, England, and the United States, held innumerable personal talks with potential investors, wrote dozens of letters, and made countless phone calls to discuss possible solutions. While all that was going on, my work as editor continued. As always I took part in the daily editorial and department head meetings, to both discuss our next edition and critique the previous one. In short, I had no time at all to write my own articles in those years. The only exceptions are a few pieces for anniversaries or memorial days.

Despite all my efforts, I failed in my attempt to save the *Jerusalem Post*. In April 1989, the paper was bought by the Hollinger International company. The group's CEO, David Radler, came to Jerusalem for an initial visit and bragged in interviews that the *Jerusalem Post* would become one of the company's flagships alongside the *Daily Telegraph*. Naturally I asked him about his plans for the paper: "I will be 65 in January 1990, I have enough vacation days saved that I can stop working tomorrow." Radler acted surprised: "What do you mean, stop? I've worked with editors who are over eighty. Of course you have to stay."

A few weeks after the takeover, he appointed Yehuda Levi, a journalist from Vancouver and an Israeli reserve officer, as president of the *Jerusalem Post*, a job that had not existed up until that point. The atmosphere in the editorial offices changed overnight. As soon as I met Levi for the first time, I knew that he had no interest in working with me. In August he came into my office and said openly: "Ari, you cast too long a shadow. I'd like for you to leave as soon as possible." He later wrote me a letter saying that he could understand how very difficult this step was for me, after all, the paper was identified with my name in the public eye.

After talking to Levi; I called Erwin Frenkel and told him the news. Then I left the newsroom; I needed time to digest the situation. When I returned, our shared secretary called me and said excitedly:

"Ari, you won't believe it. Erwin acted like a man. He said: 'If Ari has to go, I'm going too.'"

"We'll see what happens," I answered.

The next day, Frenkel had his talk with Levi. Afterwards, when I went into his office to hear what he had decided, he said sheepishly to me: "We discussed you having an opportunity to work on your idea of setting up French and Arabic weekly editions of the *Post*." He would take over the helm of the paper and they would throw me a few special projects as crumbs. Although I had suspected that he would react in that way, I was disappointed by Frenkel. Still, I warned him: "Yehuda Levi wants to become editor-in-chief and he won't tolerate anybody else at his side."

Shortly before the meeting of the board in September 1989, the first under the direction of David Radler, a petition was started stating that I must remain. The letter, signed by around one hundred employees of the paper, hung in the hall of our offices. When Radler saw it, he ordered that it be removed immediately.

A few days later, the paper's board of directors met in our Tel Aviv office. The room was full, all members of the board had come, including many people who had been named at my suggestion. Levi spoke of the upcoming changes. Key figures in the administration, including the business manager and the person responsible for advertising would have to leave in the short to middle term; the financial director was willing to keep the budget as is for the rest of the fiscal year. I will never forget how Levi then added, in a few almost thrown-away words: "And a similar thing will apply to Ari Rath." The sentence fell in an awkward silence. None of those present made the slightest sign of protest. Words can hardly describe how hurt I was by this silence. It was absolute betrayal. With effort, I managed to speak: "Could you please explain what that means?" Radler played it down: "Come Ari, leave good enough alone. We all know what it means." Then he moved on to the next item on the agenda. My colleagues knew what a hard blow this was for me. Wherever I went, they tried to hide their pity: "Hi Ari, you look great today!" They treated me like a cancer patient in the final stages.

There were still a few weeks left until my last day of work. I began by cleaning out my office. Every day, I packed boxes full of newspapers, brochures, and manuscripts into my car and at home I brought them into the basement without looking into them once. When I moved from Motza to my current apartment in Rehavia a few years ago, I took the boxes with me. To this day, I have not found the energy to go through them, surely there are a few treasures hiding there. I received my salary until the end of November, but my last day in the newsroom was Tuesday October 31, 1989.

On my last evening as editor-in-chief, I sat in my empty editorial office and listened to the evening news on the radio. The residents of the settlers' city Ma'ale Adumim were blocking the main roads between Jerusalem and Jericho in protest, because late that afternoon Palestinian youth had thrown stones at the car of a settler family. I asked the night editors who would take the story. A colleague had been called in, but half an hour later he was still not there. It could have been all the same to me, but my reporter instinct was stronger. Spontaneously, I got into my car and drove to the site of the protest. The entrance to Ma'ale Adumim was still blocked, but I found a side street that brought me to the city center. Horrified I saw smoke rising from a large yellow taxi with Palestinian plates. There wasn't a soul in sight. I took a bucket of water that I happened to find under a faucet in a driveway and put out the fire. Then I saw two frightened figures on the roof of a house coming slowly closer; the Palestinian drivers of the car, who had run away from the mob and brought themselves to safety. I went with them to the nearest police station, where we filed charges against unknown people. The police were helpful and also brought the two Palestinians home. Later they told me that they had received compensation for their taxi from the Israeli authorities as "victims of a terrorist attack." While still in Ma'ale Adumim I called in my report, stopped by the editorial offices again to say good-bye, and drove home.

◆

A few days later, I turned my back on Jerusalem. My loyal friend Peter Galliner, director of the International Press Institute, had suggested me as a participant at a conference in Moscow. The Soviet news agency Novosti was for the first time bringing together newspaper editors from the West and the Soviet Union and had also invited journalists from the opposition. The topic of the conference was freedom of the press in the era of perestroika—the economic, social and political reforms of the Soviet Union set in motion by President Mikhail Gorbachev in 1986. The journalists' focus was of course glasnost—freedom of opinion, information, and the press, which Gorbachev had introduced as the basic requirement of a democratic society. I was surprised by how openly Soviet journalists criticized Gorbachev, because despite of all his avowals of transparency, he had interfered in the naming of the editors-in-chief of the newspapers *Izvestiya* and *Pravda*. My Soviet counterparts also told us about huge conflicts surrounding the head of government, who had received very low popularity ratings in an opinion poll by the magazine *Argumenti I Fakti*. They were very surprised to hear from Western journalists that our editorials were not written by politicians, but by independent editors. The mood among conference participants was animated; in the breaks in particular there were many unofficial discussions, often about the conditions of daily life after the reforms. The biggest conflicts were between journalists from the Soviet Union and those from their former "brother countries"

Czechoslovakia and East Germany, both of which had party lines in strict opposition to the Soviet reforms.

I was surprised by Moscow. Never would I have thought that I would be received so warmly as an Israeli. For years, there had been no diplomatic relations between Israel and the Soviet Union. The highlight of the conference was a visit to the Kremlin with Yevgeny Primakov, a member of the Central Committee of the Communist Party of the Soviet Union. Although his name by birth was Finkelstein—Primakov never said whether or not he had a Jewish background—for many years he was *the* expert for the Middle East. He received us in his enormous office—there was plenty of room for all thirty visitors at the conference table. At the push of a button, the doors swung open to the adjacent assembly room of the Supreme Soviet. At the end of the official talk, I used the opportunity to ask Primakov when Prime Minister Shimon Peres would be able to travel to Moscow—I knew that the Israeli government was working towards a visit. "Tell your friends that the less pressure they put on, the more likely a visit becomes," he recommended.

My stay in Moscow, my first in the Soviet capitol, provided me with an opportunity to visit Anneli for a few days; she had just begun a post as ambassador for culture in the Finnish embassy the previous week. She picked me up at Sheremetyevo Airport and stopped suddenly in Khimki, a suburb of Moscow. We got out of the car and stood before a memorial in remembrance of the site where the invasion of the German Wehrmacht had been stopped in December 1941. I was shocked to see that Hitler's troops were only nineteen kilometers from the Kremlin when they had been halted.

I was enthralled by Moscow's wide boulevards, ornate metro stations, and theater palaces. Every evening, Anneli and I went out together; we visited the Bolshoi theater and thanks to her gift with languages, we navigated local restaurants where we ate traditional Russian food and drank vodka. I had been put up in the elegant Oktober hotel, which was then still secret lodgings for party functionaries and guests and could not be found on any map of the city. One time, when I had to ask for directions at the Intourist Office, they would not give them to me until I showed them my hotel pass. To my surprise, I otherwise had little trouble finding my way around, even though all writing—including in the metro stations—was written only in Cyrillic letters. Apparently I had learned something in Greek class at Wasa Gymnasium after all, even though my lessons lay more than half a century in the past.

When I returned to Jerusalem from Moscow one week later, I stopped in at the newspaper offices again. There I noticed a letter lying open in Frenkel's inbox. It was a request by Yehuda Levi to be admitted into the Committee of Daily Newspaper Editors—an elite circle that admitted only the editors-in-chief of Israeli papers—where for years Frenkel and I had represented the *Jerusalem Post*. My speculations were becoming true more quickly than expected.

◆

The first trip that I took under the official title of "former editor-in-chief of the *Jerusalem Post*"—a title that I still wear proudly—was in December 1989 to Germany. I wanted to see for myself the changes since the fall of the wall on November 9, 1989, even if I no longer had a newspaper that I could publish my impressions in. I flew into Tegel Airport and rented a car there so that I could get around more easily. I assumed it might be difficult to travel through East Germany. The first change I noticed since my last visit were the hundreds of East Germans and Poles buying televisions and washing machines in the stores in West Berlin. Kurfürstendamm was also overrun with people from the East who seemed overwhelmed by the superabundance in the West.

After two days at a small conference at the Aspen Institute Schwanenwerder—held, it turned out, on the lakeside property on which Joseph Goebbels had had his villa—I began my explorations. First, I got an accreditation from the East German Press Offices. The official was surprised that an Israeli journalist was interested in East German party conventions, but he gave me a press pass with no questions.

On December 16, I was present at the special convention of the East Christian Democratic Union (CDU) in the legendary Kosmos cinema on Karl Marx Allee. Eberhard Diepgen, the former—and future—mayor of Berlin was the guest speaker. Although the West CDU was not willing at the time to officially negotiate with the East CDU, because they had been part of the East German government, at the convention, Diepgen was already talking about fusion. There were intense discussions about the problem of *Koffergelder,* monies from the state kitty used by the Socialist Unity Party (SED) to finance bloc parties like the Farmers' Party or the East CDU. This strategy, I came to understand at this convention, was a propaganda stroke of genius by the communists as it enabled them to feign a democratic system with multiple electoral choices. I would never have expected to experience such an open and democratic convention just a few weeks after the fall of the wall.

The next day, I drove to Leipzig. My first stop was the Nikolaikirche, the church that had become the symbol of the protest movement. Then I visited the founding meeting of the Democratic

Awakening party (*Demokratischer Aufbruch*; DA), that had grown out of the East German civil rights movement. Wolfgang Schnur was elected president of the DA—a fateful decision since in 1990 it would be revealed that he had worked for the Stasi, destroying any future chances for the party. However the party's downfall had no effect on the career of Angela Merkel, who volunteered for the DA at its founding, soon became the party's spokesperson, and began to rise to her future position after the DA fused with the CDU in August 1990. The debates at that foundational meeting lasted late into the night.

The next morning, I drove directly to the Dynamo Hall in East Berlin, where the SED was holding its last large party convention. The hall was full to bursting; two thousand six hundred delegates and one thousand international journalists squeezed into the building. The corridors were clogged with people and you could hardly breathe for cigarette smoke—a sign of the tension felt by many participants, who were mourning the end of their party. Gregor Gysi made a passionate speech on Helmut Kohl's ten-point program, which aimed at the unification of East and West Germany. Unlike West German Federal Chancellor Kohl, Gysi believed that the reunification process would take many years. He also argued for the continuance of the SED under a new name. A special committee, open to the press, negotiated for hours over possible new names and finally agreed upon PDS—Party of Democratic Socialism. The next day, a Monday, the former official mouthpiece of East Germany, the daily newspaper *Neues Deutschland*, appeared without the communist emblem for the first time.

Unlike many of my contemporaries, I observed developments in Germany with both sympathy and equanimity. I remember well the many voices in France, Poland, and of course Israel that feared that the political changes and reunification might again give Germany a dominant position in Europe. Prime Minister Yitzhak Shamir gave a speech at the Likud party forum only a few days after the fall of the wall in which he warned against the creation of a new and powerful Germany able to threaten the security of Europe and the world. I did not share this view at all and thought analyses absurd that suggested the Federal Republic of Germany could be equated with the Third Reich. I had had so much contact with Germans over the past decades and had so often seen their earnest attempts to work through the past that I was sure that democracy was firmly anchored in Germany. Shamir, too, soon back-pedaled. Although his coalition was in the midst of a difficult crisis, he sent Foreign Minister Moshe Arens to Bonn to apologize to Kohl and assure him that the Israeli government no longer saw a united and European Germany as a threat to peace.

Epilogue
Between Jerusalem and Vienna

A few weeks before my sixty-fifth birthday in January 1990, my work at the *Jerusalem Post* had come to an end. It took me quite a while before I got over my disappointment at the betrayal of my colleagues of so many years. Against this background, I must again express my gratitude for the loyalty of my friend Teddy Kollek. Of my many colleagues and contacts, he was the only one to call and ask how I was doing. What is more, he offered me a job: He proposed that I work as a special advisor to the Jerusalem Foundation to help him with the preparation and realization of a huge event in 1996—3000 Years City of David Jerusalem. As much as I respect Kollek and his commitment to the city—the working environment of the foundation was not for me and I quit after three years.

My newly-won freedom gave me the opportunity to become more politically active. I intensified my relationships with Palestinian intellectuals and took part in many conferences as an independent political advisor and Middle East expert. I am particularly pleased to have been part of one of the first joint Israeli-Palestinian talks that, it turned out, kicked off the Oslo peace process. In the early 1990s, this initiative for a rapprochement between Israel and Palestinians was originally sparked by the Social Democratic Swedish government and its foreign minister, Sten Andersson. Early in the summer of 1991, he invited a delegation of representatives of Israel and a Palestinian delegation, including people from the PLO, to a first round of talks on a peninsula in Stockholm. Officially, the meeting was a university seminar under the aegis of the Dag Hammarskjöld chair of peace and conflict research at Uppsala University, because Israelis could only meet with members of the PLO within the framework of an academic event. Alongside Abrasha Tamir, a high-level general, and the social scientist Yochanan Peres, I was one of the members of the six-person Israeli delegation. Peres had determined through his research that even many members of the Shas party were in fact in favor of a two-state solution. The Shas party is traditionally supported by ultra-Orthodox Iraqi and Moroccan immigrants and has a reputation for being particularly conservative.

The seating plan alone for these talks proved to be a diplomatic challenge, since Israeli delegates could only be placed next to Palestinians from East Jerusalem, Gaza, and the West Bank, but not next to PLO representatives from Arab countries. In the end, the tables were placed in a U-form, so that the official PLO representatives could sit next to observers from Sweden and the United States and we could be placed across from them. Key to the success of these talks was the first meeting, at which participants had to introduce the person to their left. I was seated next to Ziad Abu Zayyad, a Palestinian lawyer and political activist from East Jerusalem, with whom I had already been friends for many years. He was seated next to Abrasha Tamir, who in turn sat next to Faisal Husseini, the son of Abdul Kader el-Husseini, a Palestinian officer who had fallen in 1948 at the battle for the Kastel Fortress. Tamir, who had fought in the same battle, praised Faisal's father as a courageous fighter and a Palestinian hero. This respectful manner created a constructive atmosphere among the conference participants.

In the evenings, we sat together and told jokes. One evening, I went with the Palestinian ambassador to Paris and an Israeli colleague to the Old City of Stockholm. We had to take great security precautions—we drove in a bulletproof car and were accompanied by three security guards—but we still enjoyed ourselves greatly. After a few days, the conference participants said good-bye almost as if we were friends. Before doing so, we had agreed with our Swedish hosts to meet again in the fall of 1991 for a meeting at which delegates would simulate peace negotiations.

We never had the chance, because in mid-July 1991, Saddam Hussein invaded Kuwait and put an initial stop to this initiative. The Palestinian leader Yasser Arafat supported the Iraqi dictator—a fatal error, because it discredited him in the eyes of the other Arab countries. At the same time, it proved to have created beneficial conditions for further peace negotiations. After the lost war, Arafat was weakened and willing to take the advice of his advisor and director of finances, Abu Alaa, to allow for first informal contact between the PLO and Israeli representatives.

In June 1992, the Labor Party won the Israeli election under the leadership of Yitzhak Rabin. The new Israeli government, with Shimon Peres as Minister of Foreign Affairs, indicated it was ready to rekindle peace talks. Rabin also dared to take on the controversial question of the settlements in the occupied territories and was, at least in word, vehemently opposed to their expansion. In Sweden on the other hand, the Social Democrats had lost the election, so that former Foreign Minister Andersson asked his Norwegian counterpart Johan Jørgen Holst to become the host of the talks between

Israelis and Palestinians. Holst tasked the diplomats Terje Røed Larsen and his wife Mona Juul with organizing official talks between the PLO and an official Israeli delegation at a chalet to the south of Oslo. These talks resulted in a significant breakthrough, because Israel signaled its readiness to recognize the PLO as the legitimate representatives of the Palestinian people. This agreement was afterwards secretly signed by Peres and Mahmud Abbas in the Grand Hotel Oslo and entered history as the "Oslo Accords," although many of the negotiations that followed took place elsewhere.

◆

In September 1993, there was an official exchange of letters between Arafat and Rabin. Holst negotiated with Arafat one entire night in Paris, arguing about one passage in which Arafat should declare himself willing to solve any conflicts that might arise at the negotiation table and to refrain from all violence. The Office of the Prime Minister in Jerusalem invited around thirty people to be present at this historic moment: politicians, government officials, and journalists, including myself. We waited for hours for the Norwegian foreign minister to arrive carrying Arafat's letter. Finally, Holst entered the room and put Arafat's missive on Rabin's desk. It was read aloud right away: Arafat declared that he would recognize the right of Israel to exist in peace and security; he also accepted responsibility for ensuring that all groups within the PLO kept this agreement. In turn, Rabin signed the prepared response, in which the State of Israel recognized the PLO as the legitimate representative of the Palestinian people. When Rabin laid down his pen, we all stood up and cheered and applauded—a memory that seems almost surreal to me today.

It is a great tragedy that when Rabin was assassinated two years later, it also meant the loss of the person Arafat had trusted and respected. Arafat was honored that the great general spoke with him eye-to-eye and repeatedly referred to Rabin as "my courageous partner for peace." I can still see the television images of September 13, 1993 clearly before my eyes. Under a cloud-free sky, Rabin and Arafat reached out their hands to one another in reconciliation on the green lawn in front of the White House.

The Oslo Accords stipulated the completion of the peace process in stages. First, in the May 1994 Gaza-Jericho Agreement, the Palestinians received autonomy in the Gaza Strip and the city of Jericho for the first time since 1967. The contract with the Palestinians made it possible to also make peace with Jordan in October 1994—an agreement that has held to this day—an event I did not want to miss. On the spur of the moment, I jumped into my car and drove towards the Red Sea, where the signing ceremony for the peace treaty was to take place outside of Eilat. I had driven this route many times, but this time I felt particularly hopeful and light-hearted because for the first time, the villages on the other side of the Dead Sea and along the border were no longer in enemy territory. The ceremony took place on a large stage erected in the middle of the desert and guarded by Jordanian and Israeli soldiers. Under the eyes of American President Bill Clinton and the American and Soviet foreign ministers, Yitzhak Rabin and King Hussein, who had met many times before, hugged one another. Then Hussein invited all official guests to his palace near Akaba to celebrate.

In December 1994, Rabin, Peres, and Arafat were jointly awarded the Nobel Prize for Peace. Rabin continued to pour all his energy into peace in the Middle East and did not hesitate to speak sharply about the Jewish settlers in the occupied territories, whom he believed were a threat to this peace. On February 28, 1995, he declared in front of the Knesset:

> You are not part of the community of Israel. You are not part of the democratic, national camp to which we in this house all belong, and there are many, many among our people who despise you. You are not part of the Zionist project. You are foreign bodies; you are errant weeds. Rational Judaism spits you out. You have placed yourselves beyond Jewish law. You are a disgrace for Zionism and an embarrassment to Judaism.

In September 1995, the interim agreement on the Gaza Strip and the West Bank was signed, partitioning the Palestinian territory into three zones, A, B, and C, over which the Palestinian National Authority and the Israeli military exercised varying degrees of control. Zone C, over which the Israeli military had the most sway, was to gradually become integrated into the area governed by the Palestinians.

My last encounter with Yitzhak Rabin was on October 24, 1995 in New York. Rabin's speech on the occasion of the fiftieth anniversary of the United Nations caused quite a stir because he praised Arafat for the courage to be Israel's partner for peace. Most of the Arab delegations remained in the assembly hall and also applauded. I believed I was a witness to a new era; moved to tears, I joined the thunderous applause. Afterwards, a small group of Israelis gathered in the rooms of the Israeli delegation and congratulated Rabin for his brave words. Clearly still agitated from his talk, he smoked one cigarette after the other. We raised our glasses for a heartfelt "l'chaim!" It was the last time I ever spoke to him.

It fills me with sadness that the path we had started on so full of hope came to an abrupt end with the murder of Yitzhak Rabin on November 4, 1995 at the hands of a nationalist religious fanatic. I would have liked to have been at the huge peace rally in Tel Aviv that had been planned on that day, but I was visiting friends in New York. I was in a shoe store in Manhattan, buying a pair of typical American flip-flops for my sister Henny, which she always asked me to bring back, when I heard about the catastrophe. I paid with my credit card, which the Afro-American salesman noticed was from an Israeli bank and so he asked me empathetically whether I was from Israel: "Is your prime minister named Rabin?" I answered in the affirmative. "I have bad news for you—Rabin was shot." I could not believe it at first, and took a taxi back to my friends' apartment. They were sitting in front of the television watching Clinton's memorial speech. He was fighting back tears and ended with the words "*shalom, chaver*"—peace be with you, friend.

Still in shock, I returned that night—as planned—to Tel Aviv. There was a dead silence in the airplane. When I arrived on Sunday afternoon, I brought my luggage to my apartment and went to the Knesset, where Rabin's coffin, draped in the blue-and-white flag and guarded by six generals, was laid out in the large square in front of the building. Thousands of people came to take their leave of him. The head of the American mission came towards me, clearly upset. We hugged spontaneously. He told me: "I'm just back from meeting Arafat in Gaza, he's also shocked and very worried about the future."

Not until this outpouring of public grief for Rabin did it become clear just how widespread hopes for peace had been throughout Israeli society. In an obituary for the German weekly *Die Zeit*, I described the mood in the country:

> They come day and night and stand in still devotion in front of the new grave on Mount Herzl in Jerusalem, covered with flowers, wreaths, and posters. They light memorial candles, write poems and letters, sing quiet songs and ask for Yitzhak Rabin's forgiveness for not supporting and protecting him on time ... They promise to continue Rabin's work and to fulfill his political legacy—peace. The silent majority in the country now offer the dead head of state that which was not granted to him in life.

Shimon Peres, who was named Prime Minister in the night of the assassination, made a grave mistake by not calling for new elections. Even the National Religious Party professed regrets at the time, and most likely the supporters of peace would have made huge gains. Instead, the situation escalated. After Rabin's assassination, the head of security services, Carmi Gillon, announced his resignation. To allow him one more accomplishment before the end of his career, Peres gave him permission to execute a high-level Palestinian terrorist. Abu Ayyash, "the engineer," had not initiated any suicide attacks for quite some time, but he had been closely watched by Israeli intelligence. A neighbor in Gaza, a collaborator who worked with Israeli intelligence, lured Abu Ayyash into a trap and his head was ripped off by a drone. The effect of this act was disastrous. Like the sorcerer's apprentice in Goethe's eponymous poem, the Israelis could not get rid of the spirits they had summoned. A whole generation of young Palestinians swore to revenge Abu Ayyash's death and to prove that they were just as powerful without their leader. Over the course of the year 1996, there were numerous, horrifying suicide bombings. Every week—usually on Sunday when many young soldiers were returning to their units—Palestinian terrorists blew up public buses, murdering dozens of innocent people. Only much too late did Arafat understand that he would have to halt these attacks, because they seriously weakened Israeli voices for peace.

To this day, the peace process has not recovered from Rabin's assassination, even if there have been various half-hearted attempts at peace over the past fifteen years. Half-hearted, because the Israeli side is not truly interested in a solution. I am almost too ashamed to remember the second peace talks at Camp David in 2000, where the Israeli delegation treated Arafat with complete disrespect. Prime Minister Ehud Barak, with his incomparable arrogance, destroyed all of the progress that had been made.

Nevertheless talks continued after the failed 2000 summit, although in the meantime there had been numerous clashes between Palestinians and Israeli military and police in the occupied territories—the so-called Second Intifada. Official delegations from both sides continued negotiating until the end of the year and even made good progress. But Barak's resignation and the election of Ariel Sharon as Prime Minister put an end to all talks.

US Senator George Mitchell, who had played a leading role in negotiating peace in the Northern Ireland conflict, was named Special Envoy for the Middle East by President George W. Bush. In June 2002, Bush introduced the "road map for peace," which had been designed by the UN, the United States, the European Union, and Russia, and which in the end produced no results. Not even the 2003 Geneva Initiative, in which leading Palestinians and Israelis worked out a detailed plan for a two-state solution, was able to revive the peace process. The initiative proposed founding a Palestinian state on the territory of the West Bank and the Gaza

Strip. The border to Israel would have been the "green line"—the ceasefire line of 1949. Around two percent of the West Bank, where the largest Israeli settlements were located, was to become part of Israel and the Palestinian state would be compensated by the same amount of land in the south. Since that left around 10,000 Israelis in settlements who would still have had to have been relocated, the Palestinians were to limit themselves to a symbolic right of return, the details of which remained a question of negotiation.

◆

I followed all of these efforts closely and with great hopes, while attempting in my private life to help to bring Israelis and Palestinians closer together. From 1998, I took part in a project in Ramallah initiated by Henning Niederhoff, the director of the newly founded Konrad Adenauer Foundation. He visited the Palestinian-ruled areas and attempted to initiate a trialogue between Israelis, Palestinians, and Germans. I shared his view that peace is only possible when all conflict parties understand the suffering of the other side. Israelis and Palestinians are both often far too fixated on their own respective narratives. Niederhoff was able to assemble a group of around fifteen participants. In the spring of 1998, we visited Israel's national memorial in remembrance of the Shoah, Yad Vashem. I was very impressed by how closely the Palestinian participants studied the exhibition, which tells the history of the persecution and execution of the European Jews by the Nazis in great detail. They were upset only by a photo of the Grand Mufti of Jerusalem next to a mass grave in the Bergen Belsen concentration camp. They felt that it gave the impression that the Grand Mufti carried responsibility for those deaths. They also criticized that the exhibition signs were only in Hebrew and English.

On a Friday in February 1999, we went with Palestinian historian Saleh Abdel Javad to Lifta and Zuba, Palestinian villages near Jerusalem that had been destroyed in 1948. He had researched the Nakba for many years at the Palestinian Birzeit University and he and his students had gathered witness testimony in the Palestinian refugee camps. 'Nakba' means catastrophe in Arabic and refers to the displacement of the Palestinian population of around four hundred and fifty villages in the Israeli part of the former British Mandate area. Many important discussions grew out of those visits. Yad Vashem, which for a time was trying to attract more Palestinian visitors, was interested in the results of our trialogue. When the new exhibition opened in the museum's new building, they had taken account of our critique. Today, there are Arabic audio guides available at Yad Vashem.

After Niederhoff returned to Germany and the Second Intifada broke out in 2000, the trialogue stagnated. Around the same time, Ziad Abu Zayyad invited me to join the editorial committee of the *Palestine-Israel Journal*, a magazine of approximately one hundred and twenty pages published two or three times a year. Founded in 1994 during the Oslo peace process, this English journal publishes in-depth reports and analyses in the areas of politics, economics, and culture to contribute to a better mutual understanding of the two peoples. Through a commitment to cooperation, this unusual Israeli-Palestinian coproduction has survived even the most difficult times of political tensions. In 2012, the magazine won the international media prize of the London Next Century Foundation for its "outstanding contribution to peace": The *Palestine-Israel Journal* "encourages peace and promotes rapprochement in this most difficult of arenas."

◆

Ever since Dave Kimche had unsuccessfully applied for the post of editor-in-chief of the *Jerusalem Post,* we had remained in contact. After he stepped down from all of his government positions in the late 1980s, he put his exceptional talent for getting along with people at the service of peace. Together with Egyptian, Palestinian, and Jordanian politicians, he founded the "Copenhagen Group," an international alliance supported by the Danish government. The group regularly hosted informal talks with Middle Eastern intellectuals in order to advance peace negotiations, which often stagnated. In 2005, he gave me a call: "What do you think about publishing an online Israeli-Palestinian newspaper?" The idea of working regularly again as an editor appealed to me and I agreed. We called our paper, which was written in English, *Partners for Peace* and very soon we found the ideal Palestinian co-editor, Ata Qaimary, a fifty-odd years old Palestinian journalist who also ran a translation agency. At our very first meeting, he told me why he was so vehement about peace with Israel. The path of terror, which he himself had taken in his youth as a member of the Palestinian Front for the Liberation of Palestine (PFLP), was a dead end. Qaimary had spent many years in Israeli prisons and had learned fluent Hebrew there before starting a family in Jerusalem and becoming a peace activist.

On our website, we published articles about Israeli-Palestinian projects and also opinion pieces from the Arab countries in favor of peace. In 2007, the Danish government stopped financing the project and we were unable to find sponsors who wanted to keep it running.

Today I can see that all of these efforts remained no more than individual initiatives. The peace process is stagnating because there are not enough people who are actively working towards rapprochement between Palestinians and Israelis. Oslo's interim solution seems to have become permanent. Living conditions for Palestinians, which were supposed to improve through these measures, have become significantly worse. When Gaza and the West Bank were under Israeli administration, the borders were open and up to 70,000 Palestinians from the Gaza Strip alone went to Israel every day to work. Today, the two countries are strictly separated. For long stretches of the border they are kept apart by an insurmountable wall. Its undeniable advantage—keeping Palestinian suicide bombers from entering Israel—has a downside that cements strife. The border makes space for many illegal Israeli settlements and cuts Palestinian villages off from their fields and orchards. The border wall, which would be around three hundred fifty kilometers long if it were straight, is today more than seven hundred kilometers long.

My whole life I have looked optimistically into the future, and despite all obstacles, I always believed the future of the state of Israel was secure. Today, I am more pessimistic than ever before. With Israel's current government, peace is further and further away. The Arab states are increasingly estranged from Israel, despite the formal existence of peace treaties with Egypt and Jordan, and further developments are difficult to predict after the Arab Spring.

Never before have nationalist and Orthodox parties had so much power in the Israeli government. Liberal and balanced voices are increasingly marginalized while large swaths of society hold racist and ultra-Orthodox views. The settlers' movement directly and indirectly dictates key government decisions. Even Supreme Court rulings that illegal settlements must be removed are often blatantly ignored. Rather than consider further disengagement, the government continues to approve new settlements on Palestinian land despite international condemnation. Palestinians crossing the border or otherwise dealing with Israeli authorities continue to be harassed and are often subject to humiliating controls. The decades-long occupation of Palestinian territory has brutalized and demoralized Israeli society. The message behind these breaches of international law is clear: The Israeli government is by no means willing to give up occupied territory and, despite lip service to the contrary, does not truly want peace. Yet the Palestinians, it seems to me, are today willing to make more concessions than ever before. In December 2011, at the Kreisky Forum in Vienna, I had the opportunity to hear an address by Mahmoud Abbas (Abu Mazen), head of the PLO and president of the Palestinian Authority.

To the surprise of his audience, Abbas conceded that "it was a mistake to reject and fight against the partition plan in 1947." Back then, the Palestinians would have received more than forty percent of the British Mandate area; today, they would be satisfied with the twenty-nine percent that remained after the 1949 ceasefire. However at least one-third of this territory is home to Jewish settlements—it is too little space for a group comprised of over four million people.

And unlike twenty years ago, today it is unclear whether a majority of Israelis would vote for a two-state solution. The Orthodox groups are more and more militant and the fanatical nationalist views of many new immigrants from the former Soviet Union, France, and even the United States are shaping the contours of Israeli society. Ever since the state of Israel was founded, the Chief Rabbinate has interfered in matters of civil society. Marriages can only be performed by a rabbi, qadi, or priest. The mayor of Nikosia in Cyprus is of course grateful for this state of affairs, because hundreds of secular Israeli couples accept his package deal every year—marriage in a civil ceremony at city hall including a champagne reception and an overnight stay in a newlywed suite.

Religious fanaticism is growing. Whoever breaks the Sabbath must now fear—and not only in Orthodox neighborhoods—that they will be attacked, either verbally or by the throwing of stones. In some cities or neighborhoods there is now even a strict separation of women and men on the sidewalks and in buses. As painful as it is for me to write this down: It is more and more difficult for me to feel at home in today's Israeli society.

◆

Pulling back from working for a daily paper has since 1990 also made it possible for me to engage, alongside my work for Israel, more closely with the country of my birth. I have taken many trips across the country and discovered, to my surprise and joy, that a new, much more open climate has sprung up after the Waldheim era.

At a reception hosted by the Austrian ambassador in June 2005, I was approached by his former chauffeur, Leo Luster. Leo himself had suffered greatly during the war and had survived both Theresienstadt and Auschwitz. He pulled me to the side to give me some friendly advice: "Ari, you're eighty years old now. You travel a lot and something could happen to you at any time. At least now give the Austrians the chance to take care of you. If I could do it, you can too." I decided on that very evening to again accept Austrian citizenship, as my brother had years earlier. A few weeks later, after

*Ari Rath and Stefanie Oswalt in Czernowitz, 2008.
Photo: Katrin Schulze.*

an expedited procedure, I received my citizenship certificate from the hands of Foreign Minister Ursula Plassnik.

I have also greatly expanded my contacts in Germany over the past twenty years. During numerous trips and in many seminars I have met many people who are actively and openly dealing with their country's Nazi past. Encounters with young people especially have given me particular joy. In the 2002/2003 winter semester at the University of Potsdam I taught a seminar on "The Fall of the Israeli Labor Movement"—a title that was provocative at the time, but in the meantime has been shown to have been prescient.

And as part of my efforts to learn more about my own family history, in 2008 I finally traveled to Ukraine to search for traces of my family in Galicia and Bukovina. All of my life I had wanted to say Kaddish at Omama Frimtsche's grave in Stryi, and also to find the house that she had left to my brother and me. I also wanted to visit Kolomyia, the city in which my father had been born, as well as Czernowitz, where family legend has it my uncle the famous rabbi had been active.

Shortly before midnight one evening in September 2008, accompanied by Stefanie Oswalt and a friend who acted as interpreter for us, I boarded the night train to Cracow. After an uncomfortable night in the sleeping car and a sparse breakfast at the train station restaurant, we continued on to the Polish-Ukrainian border, east of Przemyśl. The train stopped at a small station in the middle of nowhere, from where we walked a few hundred meters to an old Ukrainian bus. After a longer wait, the old rattletrap brought us to the Polish-Ukrainian border station and, after a three-hour drive over crumbling streets, eighty kilometers further, to Lviv/Lemberg. We took a taxi into the city center, over cobblestone streets with tram tracks running down the middle, which could have been in any Viennese suburb. Despite decades of Soviet occupation and Ukrainian rule, traces of the Habsburg monarchy are still very present in Lemberg. It was already evening when we arrived at the George Hotel, an imposing neo-Renaissance building that had been built in 1901 at the behest of Emperor Franz Joseph I. The wide grand staircase, flanked by pillars, is a remembrance of the former elegance that this hotel in the capitol of Austrian Galicia once exuded.

Before our journey, I had been in touch by email (in Yiddish) with Boris Dorfmann, an 83-year-old retired Jewish pharmacist who had often taken care of visitors from Israel. He gave his great-nephew the task of accompanying us during the week and helping us to trace my family history. Sasha had prepared for the task as if it were a Master's thesis and knew almost all of the historical and political dates pertinent to the sites on our itinerary. On the first day, we took a tour of historic Lemberg and went up to the Lviv High Castle which offers a one-of-a-kind view of the old city, the surrounding suburbs, and industrial areas. Instead of driving in the Mercedes we had been promised, on the next day we got into a rusty Lada station wagon for a trip of around one hundred kilometers to Stryi, Kolomyia, Drohobycz, and Czernowitz—place names that I had been hearing since my childhood.

The small one-story houses with wrought-iron balconies that give the city of Stryi its character were exactly as I'd imagined them. I was greatly disappointed however that we were unable to find Kraszewskiego Street, where Omama Frimtsche's house had been located; the Ukrainians had renamed all the streets. Neither was I able to fulfill my wish to say Kaddish at her grave. Under Soviet rule, the Ukrainians had razed the Jewish cemetery and put up a modern industrial park on the site. They cut up the gravestones to use as cobblestones and with a large bone mill had ground up the remaining skeletons to use as fertilizer. Not even the Nazis had thought up such horrific treatment of Jewish cemeteries.

Neither were there any remnants of the small Jewish cemetery in the old city, except for a monument in remembrance of the rabbinical dynasty that had been famous in Stryi in the Middle Ages. I took my small black Hebrew siddur from my breast pocket and prayed there for the remembrance and salvation of my Omama Frimtsche and my mother, Laura.

The only proof that the majority of Stryi's population had once been Jewish is the huge ruins of the former synagogue, whose four-meter high walls reach up to the sky, overgrown by trees and shrubs. Black graffiti guides one along the path to the ruins: swastikas and inflammatory antisemitic slogans in Ukrainian.

We only stayed a short time in Kolomyia, where my father and my uncle Jakob were born. A wealthy Jewish computer salesman who spends part of the year in China was waiting for us in the synagogue—the only one remaining of what had once been fifty in the city. He had rebuilt the shul completely with his own money.

Finally, I celebrated Rosh Hashanah, the Jewish new year, in Czernowitz, the capitol of former Bukovina. Everywhere in the city center, construction workers and craftspeople were busy improving the city's appearance for the 2012 European Cup. Even in the enormous Jewish cemetery, which holds thousands of graves that survived the war, dozens of stonemasons were working to carefully restore the headstones. In the evening, I went to the one active synagogue, where to my surprise many young men were praying. A quick glance into the siddur of the man next to me informed me that they were reading their Hebrew prayers in Ukrainian transliteration, since they could not read Hebrew. After the service, everyone received a glass of Slivovitz and we drank to the health of the new year; the rabbi greeted me warmly as a guest from Jerusalem.

I spent ten days in Warsaw and Berlin and returned to Jerusalem; sad because I had not been able to find any traces of my family and exhausted from the hardships of the journey. It was my final good-bye to the lost world of my parents.

In contrast, I had been able to reconnect to my Viennese roots. In 2010, I went to Austria for rehab to recover from the aftermath of a physical malaise. A planned stay of a few weeks in a clinic turned into months. In the meantime, I spend part of every year in the city of my birth. Only three years ago, I would never have believed that

Ari and Meshulam in their parent's apartment on Porzellangasse in Vienna, 2000.

this might one day feel like a possibility. I have been overwhelmed by the many warm people I have met in this time, who go out of their way to be helpful. I have also made many new friends. Some people I might have met eighty years beforehand, yet only in October 2009 did I meet Eric Pleskow, the successful American film producer and president of the Viennale, the Vienna film festival. Pleskow, also born in April 1924 in Vienna, grew up very near me on the Porzellangasse. It may have been due to our now negligible but then decisive age difference of eight months that we never met earlier. In August 1939, he and his family managed to flee Austria at the very last minute. An autodidact, in the United States he began working

The Porzellangasse Boys: Ari and Eric Pleskow in Vienna, 2011.

as a filmmaker's assistant at the age of fifteen. From 1951, he was responsible for European distribution at United Artists and began to produce his own films, including *One Flew Over the Cuckoo's Nest* and *The Silence of the Lambs*. His productions have won a total of fourteen Oscars. A film was shot about our late encounter, *Die Porzellangassenbuben* (the Porzellangasse Boys) and was broadcast by ORF on Austrian public television.

It gives me great satisfaction to see that there is a growing interest in confronting the Nazi past in today's Austria. There is also an increase of interest in Jewish and Israeli life and culture. Vienna has had a Jewish Museum for over twenty years, since 2009 the Hamakom Theater has been dedicated to Jewish culture and remembrance, and there is an annual Jewish film festival—hardly a week goes by without at least one high-level Jewish-themed event. The official Jewish Community has around nine thousand members and runs an elementary school, a middle school, and the Hakoah sports club. Since 2011, the Jewish Community has hosted the European Maccabi Games, attended by two thousand international athletes. Nevertheless, the shadows of the past are always present. The right-wing populist Freedom Party of Austria (FPÖ) is the third-largest party in the country and growing. Although they spew racist ideas, today they would garner twenty-five percent of the vote. Since media mirrors society, I am also worried by the *Kronenzeitung* phenomenon. The tabloid with xenophobic undertones is read by four million people daily, half of the Austrian population. Their reporting is sensationalist, superficial, and often also anti-European. In Vienna today, it is possible for the owner of a well-known Austrian retail chain to deny permission to put up a memorial plaque on one of his houses for Aaron Menczer, a Jewish educator murdered in Auschwitz, with the argument that he does not want his house to become a target for vandalism. The fact that dueling fraternities (*schlagende Burschenschaften*) are able to hold a ball at the Hofburg on Holocaust Memorial Day is in my eyes an intolerable provocation, and I will continue to support upright democratic forces that are working against such disgraces.

Among the highlights of my new life in Vienna is without a doubt having been awarded the Grand Decoration of Honor for Services to the Republic of Austria in parliament on November 29, 2011 by the president of the National Council of Austria, Barbara Prammer. Former Federal Chancellor Franz Vranitzky gave the main speech. This honor touched me deeply. At the same time I am pained, as I expressed in my acceptance speech, that I am one of very few who remain in contrast to those who were never granted an opportunity to be of service to Austria. How many thousands of

Austrian Jews of my generation, and our parents' generation, would have been more than happy to help our country achieve fame and fortune had they been given the chance?

I have experienced so many things that I had once believed impossible. My greatest wish is that I might still see my homeland dedicate itself to peace.

Acknowledgements

"Now you have the time to write down the story of your life." Those words were written on a note that my friend Peter Galliner slipped under my hotel room door in Moscow in 1989, in lieu of a good-bye. It would be another twenty years before they became true.

I have many people to thank for helping this book to see the light of day. First and foremost my publisher Herbert Ohrlinger for his trust, his patience, and his personal commitment. I am particularly honored that he edited the first chapter of the book himself, which I interpret as an expression of his esteem. I am also deeply grateful to Brigitte Hilzensauer, who brought thoughtfulness and sensitivity to the completion of the editing process.

I would like to thank the Future Fund of the Republic of Austria, in particular Dr. Kurt Scholz and Prof. Herwig Hösele as well as Anita Dumfahrt, for the generous support of Stefanie Oswalt's work.

Gertraud Auer Borea championed the project from the beginning with great enthusiasm and provided important contacts.

Without the generosity of Orit Zaslavsky, Carmel Zamir, David Brauner, and Avremel Israeli we could not have illustrated the book. Special thanks are due to Jenny Nash, who went to great lengths to find the letter that I wrote to her father from aboard the *Galilea* on November 2, 1938 in the name of our Beserlpark gang.

Judy Siegel-Itzkowich, Alexander Zvielli, and Louise Loveall from the *Jerusalem Post* were always ready to support the project with information and research.

Thank you also to Renata Schmidtkunz, Nadja Fratzl-Zelman and Peter Fratzl, Celia Isabel Gaissert, and Thea Radt, who graciously hosted us in Vienna, Berlin, and Israel. Benjamin Kaufmann was always there to help with computer problems, which I greatly appreciated.

This book never would have been written without the enthusiasm and tenacious labor of my co-author, Stefanie Oswalt. For many years she recorded long conversations with me and meticulously collected documents about my life. Her Nigerian name, Ikerimma—"a good thing is indestructible"—became our project's motto.

I would also like to express my personal gratitude to Philipp Oswalt and to Stefanie's father, Dieter Brauer. Without their support and understanding, this project would not have been possible: both of them cared for Stefanie's children during the long months in which we worked together in Vienna and Berlin, and while Stefanie conducted research in Israel.

This book is dedicated to my mother Laura, but also to the rest of my family: my deceased father Josef, my brother Meshulam and his wife Hannah, my deceased sister Henny and my brother-in-law Amitai, my nieces Orit and Carmel, and my great nieces and nephews Oren, Guy, Noga, Eden, Tal, and Ran, as well as my great-great nephew Yanai and his mother, Tali—and Paul, David, and Yael Oswalt.

Ari Rath, June 2012

Editorial Note

The idea for this book is almost as old as my friendship with Ari Rath, which began on a hot summer afternoon in 1993 in Tel Aviv, in the cool seminar rooms of the Dan Panorama Hotel, where Ari was giving an introduction to the Israel-Palestine conflict for thirty participants of an educational trip organized by the Federal Agency for Civic Education. I had just finished my Master's in History and German Studies in Munich and had gone on that trip before beginning a doctoral researcher position in Potsdam at the Moses Mendelssohn Center for European-Jewish Studies. I knew Israel from the months that I had spent on a kibbutz in 1987, I had studied the country's history and German-Jewish relations at university, and I was looking forward to meeting Israeli and Palestinian intellectuals and broadening my knowledge. I was greatly impressed by the encounter with Ari—a "political consultant" according to his card. His knowledge and his anecdotes seemed to be boundless; his humor and his Austrian charm immediately piqued my curiosity. A few days after his workshop, we met at a reception and spent the entire evening talking. Ari proposed that he visit me in Germany so that we could continue our conversation and a few months later, he actually showed up, passing through as always.

Since then, we have met regularly every few months: in Munich, Rotterdam, Potsdam, Berlin, and Jerusalem. We have gone on trips together: to Cologne and Vienna, but also more than once across Israel. In 2008, I accompanied him on his search for traces of his family in Ukraine.

In 1998, I asked Ari when he was finally going to write a memoir. "You're not the first person who's asked that question," he answered, but he had neither the time nor the patience. He immediately agreed when I proposed supporting him in the project. I began collecting articles that Ari had written in various German and Austrian newspapers, and reports and documentaries about him. I knew that he was never in one place for longer than a few days, but whenever and wherever we met, he told me stories from his life. Between 2002 and 2010, we collected around forty hours of audiotapes in this way, covering the years from his birth to the early 1980s. In 2005, the Moses Mendelssohn Center in Potsdam commissioned an anthology of his articles and essays entitled *Auf dem Weg zum Frieden* (On the Way to Peace). Our travels through Ukraine in 2008 were documented in a radio feature for Berlin-Brandenburg public radio.

Not until 2011, when Ari decided to live part-time in Austria, did we have a realistic chance of concluding the biography project, especially since the Zsolnay Verlag expressed interest in publishing the memoir and the Future Fund of the Republic of Austria promised financial support.

This book then grew out of in-depth conversations; the transcripts of our earlier conversations provided our starting point. Together, we went through them, rewording and supplementing Ari's memories with passages from some of his many articles. Many of the book's passages Ari wrote himself, others he dictated.

Although German is his mother tongue, for most of his life

Ari has spoken Hebrew, and Hebrew is the language that connects him to the people with whom he is closest. As a journalist, he wrote almost exclusively in English, only in the years after leaving the *Jerusalem Post* did he also publish as a German author. At first, returning to the German language for this book was a challenge. However the greatest challenge this book presented was the constant shifts in perspective. All of his life, Ari was a close observer of political and historical events—and of his own environment—then giving as objective a picture of these events as possible in his journalism. He very seldom wrote about his personal experiences. But in this book, he himself is the main subject, it is about *his* perspective on historical events and figures. It was not always easy to tease out these individual, sometimes painful, memories from his almost limitless store of anecdotes. We often wrangled over individual episodes—often it took days or even weeks for them to find the form that they have now taken in this book.

Stefanie Oswalt, June 2012

Afterword to the English Edition

The German edition of *Ari Means Lion* was published by Paul Zsolnay in May 2012. The media echo and the book launch in Vienna's Hofburg, attended by former Austrian President Heinz Fischer, were early signs that its publication was the start of yet another eventful chapter in the life of Ari Rath. And in fact, he toured with the book throughout Austria and Germany. Excerpts from the text were integrated into a theater production, *Die letzten Zeugen* (Last Witnesses) that caused a furor in the 2013/14 season of the Vienna Burgtheater. Directed by Doron Rabinovici and Matthias Hartmann, the play was a multi-layered portrait of the persecution of Austrian citizens in the Nazi era. The survivors portrayed sat on stage live during the production and could directly address the audience after the play. Ari Rath used those opportunities to speak words of warning. In February 2015 in Frankfurt, for example, he admonished:

> We, the survivors, stand here before you today in the evening of our lives, the last witnesses of the horrifying atrocities of the murderous Nazi regime. … Austrian Chancellor Franz Vranitzky, during his official visit to Jerusalem in 1993, wrote the following in the guest book of the Shoah memorial Yad Vashem: "The danger is not over yet—We

Federal President of Germany, Joachim Gauck and Ari in Dessau, Germany, 2014. Photo: Stefanie Oswalt.

must remain alert." That sentence sadly still holds true today, more than ever before.

On May 12, 2015, German Federal President Joachim Gauck publicly acknowledged Ari Rath's role as a voice of caution and a bridge-builder when he spoke on the occasion of the fiftieth anniversary of German-Israeli relations. Gauck opened his speech by honoring "the great Israeli journalist" who did so much to foster understanding between Israelis and Germans after the war and the Shoah. The willingness of people like Rath to trust Germans made possible the "miracle" of mutual relations—even friendships—after the Shoah.

Ari Rath enjoyed the attention and recognition that he received during his twilight years. He traveled to all corners of Austria, spoke at schools and conferences, gave interviews, and often also wrote articles and op-eds on the situation in Israel. Privately, he continued to visit friends and family across the globe even at a very old age. Thanks to his good health and the help of many devoted friends, he had no trouble navigating the malaise of old age until, on a trip to Israel in 2016, he became very ill and never really recovered.

◆

One week after his ninety-second birthday, Ari Rath died in Vienna General Hospital, surrounded until the end by political and personal associates, friends, and family. Three days later, in a ceremony attended by President of the Austrian National Council Doris Bures, he was buried in Kibbutz Giv'at Ha'Shlosha near Petah Tikva in the same cemetery as his brother Meshulam. Many years earlier, he had stipulated that he was by no means to be buried in the Viennese cemetery where his mother's grave stood. Although he was in Vienna often in his later years, Ari Rath identified as an Israeli to the end—the Jewish state was his home. His epitaph reads, in Hebrew and in English: "legendary journalist, pursuer of peace, the best friend ever."

◆

A little less than two weeks later, there was a memorial for Ari Rath in Vienna, at the Akademietheater. The former Austrian president, Heinz Fischer, and the former federal chancellor, Franz Vranitzky, praised the deceased as their friend and counselor, and as a builder of bridges, both in the Middle East and between Israel and post-war Austria. Writer and historian Doron Rabinovici wrote in his obituary:

> Ari was not silent in the face of racism. He knew that there is no better security than peace. He recognized that there can be no humane society at the cost of Jewish life, but also no Jewish self-determination at the cost of human rights. He understood that any nation that oppresses another can never be free. No piece of land is more holy than the life of the people on it. No nation is worth the cost of subjugating the population. ... He would have spoken up against populist oafs and authoritarian tyrants.

The events have also led Austrian journalist Alexandra Föderl-Schmid, winner of the Ari Rath Prize for Critical Journalism that was founded privately from circles close to the Viennese Kreisky Forum, to look back at Ari Rath's life work. Once co-editor of the *Standard* in Austria and now in the editorial team of the German daily *Süddeutsche Zeitung*, the former Israel correspondent remembered in summer 2023:

> Just a few days before his death, Ari Rath asked what Benjamin Netanyahu was doing in Israeli and what was going on with the government there. What would he say now, in light of the most right-wing government that Israel ever had? With a right-wing extremist as Prime Minister who sits not only in the government, but also as a defendant in front of a judge. He would certainly worry about its meaning for peace with the Palestinians and its impact on a the peace process, which has stalled completely. He was also always interested in developments in Austria; the rise of the FPÖ especially worried

him—and currently they're leading in the polls. We'd definitely have a lot to talk about.

Israeli journalist Noa Landau, editor of the English edition of *Haaretz* and 2023 recipient of the Ari Rath Prize, saw the situation in Israel in the beginning of 2023 as the result of developments whose first stirrings could be seen in the unfriendly dismissal of Ari Rath from the *Jerusalem Post:*

> He was the first victim of the first hostile takeover of an Israeli media outlet, designed to forcibly change its politics in order to promote a more nationalist agenda that aligns with the ruling party and its leaders. This major crossroad in Ari's professional journey also symbolizes in many ways the first out of many red flags, signaling that Israel was about to face a pivotal clash between its Jewish, nationalist, identity and those who envision it as a more liberal, democratic country.

Everyone who has ever had anything to do with Ari Rath, who has read his texts or heard his lectures, knows that he belonged to the latter group that desired a future in peace above all.

The final work on the translation of this memoir comes at a time in which Ari Rath's analyses and his political legacy have taken on dramatic relevance. Israel's domestic crises have weakened the country to the point of existential danger. In this situation, on October 7, 2023, the Islamist terrorist organization Hamas attacked the south of Israel from Gaza. On just one day, Hamas terrorists murdered over 1200 Israelis, most of them civilians, as well as resident workers from other nations. They also abducted over 250 hostages to Gaza—including children, women, and seniors. At the time of this Afterword only 123 hostages have been released. Rocket attacks from Gaza and from Hezbollah forces in Lebanon have been incessant ever since, and the population of Israel is under shock, with hundreds of thousands internally displaced. Many see Israel's very existence more at risk than ever before in its 75-year history. In the meantime, Israel is exercising its right to self-defense, though criticized and brought before the International Court of Justice in the Hague to justify its military campaign. Many Israelis, along with others around the world, feel that the violence has spiraled out of control. Israelis are desperately concerned about the remaining hostages. On the Palestinian side, the number of victims is meanwhile in the tens of thousands with thousands still missing; there, too, many civilians have been killed, and Gaza is experiencing a humanitarian crisis. The Middle East—and with it the world—is in turmoil.

How would Ari Rath have reacted to this situation? A man who was forced to flee from Austria and who put down roots in Palestine. Who helped build up and loved the land of Israel—despite all of his critique and sometimes disappointment: in Israel he felt safe.

It is unclear how the situation will develop, and it is too early for analyses and prognoses. What is clear, is that Ari Rath's voice is missing. His analytical acumen, his decades of political and journalistic experience. His wisdom and his humanity. His ability to listen, to make sense of events, to build bridges. His love of humankind and his unwavering optimism.

Stefanie Oswalt, Berlin, February 2024

Index of Names

Abbas, Mahmoud, President of the Palestinian Authority 351, 361
Abdel Javad, Saleh 358
Abed, cemetery caretaker 252
Abu Salef, Mahmoud 233 f.
Abu Zayyad, Ziad 349, 358
Adelson, Sheldon 323
Adenauer, Konrad, Chancellor of Germany 13, 159 f., 162 ff. 196 ff., 206 ff., 218, 357
Adenauer, Konrad (grandson) 165
Agranat, Shimon 278, 281
Agron (Agronsky), Gershon 149 ff., 238
Alaa, Abu 350
al-Assad, Hafez, President of Syria 246, 279
Alfred, chauffeur 34, 41 f.
Allende, Beatriz 263
Allende, Maria Isabel 263
Allende, Salvador, President of Chile 257 ff., 262 f., 265
Alterman, Nathan 222
Andersson, Sten 349
Anni, nursemaid 41
Arafat, Yasser 137, 233, 236, 307, 311, 350 ff., 356

Aran, Clara 155
Ardon, Yakov 157
Arens, Moshe 347
Argov, Shlomo 312
Assousa, George 232
Atherton, Alfred (Roy) 297 f.
Attlee, Clement 83
Ayyash, Abu (Yahya) 355

Bach, Gabriel 173
Bachir, Takhsin 280
Baharav, Shike 92
Bahr, Egon 255
Bandoli, Colonel 264 f.
Bar-Lev, Haim 85
Barak, Ehud, Prime Minister of Israel 224, 305, 317, 327, 356
Barkat, Reuven 148
Bassiouni, Mohammed 312, 316
Bauch, Luise 175
Bavli, Sarah 92
Becker, Aron 205
Begin, Menachem, Prime Minister of Israel 204, 206, 213 f., 225, 288, 290, 292 ff., 308, 313 ff., 317, 319, 321, 331
Ben-Arzi, Ephraim 117, 126

Ben-David, Chaim 164
Ben-Dor, Lea 151 f., 157, 205 f., 285
Ben-Eliezer, Fuad 285
Ben-Elissar, Eliyahu 290, 294
Ben-Gurion, Amos 201
Ben-Gurion, David, Prime Minister of Israel 12, 45, 52, 78 ff., 83, 86 f., 109, 112, 114 f., 117, 137 f., 141, 148, 157 ff., 171, 175 ff., 190 ff., *191*, 218, 221, 288, *318*, 323
Ben-Gurion, Mary 201
Ben-Gurion, Paula 191 f., 195, 197 f., 200, 204
Ben-Jair, Elazar 253
Ben-Natan, Asher (Arthur) 117 f., 120, 124, 197 f.
Bergel, Bernd 57
Berger, Beate 54
Bergson, Peter 112
Bernstein, Leonard 332
Besser, Joachim 175
Bevin, Ernest 83, 111
Birrenbach, Ida 197
Birrenbach, Kurt 196 f.
Black, Conrad 149
Blesson, Marie 23 f., 26
Blitzer, Wolf 299
Bloch, Adolpho 266, 268 f.
Blumenfeld, Erich 211
Brandt, Willy, Chancellor of Germany 213, 252 ff.
Brenner, Josef Chaim 59
Brentano, Heinrich von 162, 164
Breslau, Dave 102
Breslau, Rose 102 f.
Brilliant, Moshe 151

Brod, Max 244
Bronfman, Edgar 332
Bronka, cow stall director 74
Buber, Martin 57, 87
Burg, Joseph 302
Bush, George H. W., U.S. President 214
Bush, George W., U.S. President 356
Bushinsky, Jay 101

Calvary, Moses 64
Carstens, Karl, President of Germany 331
Carter, Jimmy, U.S. President 297 ff.
Chavkin, Hadassah 58
Christian, Gerold 331 ff.
Churchill, Randolph 220 f.
Churchill, Winston, Prime Minister of the United Kingdom 83, 220
Churchill, Winston (grandson) 223 f., 226
Clinton, Bill, U.S. President 161, 352, 354
Cohen, Evie 100
Cramer, Ernst 217 f.
Crossman, Richard 111

Dayan, Moshe 12, 67 f., 80, 116, 130 ff., 141, 147, 177, 193, 195, 199, 206, 225 f., 229, 236 f., 247, 269 f., 274 ff., 281 f., 288, 292, 295 f., 299, 302
Dayan, Ruth 196
de Gaulle, Charles, President of France 224
Dickie, Joan 200 f.

Diepgen, Eberhard 345
Dimitros, Ifrach 180 f.
Dinitz, Simcha 275
Dissenchik, Arie 167
Dollfuss, Engelbert, Chancellor of Austria 28 f.
Dorfmann, Boris 364
Dreiblatt, Joel 73
Dubček, Alexander 241
Dulles, John Foster 158

Eban, Abba 224, 244 f., 280, 305
Eckardt, Felix von 163 f.
Eckert, Bertl 70 f.
Eichmann, Adolf 45 f., 171 ff.
Einstein, Arik 241 f.
Eisendraht, Saul 260
Eisenhower, Dwight D., U.S. President 160 f.
Eisenstein, Family 61
El-Baz, Osama 297 f.
Elazar, David (Dado) 229, 281
Eldar, Akiva 239
el-Gamasy, Mohamed Abdel Ghani 295
Eliav, Lova 278
Elitzur, Michael 183 f., 330
Elon, Amos 166
Elyashiv, Vera 175
Embacher, Helga 204
Epstein, Ilse (Alizah) 61 f., 65
Epstein, Jehuda 61
Erhard, Ludwig, Chancellor of Germany 196
Erlander, Tage, Prime Minister of Sweden 137

Eshkol, Levi, Prime Minister of Israel 81, 176 ff., 187, 191, 193, 195, 197, 205, 207, 222, 224 f., 229, 240 f.
Evron, Eppi 300

Fahmi, Ismail 295
Faisal, King of Saudi Arabia 325
Farouk, King of Egypt 141
Federmann, Micky 256
Feinberg, Abe 117
Fiedler, Yakov 157
Figl, Leopold, Chancellor of Austria 122 f.
Flavius Josephus 253
Franz Joseph I., Emperor of Austria 364
Freij, Elias 235 f.
Frenkel, Erwin 152, 285 f., 339 f., 344
Fried, Bassia 16, 32, 34, 256
Fried, Dolly 16 ff., 32, 34 f., 256
Fried, Jakob 15 ff., *16*, 32, 34, 95, 255 ff., 259, 261, 366
Fried, Lore 16, 32, 34 f., 259, 261
Friedberg-Gross, Adele 30
Friedler, Jakob 314
Frimtsche, Omama 19, 21 f., *25*, 30 f., 33, 42, 47 f., 61, 63, 94, 268, 363 f., 365

Galili, Israel 224
Galliner, Peter 342
Gandhi, Indira 13, 186 f.
Gawad, Mohammed 291 f.
Gemayel, Bachir, President of Lebanon 315 f.

Genscher, Hans-Dietrich 311
Gewirzman (-Rath), Dorothy 139 f., 144 f., 152 ff., 158 f., 167 f.
Gewirzman, Fanny 153
Gewirzman, Marilyn 139, 144
Gewirzman, Maurice 138, 144, 153 f.
Gibli, Binyamin 176
Gillon, Carmi 355
Globke, Hans 210
Glück, Wolfgang 336
Goebbels, Joseph 345
Goell, Yossi 146 ff.
Goldberger, "Kuckie" 96
Goldberger (Family) 41, 96
Goldberger, Jane 96Goldman, Ralph 110
Goldmann, Nahum 219
Gonzalez, Felipe 308
Gorbachev, Mikhail, President of the Soviet Union 342
Gore, Al, senator 161
Gorenstein, Arthur (Artie) 99 f., 103
Gromyko, Andrei 113 f., 279 f.
Gronemann, Sami 57
Gross, Chaskel 30
Gross, Lalla 30
Gross, Mira 30
Grün, Avigdor 193
Grynszpan, Herschel 50
Guillaume, Günter 254
Gump, Hans Peter 39
Gupta, Oberst 184, 186
Gur, Motta 228
Gysi, Gregor 346

Hadar, Mary 269
Haile Selassie, Emperor of Ethiopia 181 f.
Halonen, Anneli 303 ff., 307, 328, 343 f.
Hamad, Jamil 310
Hansen, Niels 198
Harman, Avraham 160, 162, 166
Hase, Karl-Günther von 210
Hauer, Maria 31, 305
Hausner, Gideon 174
Helmer, Oskar 123
Herter, Christian 161
Herzl, Theodor 61, 150
Herzog, Chaim, President of Israel 21, 199, 269, 328
Herzog, Yaakov 162, 164, 207
Herzog, Yitzhak Halevy 21, 87
Hillel, Shlomo 248
Hitler, Adolf, Chancellor of Nazi Germany 16, 26, 35 ff., 42, 50, 54, 74, 79, 122, 160, 218, 241, 328, 337, 343
Hobeika, Eli 317
Holst, Johan Jørgen 350 f.
Hübner, Judith 291
Hussein, King of Jordan 225, 228, 230, 270, 273, 276, 288, 311, 324, 352
Hussein, Saddam, Prime Minister of Iraq 214, 350
Husseini, Abdul Kader el 349
Husseini, Faisal 349

Innitzer, Theodor 122
Israeli, Avremel 134

Index of Names

Jabotinsky, Vladimir 78, 112
Jhirad, Ellis 187 f.
Jick, Leon 99 f., 102
Johnson, Lyndon B., U.S. President 224
Jordan, Hamilton 300
Jung, Carl Gustav 65
Jürgens, Curt 118
Juul, Mona 351

Kafka, Franz 244
Kaltenbrunner, Ernst 218
Kamal, Ibrahim 295
Kashdan, Bruce 315
Katznelson, Berl 70, 72 f., 80
Kennen, Sy 113
Kenyatta, Jomo 180
Kessari, Itzik 134
Kimche, Dave 285, 359
Kissinger, Henry 13, 274 ff., 278 f., 283 ff.
Kital, Shlomo 296 f.
Klein, Hannes 204
Kohl, Helmut, Chancellor of Germany 214, 346 f.
Kollek, Tamar 216
Kollek, Teddy, Mayor of Jerusalem 12, 22, 45, 51, 114 ff., *115*, 162, 165, 177, 190, 192, 199, 214 ff., 234 ff., 292, 310, 348
Korczak, Janusz 47
Korn, Laura 25
Kreisky, Bruno, Chancellor of Austria 13, 137, 267, 306 ff., 361, 380
Kreisky, Paul 307, 309
Kreisky, Peter 310

Lamdan, Neville 315
Landor, David 190
Lapid, Tommy 255 f.
La Pira, Giorgio 147
Lavon, Pinchas 83, 175 f., 193, 221
Léauté, Jacques 185
Legum, Colin 280
Lesseps, Ferdinand de 296
Letelier, Orlando 258
Levi, Yehuda 339 f., 344
Levin, Chananya 290 f.
Lewin, Daniel Kurt 123
Lewis, Sam 301
Liebermann, Dora 94 f.
Liebermann, Josi 38
Liebermann, Rita (Henriette) 30 ff., 34, 38, 43 f., 62, *92*, 93 ff., 121, 250
Liebermann, Tamara 32 f.
Lolik, counsellor 53
Lubianiker, Pinchas *see* Lavon
Lurie, Jesse Zel 158
Lurie, Ted 146 ff., 158 f., 167 ff., 179, 190, 200, 205, 220 f., 226, 231 f., 234 f., 238, 266 f., 279, 285
Lurie, Zilla 220 f.
Luster, Leo 362
Lutzky (-Meir), Hannah 107 ff.

Magnes, Judah Leon 87
Malik, Adam 244 f.
Marcuse, Herbert 328
Masaryk, Jan 113
Masaryk, Tomáš G., President of Czechoslovakia 113
Mboya, Thomas 179 f.
Mehta, Zubin 229

Meir, Golda, Prime Minister of Israel 12, 108 ff., 147, 151, 179, 182, 189, 197, 201, 205, 210 f., 237, 240 f., 252, 254, 267, 270, 275, 277 f., 281 f., 292, 295, 307
Meir, Meira 109
Meir, Menachem 108 f.
Menczel, Mrs. 49
Menczer, Aron 46 f., 53, 369
Mercsanits, Renate 28
Merkel, Angela, Chancellor of Germany 346
Meroz, Jochanan 327 f.
Meroz, Vicky 327 f.
Meyer, Armin 166
Milson, Menachem 311
Mishcon, Victor, Lord 288
Mitchell, George 356
Mizzi, cook and housekeeper 21, 40
Modak, Frida 258, 265
Morpurgo, Channah 69
Morpurgo, Jehuda 69
Moses, Yochanan 138 f.
Mubarak, Hosni 295, 297
Myerson, Golda *see* Golda Meir

Nagel, Willy 139
Nasser, Gamal Abdel, President of Egypt 141, 222 f., 246
Navon, Yitzhak, President of Israel 82, 148, 162, 165, 177, 190, 192, 199, *199*, 317 f.
Neeman, Adi 319
Neeman, Amitai 272
Nehru, Jawaharlal, Prime Minister of India 186 f.

Netanyahu, Benjamin, Prime Minister of Israel 323
Neumann, Erich 65
Neumann, Julia 65 f., 89
Niederhoff, Henning 357 f.
Nusseibeh, Anwar 231 ff.
Nyerere, Julius, President of Tanzania 180

Obote, Apollo Milton, President of Uganda 180
Ofner, Francis 205 f.
Ohnesorg, Benno 217
Olmert, Ehud, Prime Minister of Israel 238
Oren, Mordechai 131 f.
Oron, Benni 263

Pai, Nath 136
Palach, Jan 243
Palme, Joachim 137
Palme, Olof 13, 136 f., 308
Papánek, Ján 114
Pauls, Rolf Friedemann 197 f., 208
Pech, Maria 121 f.
Pech, Walter 121 f.
Peled, Nathan 274
Peres, Shimon, Prime Minister of Israel and President of Israel 12, 81, *82*, 147, 177, 190, 193, 196, 199, 236, 254, 282 f., 343, 350 f., 355
Peres, Yochanan 349
Perón, Juan, President of Argentina 266
Perski, Shimon *see* Shimon Peres

Index of Names

Pichler, architect 16 f.
Pinkus, Louis 205
Pinnes, Dan 113 f.
Plassnik, Ursula 363
Pleskow, Eric 367, *368*
Pollak, Hans 37
Pontecorvo, Schmuel 69
Prammer, Barbara 369
Premchand, General 186
Premchand, Preminda 186, 188
Preminger, Erich (Eli) 53
Primakov, Yevgeny 343
Primor, Avi 329

Qaimary, Ata 359
Qualtinger, Helmut 330

Rabin, Yitzhak, Prime Minister of Israel 12, 85, 215, 222, 229, 236, 241, 282 f., 285, 305, 329, 350 ff.
Rabinowitz, Malka 168 f.
Radler, David 149, 339 f.
Rappoport, Asariah 222
Rath, Ernst Eduard vom 50
Rath, Henny 40, 62, *92*, 93, 95, 97 f., 129, 144, 272, 319, 354
Rath, Josef 9, 14 f., *16*, 20 ff., 30 ff., 38, 40 ff., 47, 50, 62 f., 65 f., *92*, 93 ff., 116, 121, 144, 154, 159, 219, 249 ff., 256, 273, 305, 364, 366
Rath, Laura 9, 14, 17 ff., 25, 30 ff., 64 ff., 118, 120, 250, 252, 365
Rath, Malcia 31
Rath, Meshulam (Maximilian) 9, 15, 17, *18*, 20, 23, 27, 29, 31, 33, 38, 40 ff., 46, 49, 52 f., 66, 90, *92*, 93 f., 96, 110, 129, 252, 256, 263 f., 270, 305, *367*, 379
Rath, Meshulam, Rabbi 20 f., 31, 153 f.
Rath, Moses 21
Rath, Orit 129
Rath, Surka 20, 31, 154
Rauch-Kallat, Maria 336
Ravenna, Nurit 69
Renen, Ariel 156
Reuel, Yaacov 152
Røed Larsen, Terje 351
Rogoff, Florie 110
Rommel, Erwin 66 ff.
Roosevelt, Franklin D., U.S. President 95
Rosenfeld, Shalom 166 f., 232 f.
Rosenne, Meir 294
Rothberg, Roy 132
Rothschild, Dave 169
Rotkopf, Menachem 92
Rottenberg, Federico 266
Rubinstein, Amnon 278
Rubinstein, Arthur 222

Sabbath, Josef 34
Sadat, Anwar, President of Egypt 13, 183, 246 f., 278, 280, 288 ff., *289*, 321
Safadi, Anan 234 f., 279, 289, 291, 293 f.
Sapir, Pinchas 195
Savir, Zvi 97
Schier-Gribowsky, Peter 175
Schiff, Seev 179

Schmidt, Helmut, Chancellor of Germany 210 ff.
Schnitzler, Arthur 40
Schnur, Wolfgang 346
Schocken, Gershom 168, 322 f.
Schocken, Salman 322
Schubert, Franz 23
Schuschnigg, Kurt von, Chancellor of Austria 28 f., 36 ff.
Schwarz, Arthur Zacharias 22, 51
Selbach, Josef-Wilhelm 164 f., 207
Sermonetta, Baruch "Chichio" 69
Seyss-Inquart, Arthur, Chancellor of Austria 36, 38, 218
Shagrir, Micha 272
Shalev, Mordechai 275
Shamir, Yitzhak, Prime Minister of Israel 331, 347
Shapira, Yaakov Shimshon 176
Sharett, Jakov 87
Sharett (Shertok), Moshe, Prime Minister of Israel 80, 87, 109, 117, 131, 138, 151, 177
Sharon, Ariel, Prime Minister of Israel 204, 241, 313 ff., 319, 356
Shasar, Salman, President of Israel 80
Shastri, Bahadur, Prime Minister of India 187 f.
Sheck, Seev 212
Shemer, Elisha 131
Shertok, Moshe *see* Moshe Sharett
Shinnar, Felix 196
Shinnar, Mike 208
Shkolnik, Levi *see* Levi Eshkol
Shubinsky, David 103
Shubinsky, Sam 103 f.
Shul, Ze'ev 157
Siilasvuo, Ensio 280
Silva Henríquez, Raúl 258
Simon, Ernst 57
Sindelar, Matthias 33
Singer, Pauli 37
Slánský, Rudolf 131
Soames, Mary 220
Sokolov, Nachum 150
Spranger, Otto 29
Springer, Axel 215 ff.
Springer, Friede 217
Stalin, Joseph, Soviet Premier 136
Stefan, Franz 35 f., 336 f.
Steiner, Herbert 37
Stercken, Hans 174 f.
Stoessel, Mrs. 48
Sultz, Elisha 134

Tamir, Abrasha 349
Tamir (Wolkowsky), Alexander 174
Tanner, Edi 138 f.
Teichholz, Herr 120
Tohamy, Hassan 288
Tov, Moshe 257
Turujman, Saleh 324 ff.
Tziporah 128 f., 139 f.

Überall (Avriel), Ehud 45
Ucko, Sinai 46 f., 62
Ullmann, Hanni 54
Urieli, Perez (Franz Hainebach) 55 ff., 71
U Thant, Sithu 223

Veil, Simone 214
Ventura, Schaul 69
Völkel, Bruno 25
Vranitzky, Franz, Chancellor of Austria 220, 335, *335*, 337, 369, 377 ff.

Waldheim, Kurt, President of Austria 11, 123, 279, 329 ff., 337 f., 362
Weichmann, Herbert 211
Weiner, Eva 48, 96 f.
Weiner, Margit 96 f.
Weingarten, Murray 99 f.
Weinreb, Schraga 60
Weiss, Charley 188, 231
Weitz, Sala 123
Weizmann, Chaim 78, 112
Weizman, Ezer 295 f., 298, 302, 305, 325 ff.
Weizman, Ruma 327
Weizsäcker, Marianne von 328
Weizsäcker, Richard von, President of Germany 328 f., 332
Welles, Orson 120

Wilson, Harold, Prime Minister of the United Kingdom 224
Wolkowsky, Alexander *see* Alexander Tamir
Wraneschitz, caretaker 121

Yadin, Yigael 253
Yanai, Yaakov 116 f.
Yaron, Amos 316 f.
Yisraeli, Yosef 126
Yovel, Yirmiyahu 272

Zafir, Tuvia 319
Zeilinger, Boris 41 f., 44
Zelman, Leon 330 f.
Zertal, Idith 239
Zilzer (Elizur), Michael 77
Zippori, Mordechai 314
Zuk, Assaf 75
Zuk, Avri 74 f., 78, 134, 141, 143, 155 ff., 249
Zuk, Jaffa 75
Zuk, Tami 75
Zuk, Yuval 75

Photo Credits

Facsimile and pages 16, 18, 25, 27, 82, 92, 115, 127, 191, 367 © Estate of Ari Rath.

Page 76 Public Domain.

Page 88 © Kibbutz Hatzerim Archives.

Pages 147, 150 Public Domain.

Pages 199, 287 Dan Hadani Archive, The Pritzker Family National Photography Collection, The National Library of Israel Dan Hadani Collection, The Pritzker Family National Photography Collection.

Page 289 © Moshe Millner / Government Press Office, Israel.

Page 318 © David Brauner.

Page 335 via CC-BY-SA 4.0 Bibliothek am Guisanplatz. Photo: Walter Rutishauser.

Page 363 © Katrin Schulze.

Page 368 © neuland&medienGmbH Wien, 2012.

Page 378 © Stefanie Oswalt.

www.ingramcontent.com/pod-product-compliance
Lightning Source LLC
Chambersburg PA
CBHW052048230426
43671CB00011B/1828